CHANGING CONCEPTIONS
OF PSYCHOLOGICAL LIFE

The Jean Piaget Symposium Series
Available from LEA

CHANGING CONCEPTIONS OF PSYCHOLOGICAL LIFE

Edited By

Cynthia Lightfoot
Penn State University

Chris Lalonde
University of Victoria

Michael Chandler
University of British Columbia

LAWRENCE ERLBAUM ASSOCIATES, PUBLISHERS
2004   Mahwah, New Jersey   London

Lawrence Erlbaum Associates, Inc., Publishers
10 Industrial Avenue
Mahwah, New Jersey 07430

Cover design by Kathryn Houghtaling Lacey

Library of Congress Cataloging-in-Publication Data

Jean Piaget Society. Meeting (30th : 2000 : Montréal, Québec)
   Changing conceptions of psychological life / edited by
   Cynthia Lightfoot, Chris Lalonde, Michael Chandler.
      p. cm.
   Includes bibliographical references and index.
   ISBN 0-8058-4336-1 (cloth : alk. paper)
   1. Self—Congresses.   I. Lightfoot, Cynthia.   II. Lalonde,
   Christopher A.   III. Chandler, Michael J.   IV. Title.
BF697.J36   2004
155.2—dc22   2003063128
                                             CIP

Books published by Lawrence Erlbaum Associates are printed
on acid-free paper, and their bindings are chosen for strength
and durability.

Printed in the United States of America
10   9   8   7   6   5   4   3   2   1

Contents

PART III: SELF, MIND, AND CULTURE

PART IV: THE SOCIAL CONSTRUCTION OF SELF

Preface

It's in all the papers. Ninety-six years, fifty-some films, and one true love to her credit, Katharine Hepburn died yesterday. She was, in the words of one admirer, "an inestimable self;" someone who "reminded us again and again that self is a gift not to be doubted or squandered or pawned for less that it's worth."[1]

If the eulogy reveals anything about Hepburn, it speaks volumes about our folk beliefs of having and valuing and being true to our selves, and the consequence of it all for directing our lives. Selves, it would seem, should be taken seriously, particularly by anyone who holds to the prospect that they are beacons of knowledge and action.

This book stands as commentary on that sentiment. It is a product of the 30th Annual Meeting of the Jean Piaget Society, which convened in Montréal, Canada, in June of 2000. The contributing authors constitute the original cast invited to Montréal to speak on the theme of how individuals come to construe psychological lives—their own and others. Their concerns, more specifically are how our sense of ourselves—who we are and how we think—emerges developmentally, culturally, and historically, and the implications such constructions have for personal, social, and political change. Together, the authors compose an international and interdisciplinary group of scholars already well regarded for their work on topics as diverse as adolescence, language, aging, romance, and morality. Their particular accomplishment for this special project was to pin their expertise to the cotter assumption that each of us understands ourselves as moral and epistemic agents, as authors and narrators of our own lives, and as choosers and construers of our own experience.

We have organized the book around four major themes that we will outline in a moment. There are, however, recurrent issues and sentiments spanning the sections that create their own level of discourse about selves and minds, and how they have been and ought to be studied. Throughout the book, for example, the reader is invited to reflect on the inadequacies of traditionally narrow cognitive approaches to conceptions of psychological life. By turns the authors take issue with views that settle myopically on that particular version of self and mind first fashioned and celebrated during the Enlightenment. Our authors argue that the shopworn account of mental life as objective, reflective, stable, detached, and coherent turns up an individual so devoid of desire, motive, commitment, and feeling—so anemic of personality—that it can hardly rise from the sofa, much less engage in those forms of action that we commonly take as instrumental to the pursuit of knowledge and collective life.

As their criticisms converge to undermine classical cognitive approaches, so too do their endorsed alternatives together present something of a map for how to continue. The reader will find in these pages a call to feed conceptions of mental life on the lush and shifting fields of attachments and felt experience, epiphany and power, drama and genre, and the possibility engendered by sheer coincidence. Explorations of a more connected mind and a more convivial self are promised to bring to light possible solutions to the long-whiskered and doggedly difficult problems of relating thought and action, unity and diversity, agency and duty.

The first section, *Self as Known and as Experienced*, includes work that is principally concerned with elevating the position of our experience of ourselves in constructing who we are. Agusto Blasi, for example, derides more traditional approaches for casting mental life in strictly representational terms. Such approaches, he argues, result in a reductive, "hyphenated self" that is no more than the sum of its constituent parts of self-perceptions, self-images, self-concepts, and self-evaluations. There is no place here for an active agent to manage and care for and lay claim to the various perceptions, images, concepts, and evaluations to which it is tagged; no place for the felt unity of agents and their own actions. He proposes that the basic self, that is, the self that is foundational to constructions of who we are, is experienced in the course of intentional action. Intentional action, he suggests, defines a context of "being present to oneself." Such presence requires consciousness of our selves as agents; it conveys to us our own subject-hood.

Donald Polkinghorne pursues a similar course in his revisionist narrative approach to personal identity. Although generally sympathetic to narrative theory's emphasis on how conceptions of self are affected by the language and stories in which they are articulated, he argues, like Blasi, that any account that fails to address the role of identity *as experienced* is itself a story only half-told. Polkinghorne and Blasi part ways, however, on the nature of that experience and the details of its generative power. Drawing from the theories of Ricoeur, Gadamer, and Merleau-Ponty, Polkinghorne maps out a three-part solution of prefiguring, configuring, and refiguring that forms the hermeneutic circle of identity development. The solution begins with the prefigured *life as lived*, an unreflective, nonlanguaged, unfinished "presence of oneself to oneself," which becomes transformed through story, plot, and genre. Once configured through narrative, self-stories become subject to interpretation and evaluation, that is to say, they become "refigured" and appropriated as our own in ways that fundamentally alter life as lived.

Larry Nucci is also concerned with matters of experience and agency, particularly in their relevance to moral life. He calls for a *contextualized-structuralism* to lay to rest the classical Kohlbergian perspective and all its unsettling accoutrements, principal among them the lack of consanguinity of stage, thought and action. In a more spectral, contextualized light, moral action draws explanatory power from social categories, cultural traditions, and hierarchical relations, as well as from who we are as individuals apart from, and as active interpreters of all such categories, traditions and relations. A contextualized-structuralism, on Nucci's account, holds value for defining and exploring "moral openness"—that is, our orientation towards and proclivity to hear and respond to the moral voices in our life-worlds. This openness maps the high road to moral and personal change.

Chapters comprising the second section, *Self and Mind*, share as a focal concern the joinery presumed to exist between conceptions of self and conceptions of mental life. However, each offers more expansive views that permit the inclusion of the dynamics of temperament, attachment, personality, and regulation. Beginning with the premise that mind constitutes a form of self-awareness about thinking, Andreas Demetriou addresses the problem of self-integration: what accounts for the felt unity of a self that is naturally diverse in abilities, characteristics and tendencies? Drawing theoretic inspiration from dynamic systems and modularity approaches, and informed by his own empirical data, he sets forth for consideration a three-tiered model intended to capture both the dynamic (motivational and emotional) and cognitive representational components of a "hypercognitive system" that underlies our sense of ourselves as unified and integral.

Although operating within the radically different perspective of Eriksonian identity theory, David Peterson, James Marcia and Jeremy Carpendale share Demetriou's vision of an integrated study of identity, cognitive, and epistemic development. Their study provides strong evidence for the claim that identity and epistemic development are both moved forward through a process of exploration which is itself mediated by the developing child's attachment history.

In the third contribution to this section, Louis Moses and Stephanie Carlson propose and provide supporting empirical evidence that self impacts mental life through the "non-obvious route" of self-regulation. They argue, in particular, that self-regulation—the ability to hold one's own salient perspective in abeyance in the face of competing possibilities—is the growth medium for the emergence of preschool children's theories of mind.

Contributions to the third section, *Self, Mind, and Culture*, are all concerned with the cultural contexts that frame developing conceptions of self and mental life. Dorothy Holland presents an historical analysis of how anthropology has, in the past 20 years, backed away from essentialist accounts of selves and cultures in order to articulate "social practice" theories of identity development. In the light of contemporary theorizing, identity is understood to be historically produced and mediated through the artifacts of culture—census forms, curricula vita, diagnostic manuals, and other genre. Her own "sociogenic" revision to social practice theory, illuminated in an analysis of women's constructions of romantic identity, interprets culture genres as tools of self-construction that are constrained by relations of power.

David Moshman's contribution resonates with several recurrent themes in this book. His general aim is to account for the consistency between the theories that we have about ourselves, and our actions within specific cultural and historical contexts. Theories, he argues, initially implicit in behavior, increasingly become explicit objects of consciousness that alter who we are. Theories are us. Interpreting the genocide in Rwanda as an issue of ideology and identity, rather than as an issue of tribal and racial differences, Moshman builds a case for viewing identity as theory and a commitment to being a particular kind of person.

Chris Lalonde and Michael Chandler set themselves the task of explicating exactly how individuals resolve the paradox of personal persistence, that is, how they face the challenge of understanding selves as continuous through time despite life's inevitable flux and change. Arguing that a sense of personal persistence is a "generic design feature or systems imperative" of self-hood, they trace two distinctive solutions to the problem of self-continuity, one reaching inward to some constant core protected from the turbulent surround, a second solution reaching outward through an expanding net of "relational" or "narratively-based" connections that bind the present self to its history and its imagined future. When pressed to confront the paradox of personal persistence, Western-European adolescents lean heavily on the first solution, whereas Native American adolescents favor the latter, suggesting that culture figures importantly into developing of conceptions of self.

Our fourth and final section, *The Social Construction of Self*, situates conceptions of mental life directly and dramatically in the social contexts of their making. The contributions are replete with references to persons as protean, contingent participants within dynamic fields of joint action. Theodore Sarbin argues that social identity is an answer to the question "who am I?" But because we live in a storied world, the question is more appropriately phrased in poetically nuanced terms: "in what story or stories am I taking part?" Although the personal pronoun figures into any answer—*I* am a performing arts enthusiast; *I* am a servant of the Lord—Sarbin argues that our conceptions of self, the meanings of who we are, ride ultimately on the predicates our pronouns carry in their own wake.

Rom Harré's chapter focuses likewise on the identity shaping power of language, discourse and, particularly, personal pronouns. Following Wittgenstein, he argues that selves are jointly constructed in virtue of donning public masks appropriate to the local milieu. It is on this account that pronoun systems are of special importance to personal identity: they serve to locate self-singularities in space and time.

And, finally, a provocative chapter by Amélie Rorty who disavows as misguided any notion of working out versions of persons as integrated, unified, singular, or coherent. Attenuated across fields of dramatic action, contradiction, and revolution, selves, like calla lilies, are suitable to any occasion. We are each a pocketful of "identity markers," character-forming patterns of cognitive and motivational proclivities produced as our situations demand. That these identity markers are often dug out along with odd bits of laundry lint, matchbooks, or last week's grocery list just goes to the point of our immapable futures, and our readiness to make fire.

All told, the reader will find in these pages programmatic efforts variously attuned to selves and minds as dynamic and structured, present and represented, felt and known, nonlanguaged and storied, embodied and theorized. There is paradox aplenty here. And for that we must be grateful.

—*Cynthia Lightfoot*
—*Chris Lalonde*
—*Michael Chandler*

ENDNOTE

[1]Verlyn Klinkenborg, *NYT*; July 1, 2003.

Part I

SELF AS KNOWN
AND AS EXPERIENCED

Neither Personality nor Cognition: An Alternative Approach to the Nature of the Self[1]

Augusto Blasi
University of Massachusetts Boston

The use of the term *self*, in its nonhyphenated form, has increased exponentially in recent psychological writings. However, referent and meaning are still imprecise and ambiguous. There seem to be two main referents. Sometimes "self" is used either as synonymous with oneself, the concrete person, or as equivalent with personality, as defined by temperamental and behavioral traits, or perhaps by salient psychological characteristics. The most frequent referent of the term, by far, is the subject-as-known, or the product of self-cognition. I argue here that both these uses of the term are somewhat inappropriate; I then attempt to define a domain of psychological functioning, to which the nonhyphenated "self" should be properly and unambiguously applied. It is not my intention to write about language and to construct an argument about semantics. In a discipline where agreement is rarely found, and only on the basis of empirical evidence, a discussion about the proper use of words is not likely to convince many people. My main intention is positive and substantive, namely, to point to, and clarify a set of psychological processes, to which the label, self, clearly belongs, and from which the self as object of cognition should be carefully distinguished. This domain of functioning, although essential to the understanding of specifically human characteristics, has been, at least from a theoretical perspective, seriously neglected, and one reason for the neglect is the quasi monopoly that the cognitive self has acquired in psychological discourse.

Looking at the prevalent uses of the term, not much needs to be said about the practice of referring "self" to the subject of personality traits. Most of us would agree that "self" carries a strong connotation of reflexivity and conscious subjectivity. Therefore, its application to behavioral, objectively observed characteristics, salient or not, can only be interpreted as a result of confusion, or, more likely, of terminological carelessness. For this particular meaning a much richer and far more precise vocabulary is readily available.

By contrast, the cognitive use of the term has behind it a long tradition of careful conceptual differentiations, theoretical elaborations, and empirical research. The rather successful attempt to absorb all other meanings of "self" and to monopolize the theoretical and scientific discourse on this topic requires the most attentive consideration. In modern psychology the story begins with William James' (1950) distinction between self as object or as known and self as subject or as knower. James' treatment of the self is richer and much subtler than this simple, by now standard, dichotomy suggests. It is also far less cognitive than the labels imply. In fact, he seems to adopt emotional responses and actions as important criteria for what belongs to the self. But James made several moves that eventually led psychologists toward what I consider to be a dead end: he couched the distinction in cognitive terms; recognized only two alternatives—the direct object of reflection and introspection (including the "innermost centre," or the "self of selves") and what is not empirical at all—thus neglecting the possibility of an immediately experienced self; and therefore accepted only the former as appropriate object of psychological research. This cognitive and reflective orientation was reinforced by Epstein's (1973) influential paper, in which the author, having raised the question about the nature of the self (without hyphenation), argued that it simply is the theory, or a coherent organization of beliefs, each person has about himself or herself; this concept would account, neatly and without residues, for all reasonable meanings we could give the term. The variety of cognitive aspects psychologists have been focusing on in studying the self go beyond Epstein's central point, but the cognitive approach has become almost the accepted paradigm in self psychology. In summary, contemporary psychologists went one important step further from W. James: they collapsed the two kinds of self of James' distinction and proclaimed that the self can only be the self as known in all its cognitive varieties—self-perceptions, self-images, self-concepts, self-schemata, self-narratives, and, of course, self-theories. I refer to this concept as *representational self* or *cognitive self*.

Briefly, in what follows I try to show that: (a) there is a nonrepresented self, captured, indirectly, in every immediate experience, but primarily in the very process of acting. I variously refer to this meaning of "self" as lived self, subjective self, experiential self, or simply self; (b) this self is the foundation for the attitudes of self-valuing and self-caring, giving origin to a whole series of self-emotions; (c) the immediately experienced self grows through self-appropriations, and not through the accumulation and the organization of knowledge and cognitions about oneself; as a result, (d) the nature of self-knowledge and its relation to the development of the self need to be thoroughly reconceptualized to emphasize the role of conscious and agentic processes.

CARING ABOUT THE SELF AND MANAGING THE SELF

Toward the end of his life—improbably, as some might say—Michel Foucault became interested in the contemporary emphases on the self. He was not concerned with the psychological aspects of the phenomenon, but with its philosophical and political implications. He felt that the specific forms of the self, as we now experience it, make us particularly vulnerable to the manipulative and freedom limiting strategies of cultural power games. He also felt that the most effective way of protecting ourselves would be to become aware that the self we experience does not have ontological status, is not therefore inevitable, but has its own genealogy. The modern self, then, would be the result of cultural-historical transformations, and still contains traces—thematic traces—of very different forms of self experience in ancient times. Therefore, in his last work on the history of sexuality (particularly 1985, 1986), he set out to describe and interpret the culture of the self during 8 centuries of Greco-Roman history, from Hellenistic Greece to the first centuries of imperial Rome and early Christianity.

What matters for the present discussion, quite independently of Foucault's ideological concerns, are the observations of people's attitudes and behaviors toward themselves, gathered from a variety of historical, philosophical, and religious documents. There was, then, in many people a real "conversion" to the self—that is, a sharp focusing of attention to, and the establishment of an intense relationship with one's self, one's soul. The core attitude of this relationship was care and concern—for its wealth, well-being, and perfection. Foucault traced this attitude back to Socrates' words, as reported in Plato's *Apologia*:

> Are you not ashamed that you give your attention to acquiring as much money as possible, and similarly with reputation and honor, and give no attention or thought to truth and understanding and the perfection of your soul? ... This is what my God commands .... I spend all my time going about trying to persuade ... to make your first and chief concern not for your bodies not for your profession, but for the highest welfare of your soul .... (1963, 29e-30a)

As revealed in this and many other texts, the basic characteristics of the "conversion to the self" were the realization of the supreme importance of certain core aspects of oneself (soul, or spirit); constant attention to these aspects, concern for their health and integrity, active care for them, for their own sake and not because they may be instrumental to achieving other goals, such as wealth or career, social reputation and respect; finally, an attitude of active engagement, careful management, persistent work, aimed at cutting and pruning, controlling what is excessive and damaging, molding one's imagination, emotions, and behavior. A frequent ideal objective was to become sovereign of oneself, to achieve perfect mastery of one's emotions and passions, and to be completely self-possessed.

The approach of active care to the self was concretely expressed through various practices, that Foucault calls "technologies of the self." These practices, frequently compared to athletic exercises, are classified by Foucault (e.g., 1997) under several categories: some strategies were aimed at learning and memorizing special texts of wisdom, that one could use to see the real meaning of events or to control sudden emotions; other practices were aimed at freeing oneself from unwarranted anxieties. For instance, one would systematically and vividly imagine extremely upsetting events, in order to understand that, as such, they are not evil or true misfortunes, and that it's only our misplaced anxieties and false opinions that make them seem so. There were exercises aimed at establishing and testing one's independence from the world, and at mastering one's body, emotions, and desires: for example, abstaining from favored foods or from sex; enduring privations, fatigue, or sleep. One practice, particularly important among the Stoics and the early Christians, was to vividly imagine one's death as a present event.

Where is the self in this complex of attitudes and practices? For Foucault—on this he agrees with many others[2]—the self does not reside in the object of one's attention or in the product of one's self-cultivation, but consists of a special kind of relationship that a person establishes with oneself. In its focused intensity, assiduous attention, and strenuous work to achieve emotional control, self-mastery, and autonomy, there is a heightened self-consciousness and sense of subjectivity; the subject, previously immersed in action and experience, comes into relief, and the self originates.

Although limited to a specific period of cultural history, the attitudes described by Foucault, far from being alien to us, resonate with our experience and with accounts from very different cultures and different times. Of course, there are important differences—in the way the self or the soul is conceptualized, or in the ways its preciousness and unconditional worth is understood; in the goals to be achieved; and in the specific practices for reaching these goals. Foucault himself distinguishes secular and religious orientations; he notes the crucial difference between seeing the soul as supremely important because it contains the imprint of God, and seeing it as a harmonious work of art, entrusted to one's work and diligence. Similarly, the superficially more passive Eastern approach to self-perfection, as reflected in Buddhism, Yoga, Taoism, and Hinduism, is indeed very different from the strenuous individualism of Emersonian variety, which is very different from the aesthetic preoccupations of various utopian movements, such as, in Jungian psychology, or in the many contemporary versions of the human potential movement. And yet it is possible to abstract from the differences certain common elements: a distinction between the essence of one's being and other superficial aspects; the belief that the former is unconditionally worthy and supremely important; and a tendency to care for this "soul," attend to it, and work for it. In the interviews that I and my collaborators conducted with well-educated, middle class, American groups, both religious and secular, a sizable number of adults were found who do indeed distinguish a core part of themselves, frequently identified with those values and ideals to which one is deeply committed; are concerned with protecting this core identity from potentially corrupting influences, and try to actualize it in daily choices and decisions; who examine themselves to check their fidelity to their commitments, and would suffer distress and guilt for what they consider to be self-betrayals (Blasi & Glodis, 1995; Shindler, 2001).

This type of self experience based on an attitude of care for the self, desire for integrity, and assiduous work on oneself, is not universal, but seems to depend on historical and economic conditions, culturally accepted ideas, and on individual development. Even so, it cannot be denied that it constitutes a significant slice of human experience and behavior, alongside the more contemplative experience of cognitive self-construction and self-knowledge. Like the latter, the former are data that need to be explained. And yet observations like those reported by Foucault and many others have been completely bypassed by the theoretical perspective that views the self as representations and the product of cognitive processes. In fact, it is very difficult to imagine, at least for me, how, starting from cognitive self-representations, one could *theoretically* explain the attitudes of care for the core self, and the active, responsible management of the self. These aspects of human functioning are not aimed at contemplative knowledge; they are aimed, instead, at self-control and self-change through focused, intentional, agentic processes. The problem is especially serious when one conceptualizes the construction of self-representations, as is frequently done, as a result of nonintentional, more or less automatic, frequently nonconscious information processing operations.

THE SELF IN INTENTIONAL ACTION

Foucault believed, as many others do, that the self he described is a result of, and contingent to, cultural and historical circumstances. But one can still ask: what makes this intensely focused relationship to oneself possible? It is easy to accept the role of cultural expectations and ideas, for example, in determining certain beliefs about the supreme importance of one's soul. But how does a person grasp that the self he or she cares about is his or her own? Why does he or she care about his or her own self and not so much about the self of other people? Foucault was not interested in these questions, but psychologists should be. I would argue that a different kind of self experience—less direct, more implicit, more embedded in concrete actions and in the relations people have with other objects—is present also when there is no evidence of a focused relation to oneself, and that this very basic, immediate self is the condition for the possibility of the experiences described by Foucault, and also for the possibility of self-knowledge. In thinking about this basic self, the notion of consciousness is both necessary and misleading. This notion, in fact, is highly ambiguous; in addition, it may be so closely identified with cognition as to lead one to the unwarranted conclusion that the self can only be found in cognitive reflection. In reality consciousness is neither a necessary nor an exclusive feature of cognition. There are cognitive processes as well as representations that are not conscious. At the same time, there are nonrepresentational processes that are conscious. A central kind is intentional action.

As each of us can easily realize, in every intentional action there are certain aspects of which we are directly and focally aware. Primary among them is what the action is about, its immediate goal: for instance, as I write, I am aware that I am writing, that I am trying to select the appropriate words; I am also aware of what is at the margins of my action: the clutter on my desk, the light, the color of the room, and so on. But our consciousness of acting is not exhausted by the goal we intend, the mental processes that we pursue, and the context in which the action takes place. There are other aspects in our consciousness. In fact, these aspects are an essential part of it, although we are rarely aware of them in the moment of acting: for instance, that *I* am acting, that the action originates *within me,* is to some extent *under my control,* and is therefore *mine.* In summary, in every intentional action, there is a nonfocal consciousness of myself as agent, as owner of the action, and of the action as mine. I am suggesting, then, that *the basic self is what is experienced immediately but nonfocally in the very process of acting, every time there is intentional action*. Its two major features—at least those I wish now to emphasize—are agency (the immediate sense that the self is a source of, and controlling action) and mineness (the immediate sense that this action belongs to the agent self). I think this is incontrovertible. It is this aspect of experience that defines experience as experience and determines subjectivity.

It seems also incontrovertible to me that intentional actions are on the side of in-the-world-factuality and not on the side of cognitive representation; as such, they do not represent anything, although some kind of representation of the goal is required for an action to be intentional. As Russell (1996) puts it, "subject-hood rather than representation is the core feature" (p. 20). At the same time, intentional action essentially differs from other movements in space, precisely because it involves the consciousness of self as agent, and therefore subjectivity. This difference, it is important to note, is not a result of adding some kind of mental representation of oneself to spatial movement. Experience of self is part-and-parcel, one with, intentional action. There is only one reality, but a reality that is both physical-in-the-world and subjectively conscious; this kind of consciousness is like the mental lining of intentional action, or the mental side of a physical coin. This experience is unique and totally unlike the perception of external objects, including external bodies. Prior to the construction of conceptual categories, it establishes a primitive but fundamental sense of ownership and mineness.

Philosophers and those psychologists who recently have been investigating the infant self struggle to find appropriate terms that could convey, or simply not distort, the unique features of immediate consciousness of self in action. For instance, they write of primary consciousness (as opposed to reflective self-awareness); perceptual or preperceptual awareness (as opposed to conceptual or representational knowledge); consciousness of self; existential self (opposed to categorical self); situated self (opposed to identified self); self experienced from the inside; and so on (cf. Bermudez, Marcel, & Eilan, 1995; Rochat, 1995). Perhaps the metaphor of presence—of being present to oneself in the process of acting—best conveys the total unity and the lack of distance between the agent self and the action, and thus the noncognitive nature of the subjective self.

How do we know that the self is indeed in consciousness, and yet is not originally a concept or a representation? What is the evidence for this kind of proposition? There are two arguments. The first and most powerful is that this is in fact the way we experience ourselves every time we are involved in intentional action, namely, through the immediate consciousness of us acting and owning the action. The second, a kind of transcendental argument à la Kant, is that, if the only way we could reach the self were through conceptual mediation and reflection, then no subjectivity, no first-person knowledge would be possible, and the overall character of human experience and knowledge, not to speak of language, would be lost.[3]

THE EARLY SELF: THE SUBJECTIVITY OF DESIRE

One central question that psychologists involved in studying the infant self have been trying to answer concerns the age in which the earliest self experience can be assumed to be present. From the perspective of my discussion, however, answering this question is not so important. Instead it is important to point out certain special characteristics of the early self. In particular, I wish to emphasize two early characteristics that, in my view, mark all later self experience. One is that the *early self is bodily through and through*. This is true of all of us, but is particularly true of infants. I don't simply mean to say that the infant self is exclusively grasped through the body and physical action, which of course is true. What I wish mainly to emphasize is that in infancy the "mental"—the minimal awareness that is necessary for experience—is not yet abstracted and isolated from its material content through reflection and the objectification of concepts. This early self, then, will provide the content for later cognitive and conceptual activity, for the progressive construction of the self as object; for now, however, it is reality waiting to be known. This temporal separation of the subjective self as lived reality and the objective self as known reality, the distancing of the latter from the former, will characterize any later effort of each person to know oneself.

The second characteristic is that the infant self is mostly experienced as a desiring self. Early in life, instinctual tendencies, impulses, and needs may be passively experienced as something impersonal occurring in a localized within. However, as soon as the impulse generates intentional action, determining the goal that subtends it, the impulse is taken over and appropriated by the agent, and is transformed into a desire or an early form of willfulness. At this point the self is not only experienced as the agentic source of action but as a wanting self. The experience of intending, desiring, and trying sharpens and clarifies the sense of mineness, for instance, by setting into operation dynamics of resistance and conflict: resistance of the body to the child's intentions; and resistance of the child's desire and will to the limits coming from other objects, and also from the interferences and demands of other people. In summary, in the early development of the subjective self, and forever after, there is the convergence of two central aspects characterizing the self—the experience of mineness in agency and the experience of mineness of desire. From very early on, the frequent and intense experience of desire is shot through with the characteristic of ownership and possession. In humans, these events are no longer impersonal, but are colored by possessive subjectivity. Vice-versa, possessive subjectivity always has the quality of self-interest, involvement, engagement, wanting-for-oneself.

Perhaps there is no need to underline that the desiring self, like the actions that it motivates, is not a matter of cognitive representation, but is on the side of factual reality. This, I think, is an important point. Philosophers frequently stress that cognition, as such, does not motivate, but this is a truth that cognitive theories, including cognitive theories of personality, tend to forget. The temptation is always there to try to transform desires, attitudes and stances, interests and values, into representations. Specifically, all cognitive approaches to the self, attempting to reduce the self to self-concepts and self-theories, eventually encounter a crucial problem: to explain how and why people care about, have special emotions for, whatever concerns them, simply because it concerns them. Why do I care about my abilities and not about yours? Why should I care about my self-concept? Why am I concerned about the health and integrity of my core identity—my soul—to the point of carefully shaping my behavior, and controlling my wishes and impulses? In my opinion, to the extent that the self is reduced to cognition, these questions have no answer. I do not believe that all motives are self motives. I do understand cognitive motives: the need of asking questions, of finding answers, of organizing knowledge in a logical way; the need to avoid inconsistency, and so on. I do appreciate the attraction that an elegant and coherent theory has for us. But why should it matter whether the theory is mine or somebody else's? Or whether the theory is about me rather than about a patient I am seeing in therapy? The answer, I think, is that our self is the subject of desires, wanting to satisfy them in action; and that the self and its desires are real facts and not constructed representations.

THE DEVELOPMENT OF THE SELF:
PROCESSES AND MILESTONES

One could readily accept that the origin of subjectivity is indeed intrinsically tied to intentional action and the immediate consciousness of agency that it comports, but then argue that all later developments of the self are cognitive constructions, grafted, so to speak, onto the initial contentless point of subjectivity. If this were the case, what really matters about the self, its characteristics and its contents, could only be cognitive. But I do not believe that this idea actually captures the way the self develops from the beginnings of subjectivity. Rather, I think that the self-as-subject has its own developmental sequence and its specific developmental processes. Cognitive processes and knowledge are important, indeed necessary factors in the development of the self. However, neither the developmental transformations of the self, nor the processes by which they are accomplished, are, as such, intrinsically, cognitive.

Each one of us is born and grows up in specific geographic, social, cultural, and historical contexts and functions psychologically within an organismic environment—a body, a set of needs and impulses, perhaps certain physiologically based temperamental characteristics. Strictly speaking, in early infancy none of these features are ours, belongs to us. We could even say that we are entirely under the control of, and, in this sense, are owned by, what is around and within us. With the origin of the self in intentional action, the relations with our physical and social environment begins to be reversed. In becoming agents, we begin to own our actions and slowly begin to control our movements. In agency, the subjective self feels the owner; the sense of mineness is its central feature. I would argue that the development of the self continues by progressively extending the sense of mineness and of ownership. But "mine" may have two different meanings: of having or possessing, for instance, an object or even a person; and of being, identifying with, for instance, a set of goals or certain values. These two meanings are involved in two sets of processes, that I simply label, here, *self-mastery* and *self-appropriation*. Both are important for the development of the self, but in different ways. And yet these processes are not independent of each other or completely distinguishable, except at the conceptual level. Most frequently it is difficult to tell where one ends and the other begins. Rather, they work together and influence each other.

Self-mastery involves the conscious and intentional attempt of slowly taking possession of, "colonizing," different aspects of oneself—one's actions, but also one's emotions, impulses, and tendencies. Strictly speaking, the aspects that one ends up controlling and possessing may never become a part of the subjective self. At times, the attempt to master these aspects may be guided by the wish of rejecting them. The Stoics and early Christians described by Foucault (1986) attempted to master, through laborious exercises, their desire for earthly possessions, their fear of social rejection, or their anger, precisely because they had rejected these tendencies from their sense of self. Even so, the process of self-mastery would lead to the expansion and transformations of the agentic aspect of the self-as-subject, both its objective achievements and the subjective experience that goes with them. On one hand, the child becomes increasingly capable to control impulses and regulate the feelings and the expressions of emotions, is better and better able to respond to social requests, to feel a sense of obligation, to make promises and to responsibly keep them, to commit him or herself to various projects. On the other hand, the subjective experiences associated with these achievements increasingly differentiate and characterize the sense of self: the sense of being in charge, of being responsible, of being committed, the sense of mastery and self-esteem are different ways of experiencing subjectivity. These developmental milestones of the agentic self should be distinguished from organismic regulatory processes. The latter processes are present from the earliest development, but are more or less automatic, nonintentional, nonconscious. By themselves, they could never lead to the sense of mastery, of responsibility, and commitment.

APPROPRIATION AND SELF-APPROPRIATION

By "appropriation" I am referring here to processes that go in opposite directions: toward what William James calls "welcoming and rejecting" (1950, e.g., p. 277),[4] appropriating or owning and disowning, acknowledging certain characteristics as one's own, while treating others as alien and foreign. We may not understand theoretically how appropriation works and how it produces its powerful effects. But there is no doubt that the process, in its dual orientation, is common and its consequences are indeed important. All of us have the experience of treating the many, and equally real, aspects of our personality differently with respect to our sense of self. All actions that we perform feel ours. Most, however, are taken for granted and treated as routine occurrences, as simply constituting the background, the texture of our daily living. Some, by contrast, perhaps because of their meaning and their relation to specific goals, are particularly wanted and cherished, appropriated to our sense of who we are; others, finally, are disowned and rejected, perhaps because they do not fit with the image we have of ourselves, or because they contradict the values with which we identify and that we want to pursue in life.

To have a clear sense of the powerful role of appropriation it is sufficient to consider the process of socialization. Relatively early in his or her development, the child begins by appropriating his or her parents' requests; later he or she appropriates household or school rules; then the duties connected to his or her various roles, and eventually moral obligations. The child does not simply know what his or her social expectations are, but transforms at least some of them into expectations and wishes of one's own. At this point, norms and duties are translated into a sense of personal obligation. Within this social context, the child appropriates his or her actions—the child's intention for acting, his or her decisions, the reasons by which he or she was guided, and the consequences that his or her action produced. Of course he or she *knows* that an action occurred and that he or she was its physical cause. But the terms, "learning" and "knowing" are utterly insufficient to suggest what is happening in these cases. In fact, even when one learned the social expectations concerning responsibility, the possibility is always open of disowning one's action, of denying one's intention, of blaming others or the circumstances. By appropriating one's actions, a person feels socially responsible and perhaps publicly accountable. One may feel the responsibility to confess, to avow one's fault, to redress the damages caused by his or her actions, to try what one can to control impulses and change behavior. Similar accounts can be given for many other aspects of human functioning.

Appropriation, then, is the more or less conscious taking-over of various aspects of oneself as one's own property; it works jointly with, and is conditioned by, the previously described process of self-mastery. *Self-appropriation*, as I am using the term here, is a special form of appropriation, whereby an aspect is not simply owned but is integrated in the sense of who one is. It has to do with being rather than with having. Self-appropriation, then, covers the domain of self-images, self-concepts, and self-schemata. But it differs from these cognitive processes in at least two respects: it implies a more or less conscious selection among what is known about oneself, and consists of welcoming (or rejecting) the selected contents, and wanting to identify oneself by them (or in contrast to them). Of course, I know that I am all the things that I realize are true of me, but I want only some of them to be really me.

James (1950, p. 291) had already observed how human beings are capable of even disowning their own bodies, sometimes regarding them "as prisons of clay which they should some day be glad to escape." If this is the case for one's body, it is even more so for other aspects. For instance, both Don Juan and St. Anthony, the desert anchoret, experienced and knew to harbor sexual desires. But they did not appropriate these desires to their sense of self in the same way: Don Juan treated them as an important, welcomed, part of his being; St. Anthony looked at them as cancer-like growths in his body, and rejected them from the sense of who he wished to be. A more common example concerns gender identification (but similar observations can be made with regard to national or religious affiliations, one's work and other social roles, and also about the emotions we experience, the behavioral tendencies and traits we detect in us, or the norms we are in fact following). Soon in his life a boy learns that he is a boy: he knows the meaning of the word, boy, the basic identifying characteristics of boys, and also knows that he has these characteristics. But he does not choose to be a boy. In this context, choosing and wanting make no sense to him: you do not choose the reality in front of your eyes; it simply is. This child has the self-concept of boy, but did not appropriate his boyhood to his sense of self. In growing up, unlikely as it might be, this person may continue to relate to his gender in the same neutral way, as a characteristic that is just there and about which he has no special feelings. More probably this person will like being a male and the characteristics and expectations that go with his gender; he may even take his maleness as the core of the subjective sense of himself, organizing his judgments and values, attitudes and decisions. At this point, what was a fact of his nature is no longer just an objective fact, but is subjectively chosen and wanted as what defines him. But it is also possible for yet another man, although acknowledging the inevitable fact of his maleness, to reject it, wishing that he were not so constituted; he may perhaps attempt to diminish its effects, for instance, by assuming body postures and mental attitudes that are contrary to the male social stereotype.

These are some of the experiences of self-appropriation and some of the ways this process contributes to the construction of the self. But to describe is not the same as to explain or to theoretically understand how self-appropriation works, under what conditions it is effective to change a person's behavior, or what its limits are. I do not have a psychological theory of self-appropriation. But I think it is important to sharply distinguish the conception I am offering from two very different perspectives, one that understands this process to be cognitive, and the other that sees it as a defensive strategy. Sometimes, particularly in the context of social constructionist theories inspired by Vygotsky's ideas (cf. Cox & Lightfoot, 1997; Valsiner, 1997), appropriation and self-appropriation are seen as akin to cognitive assimilation, namely, as an active approach to grasping reality and integrating it in one's cognitive structures. Once again, the issue is not about words, but about the specific meanings attached to them. All these terms—active, appropriation, assimilation, internalization, and so on—are highly ambiguous and need to be carefully defined.

As I see it, there are two fundamental differences between self-appropriation, as I am using the term, and cognitive assimilation, as, for instance, is understood in Piagetian theory. First, self-appropriation is agentic, cognitive assimilation is not. Cognitive assimilation may be said to be an active process, because it involves the transformation of reality on the part of the organism and indicates the organism's contribution in the interaction with the environment. But this process, whether at the biological level or at the cognitive level, is not guided by conscious intentions; it simply happens within us. This is not to say that cognitive accounts of self-construction do not rely, at the descriptive level, on conscious and intentional processes. Interesting examples can be found in Moshman (1999) and Berzonsky (e.g., 1989). One should ask, however, whether these accounts have the theoretical tools to explain what is being described. My answer is that they do not: once the subjective agentic self has been bracketed from cognitive theory, one cannot smuggle it in through the back door.

The second and more important difference between cognitive assimilation and self-appropriation is that the former functionally aims at *understanding* as adequately as possible what is—in this case, one's own psychological reality—while self-appropriation aims at *molding* the psychological reality that we know to be ours. As already mentioned, we do not appropriate to our self all that we understand about ourselves. What we select for self-appropriation is not *factually* more real, nor necessarily better known or better understood than the many other aspects of our personality that remain in the background; vice-versa, what we disown and reject from our sense of self is not *factually* less real than the rest of our personality. In fact, frequently the opposite is the case. Therefore, knowledge of what is factually a part of us, or theories by which we organize and explain the many characteristics that factually are ours, cannot offer the key for self-appropriation or for the sense of self that is constructed by it. Vice-versa, the aspects that we self-appropriate are not selected in order to arrive at a better, more comprehensive, more logically consistent, understanding of our factual psychological reality. Rather, we appropriate certain elements in order to shape and modify the reality of who we are, and not simply its representation.

A very different view, frequently found among psychoanalytic schools and in certain more skeptical quarters of social psychology (e.g., Greenwald, 1980), accepts the motivational and dynamic nature of self-construction, but interprets the acts of self-appropriating and disowning as leading to cognitive distortions and self-deception, and as motivated by the narcissistic need to believe that we are better than what we actually are, the desire to protect our self-esteem, or a defensive rejection of responsibility and guilt.

I would not deny that these and similar processes exist and have a powerful role in creating a distorted image of oneself. At the same time their effect may not be as pervasive as these theories suggest. Judging from our interviews (e.g., Blasi & Glodis, 1995; Shindler, 2001), it is clear that many people acknowledge that the characteristics they reject are as factually real as those they appropriate. In fact, they may acknowledge that an ideal, chosen as central to the sense of self, is more of an inspiration than a pervasive reality in their lives, whereas the rejected characteristics are factually, and perhaps painfully, very real. In these interviews one may even observe the expression of a degree of wariness about the ever-present possibility of self-deception. In a way, it may be just this tension—between what one is and what one wishes to be and appropriates to the sense of self—that guarantees the authenticity of self-appropriation. Self-deception and genuine self-construction seem to move in opposite directions and aim at opposite states: the former produces isolation, compartmentalization, and lack of awareness; the latter leads one toward responsible integration and self-consistency.

A more plausible approach to self-appropriation was elaborated by Frankfurt (e.g., 1988) in a series of writings aimed at clarifying the questions of what it means to have a will, how one constructs it and thereby defines and shapes one's identity. Frankfurt centrally relies on the human capacity for self-reflexivity, by which people establish a hierarchy of *self-possessions*. He is not referring to metacognitive processes, Piagetian second-order operations, or the reflective construction of self-concepts or self-theories about oneself. For him the self has to do with the structure of the will, and the will is structured through appropriation and rejection of one's characteristics. Whatever their origin—biological or social—these characteristics (desires, motives, inclinations, traits) are given facts about people's lives. But people have the capacity to desire to have or not to have some of these characteristics (second-order desires); they may even want for these second-order desires to be effective in determining one's actions and ordering one's life (second-order volitions). Sometimes we assent and identify with some of our inclinations and desires to the point that we totally (and not simply contingently and pragmatically) reject objects, actions, and desires that are in conflict with them. In this context Frankfurt adopts the expression, caring-about and being concerned with (note the similarity with

Foucault's language). Caring about the objects of certain desires identifies us with our desires, and in addition extends our will into the future through commitment: we make ourselves instruments in pursuing our projects and vulnerable to their losses. In mapping his area of study, Frankfurt convincingly argues that the questions about what we care about form a separate and different set of questions from those concerning knowledge, what to believe, and those concerning ethics, how to behave. Of course, he writes as a philosopher. But a psychological approach to the self cannot ignore the validity of the phenomena he describes and the appropriateness of the language of desire, will, caring-about, and concern.

THE CASE OF IDENTITY

Identity may rightly be seen as the highest developmental transformation of the self. But identity is also what is most frequently understood in cognitive terms: sometimes as the sum total of one's self-concepts, sometimes as a more or less consistent organization of self-concepts or schemas; sometimes as the subjectively salient or important self-concepts; sometimes as a theory about oneself. More recently, identity has been defined as a coherent story a person tells about him or herself (e.g., by McAdams, 1990). Here I limit my observations to the narrative approach to identity. Clearly the autobiographical story has several advantages over other cognitive products as a representation of oneself: first of all it involves a selection, frequently conscious and intentional, among autobiographical materials; in addition this information is organized, also from a subjective perspective, in order to stress overall personal meanings; the organization of an autobiographical story emphasizes the continuity among one's past, present, and future, and follows the basic pattern of human life; in doing so, it provides the person with a clear sense of sameness over time and across actions, situations, and choices. As Erikson (e.g., 1959) recognized, these characteristics—subjectivity of interpretation, selection, coherence, sameness, and continuity—seem to be important for personal identity.

But serious questions arise when one tries to understand identity through narrative: Would any story about oneself, even a very coherent one, do what identity is expected to do? Shouldn't the story-as-identity have a relation to the person's life, his or her commitments, his or her projects? Is it not possible that the story we tell about ourselves only satisfies our needs for coherence, for self-exculpation, for self-esteem, and so on, rather than helping us to locate and carve out a space in which our lived relationships, work, and guiding values acquire cultural and historical support? Ultimately there are fundamental differences between a story about oneself and identity: one is the construction of a representation, the other the construction of a life. It is one thing to say that telling one's story is instrumentally essential for the construction of identity, or that one's story reflects one's identity; it is altogether another thing to claim that identity *is* a story.

Perhaps the differences between a story and identity can be condensed around one question, concerning the senses in which one can speak of truth for a story and for identity. A story is true by reference to events that exist independently of it. By contrast, the selection by which identity is constructed is *made true* by the person's investment in it and commitment to it. A person's commitment to his or her ideals validates and authenticates the selection and appropriation of these same ideals as one's identity; at the same time, the validity of these ideals legitimizes their selection as one's identity and one's commitment to them. In summary, identity is true because it is lived in the course of one's life through one's commitment, affective engagement, responsibility, and attention to avoid self-betrayals. In this way, identity is experienced as authentically and individually one's own, the ultimate self-possession. But this is definitely not the case of stories. Once again, a story, like concepts and self-concepts, is a cognitive product. Identity, a late transformation of the subjective self, is not primarily cognitive: its substance and texture consist of self-processes—appropriation, affective investment, responsibility, and commitment.

The self-creating truth of identity can be conveyed by Ricoeur's (1993) example of "keeping one's word." Giving and keeping promises, making and maintaining commitments demand a real kind of sameness, even when the individual's behavioral characteristics have objectively changed. It is not simply a factual sameness—as it can be equally observed in the continuity of a chair, of a plant, and of a young infant; it is a sameness that is subjectively created in the very act of giving a promise or making a commitment. According to Ricoeur, four interrelated characteristics are involved in any person's ability to maintain promises and commitments: The identity of the subject (as opposed to trait consistency); the relation of promising to agency, the sense, namely, that one is the source of both the action of promising and those actions by which the promise can be fulfilled; a sense of ethical responsibility, tying the agent to his or her community; and finally a narrative by which the subject relates to one's character or to the unfolding of personality. The sameness of the person giving his word is produced in the very act of promising, by personal investment in, and self-appropriation of, the promise. Self-knowledge is involved in both keeping a promise and identity; a self-narrative may be required; but we are here within the domain of the self-appropriating subject.

SELF-COGNITION AND SELF-KNOWLEDGE

This chapter has focused on one type of relation that a person can have with him or herself, defined by an active care that is expressed through self-control, self-mastery, and the molding of one's self. But it is possible to relate to oneself in another, more contemplative, way: by trying to determine what one's characteristics are, or to discover one's emotional tendencies, needs, motives and sensibilities, in sum, by pursuing self-knowledge. Should we say, then, that the self, born of the relation one has with oneself, is after all the product of cognition? I think not. Here too I argue that the self, although necessarily related to cognition, is partially independent of it; in fact, that the inverse relation obtains, that knowledge and self-knowledge cannot be achieved without the self and its operations.

But it is useful to start by distinguishing between cognition and knowledge. This distinction is not so common and may be somewhat idiosyncratic, but is far from being arbitrary. By cognition I am mainly referring to the discrimination and the organization of experience and reality by applying to them one's conceptual apparatus and logical structures. These processes are present from the earliest age and frequently occur automatically, independently of conscious intentions. Although the child's interactions with the environment may be guided by conscious goals and intentions, the construction of conceptual tools frequently happens unintentionally and nonconsciously. This is also true of the construction and use of self-concepts and self-schemata. By contrast, *knowing* and *knowledge*, as I use the terms here, are what one does and what one finds, when one asks about the world and oneself the questions, What is this? Is this really so? These questions—they range from the early unverbalized curiosity about the object in itself to the later critical reflection aimed at grounding judgments in evidence—naturally lead to judgments about reality and define what I call the project of knowing. The term *project* is meant to convey the agentic, intentional, and conscious pursuit of a special interest in knowing, even more than the systematic and long-term nature of the acquisition of knowledge (Blasi, 1982).

Of course, cognition and knowledge are closely related to each other and feed on each other: the project of knowing cannot even begin without the application of conceptual categories and logical schemata; vice-versa, knowledge may eventually lead to the conscious construction of new categories and the reorganization of one's conceptual and logical system. All this is well known. In fact, in recent years, there has been considerable interest in extending the study of cognition to those processes and attitudes that are required to arrive at a reflective and critical knowledge (cf. King & Kitchner, 1994; Kuhn, 1999; Moshman, 1998). In these writings one frequently finds the language of agency: the knower recognizes this or that; he or she justifies knowledge; has the intention to conform to epistemic norms; exercises deliberate control and application of inferences; is guided by the ideal of objectivity (these expressions were taken from Moshman, 1999). In my opinion, however, it is not sufficiently appreciated that these and similar practices cannot be understood without explicitly recognizing for the subjective self a central role in the project of knowing. Perhaps we do not fully realize that there is a real break between cognition and knowledge, that the theoretical assumptions that are useful for understanding cognitive processes and conceptual-logical development become inadequate and even misleading when they are extended to the explanation of judgmental and critical processes, in which conscious self-direction is essential.

Naturally asking questions about an object (by contrast with discrimination and categorization) presupposes a conscious separation of the subject from the object, therefore the consciousness of one's self in action.[5] But the continuing importance of the subjective self for knowledge becomes obvious, when one considers that the term *judgment* is not used metaphorically in the context of knowledge. A judgment is not a response or an output, but a statement, a stance, of the subject about an object. In its full meaning, the knower is literally a judge: as such, he or she is and should feel responsible for what he or she claims to be true; he or she is witness for the truth and a guarantor that the object is as he or she claims it to be (Blasi, 1983). Even when knowledge is arrived at socially, through communication and discussion, one cannot relinquish one's personal responsibility for what one believes to be true. As already discussed, responsibility requires ownership and appropriation, and these are processes of the subjective self.

Additionally, the pursuit of knowledge is not always calm and serene, but takes place in a context of conflicting interests. The relation of cognitive processes and conceptual-logical structures to the project of knowing is not as tight as one may think, when cognition is understood according to systemic models; knowledge does not derive automatically and necessarily from concepts or logical structures, or even from reflecting on the tools and strategies one uses. To put it differently, failures of knowing are not simply a result of insufficient competence, errors, or logical fallacies. Rather, cognitive processes and conceptual structures are tools that can be used for various and divergent purposes and can be subordinated to projects that have little or nothing to do with the truth. For instance, one could bring concepts together for practical goals, or for playful and aesthetic purposes; one could use concepts and logic for persuasive and manipulative purposes, as is frequently done in advertising; one could engage in discussions concerning scientific propositions mainly to satisfy one's ambition and one's need for power. One important project in all of us is defensive, aimed at protecting ourselves from anxiety and from possible blows to our self-esteem: in this case, the cognitive armamentarium may be used to screen the truth out and to deceive ourselves (Blasi, 1983).

In summary, pursuing knowledge is intentional and is sometimes guided by conscious choices, including the choice to sacrifice for it the satisfaction of other needs. Therefore, one owns and feels responsible not only for one's judgments, but also for the laborious activity that led to them. If this is true of knowledge in general, it is particularly so for self-knowledge. Here, in the unity and privacy of self-consciousness, distinctions among experiences, needs, or interests, are murky and ambiguous; needs are felt more intensely and conflicts among projects more sharply; self-deceptive strategies are more likely to occur. The project of self-knowledge, then, is more likely to be successful, if the subject engages in a double appropriation: if, on one hand, one values self-knowledge to the point of making of it one's own project, perhaps gives to it a place in the sense of oneself, and feels centrally responsible to pursue it. On the other hand, as Fingarette (1969) cogently argued, many instances of self-deception are a result of the inability to fully own those aspects of oneself—action, decisions, desires, tendencies—that cannot be consciously integrated in the sense of self. In this case, pursuing self-knowledge with care and attention requires being open to one's personal reality, and therefore its acceptance and appropriation by the self. Once again, responsibility and appropriation are operations of the subjective self. To the extent that self-knowledge is dependent on them, to that extent it is dependent on the self.

A CONCLUDING THOUGHT

In this chapter I contrasted two very different conceptions of the self. According to the first, the story starts with cognition, the processes of organizing the world of objects through mental representations. Eventually cognition becomes reflective, differentiating the individual organism from the rest of the environment: here the self originates as one represented object among other objects of representations. About this self, more and more concepts are constructed and are organized in increasingly complex ways, and according to a variety of schemata, including the narrative schema. Here the self is one sub-heading within cognition, which is one chapter of personality functioning. According to the second conception, the story begins with the self, present in the immediate experience of agency and mineness. This subjective self is all pervasive, extending as far as experience and intention go: it underlies and supports physical actions, choices, decisions, and projects about the world of objects and about oneself; it also underlies all cognitive activities that are consciously directed, including those aimed at oneself. The subjective self grows and becomes increasingly differentiated, without ever losing its subjective quality, through mastery, appropriation, and self-appropriation. The ideal goal is autonomy, individuality, and an identity rooted on a hierarchy of commitments.

The advantage of the first approach is that a great deal is known about cognition: the way its different components operate and how they interact with each other; what are its products and how they are organized. Its serious drawback is that cognition does not and cannot explain (beyond descriptive accounts) central human characteristics that are undoubtedly related to the agentic aspect of the subjective self: among them are self-control and self-mastery, responsibility and commitment, independence and autonomy. I am referring here to the actual operation of these characteristics, not to the way they are understood. To wish to explain agency by relying on cognitive representations is a bit like wanting to explain the flying of a bird from the knowledge of its anatomy: one could have a very accurate computer representation of the anatomy of the wings and the rest of the body, but the "bird" will not fly.

One weakness of the account of the self that I proposed is that, as soon as one goes beyond self-cognition and self-understanding, all sounds mysterious and evanescent. We are afraid—this was James' fear—of being brought back to metaphysical ghosts. But this weakness is only apparent, a result of the idea that, to explain the self, we need to go beyond the domain of experience. In my view, a theory of the self only requires the understanding of three cornerstones in their mutual relationships: the indirect and immediate experience of agency and mineness in the very moment of acting; the central processes of appropriation and self-appropriation—their determinants, individual differences, and consequences; and, in particular, establishing the connection between these processes and the variety of self-traits, such as control, responsibility, sense of inner unity and identity, sense of separateness from others and of individuality. This work has yet to begin. This chapter can only suggest the direction.

ENDNOTES

[1]A version of this chapter was presented at the Jean Piaget Society Conference, Montreal, June 1, 2000.

[2]For instance, Kierkegaard wrote: "The self is a relation [i.e., a synthesis of body and soul] which relates to its own self .... The self is not the relation but consists in the fact that the relation relates itself to its own self ..." (1954, p. 146). Namely, "he has himself as a task, ... to order, cultivate, temper, enkindle, repress, in short to bring about a proportionality in the soul, a harmony ..." (1959, p. 267).

[3]James Russell (1995, 1996) strongly emphasizes that agency can only be known from the inside, not from the outside by coding and parsing the actions of agents. He allows that such coding is in principle possible, and that it is plausible that very young infants are endowed with tools to classify behaviors as intentional and nonintentional, purely on the basis of externally observed characteristics. But this is not the same as, nor would it yield, a conception of agency, "because this conception depends on the experience of trying to achieve goals and of being in control of one's body .... It is an experience no less than, say, pain is an experience .... A creature that never felt pain could accu-

rately code pain behavior, but its conception of pain would be empty. The parsing of agency by our imagined system would be similarly empty" (Russell, 1995,
p. 143). Similarly, experiencing agency, or experiencing self, is not a matter of
ascribing predicates. "When a baby of four months extricates its rattle from the
rungs of its cot, it is experiencing agency [and self], not ascribing predicates"
(ib., p. 144).

[4]The concept of appropriation plays a central role in W. James' (1950) account of the self. But James uses the term for two different purposes and endows
it with two very different, and I believe incompatible, meanings. In one context,
appropriation is used to explain the variety of objects that end up being associated with the empirical self and constituting the material, social, and spiritual
selves. In another context, appropriation is used to explain the unity and the
continuity of experience, if one can assume, as James does, that there is no single central unifying subject, but only the stream of separate moments of awareness. The first kind of appropriation is presented as a basically conscious,
agentic act of choice—what he describes as welcoming and rejecting. The second, instead, is presented neither as a choice, since all past moments of the
stream are successively inherited by the following ones up to the present moment, nor as a process of which we are aware. In this second meaning, appropriation is not an experience but is inferred from the experience of unity of
thought. It is quite a feat for James—motivated by metaphysical preoccupations
—to try to explain agency without any agent. In any event, it is clear that James'
account of the self is far from being cognitive.

[5]Piaget was very clear about the central importance for cognitive development of overcoming egocentrism through decentration. But he tended to view
these processes as establishing distinctions among cognitive objects and to deny
any cognitive role for subjectivity. He seemed to believe that objectivity, the goal
of knowledge, can only be arrived at by progressively controlling and eliminat-
ing the intervention of the subject in the cognitive process. He did not quite
grasp the importance for the task of knowing of responsibility and personal
commitment, that is of the subjective self.

REFERENCES

Bermudez, J. L., Marcel, A., & Eilan, N. (Eds.). (1995). *The body and the self.* Cam-
bridge, MA: MIT Press.
Berzonsky, M. D. (1989). The self as a theorist: Individual differences in identity for-
mation. *International Journal of Personal Construct Psychology, 2*, 363–376.
Blasi, A. (1982). Kognition, Erkenntnis, und das Selbst (Knowledge in social cogni-
tion: The role of the self in the acquisition of social knowledge). In W. Edelstein &
M. Keller (Eds.), *Perspektivität und Interpretation* (pp. 289–319). Frankfurt am
Main: Suhrkamp.
Blasi, A. (1983). The self and cognition: The roles of the self in the acquisition of
knowledge, and the role of knowledge in the development of the self. In B. Lee &
G. G. Noam (Eds.), *Developmental approaches to the self* (pp. 189–213). New York:
Plenum Press.

Blasi, A., & Glodis, K. (1995). The development of identity. A critical analysis from the perspective of the self as subject. *Developmental Review, 15,* 404–433.

Cox, B. D., & Lightfoot, C. (Eds.) (1997). *Sociogenetic perspectives on internalization.* Mahwah, NJ: Lawrence Erlbaum Associates.

Epstein, S. (1973). The self-concept revisited, or A theory of a theory. *American Psychologist, 28,* 404–416.

Erikson, E. H. (1959). Identity and the life cycle. *Psychological Issues, 1* (special issue).

Fingarette, H. (1969). *Self-deception.* London: Routledge & K. Paul.

Foucault, M. (1985). *The use of pleasure.* New York: Pantheon Books.

Foucault, M. (1986). *The care of the self.* New York: Pantheon Books.

Foucault, M. (1997). The hermeneutics of the subject. In P. Rabinow (Ed.), *Ethics, subjectivity, and truth. Essential works of Foucault* (Vol. 1, pp. 93–106). New York: The New Press.

Frankfurt, H. G. (1988). *The importance of what we care about: Philosophical essays.* New York: Cambridge University Press.

Greenwald, A. G. (1980). The totalitarian ego: Fabrication and revision of personal history. *American Psychologist, 35,* 603–618.

James, W. (1950). *The principles of psychology.* New York: Dover Publications. (Originally published 1890)

Kierkegaard, S. (1954). *The sickness unto death* (W. Lowrie, Trans.). New York: Anchor Books. (Originally published, 1849)

Kierkegaard, S. (1959). *Either/Or, Vol. II* (W. Lowrie, Trans.). New York: Anchor Books. (Originally published, 1843)

King, P. M., & Kitchener, K. S. (1994). *Developing reflective judgment: Understanding and promoting intellectual growth and critical thinking in adolescents and adults.* San Francisco: Jossey-Bass.

Kuhn, D. (1999). Metacognitive development. In L. Balter & C. S. Tamis-LeMonda (Eds.), *Child psychology: A handbook of contemporary issues* (pp. 259–286). Philadelphia, PA: Psychology Press/Taylor & Francis.

McAdams, D. P. (1990). Unity and purpose in human lives: The emergence of identity as a life story. In A. I. Rabin, R. A. Zucker, R. E. Emmons, & S. Frank (Eds.), *Studying persons and lives* (pp. 148–200). New York: Springer-Verlag.

Moshman, D. (1998). Cognitive development beyond childhood. In W. Damon (Series Ed.), D. Kuhn & R. Siegler (Vol. Eds.), *Handbook of child psychology: Vol. 2. Cognition, perception, and language* (5th ed., pp. 947–978). New York: Wiley.

Moshman, D. (1999). *Adolescent psychological development. Rationality, morality, and identity.* Mahwah, NJ: Lawrence Erlbaum Associates.

Plato. (1963). Apologia (H. Tredennick, Trans.). In E. Hamilton & H. Cairns (Eds.), *The collected dialogues,* Bollinger Series LXXI. Princeton, NJ: Princeton University Press.

Ricoeur, P. (1993). Self as *Ipse.* In B. Johnson (Ed.), *Freedom and interpretation. The Oxford Amnesty Lectures 1992* (pp. 103–119). New York: Basic Books.

Rochat, P. (Ed.). (1995). *The self in infancy. Theory and research.* Amsterdam: Elsevier.

Russell, J. (1995). At two with nature: Agency and the development of self-world dualism. In J. L. Bermudez, A. Marcel, & N. Eilan (Eds.), *The body and the self* (pp. 127–151). Cambridge, MA: MIT Press.

Russell, J. (1996). *Agency: Its role in mental development.* Hove, England: Lawrence Erlbaum Associates.

Shindler, C. P. (2001). *Integration of religious commitment in personality: Its relation to ego development and cognitive complexity.* Unpublished doctoral dissertation, University of Massachusetts, Boston.

Valsiner, J. (1997). *Culture and the development of children's action: A theory of human development* (2nd ed.). New York: Wiley.

Chapter 2

Ricoeur, Narrative and Personal Identity

Donald Polkinghorne
University of Southern California

People undergo constant change throughout their lives. They change physically from a babe in someone's arms to a robust adolescent to a less robust elder. Throughout their life they engage in a multitude of various activities, think all sorts of thoughts, and undergo changing moods and emotions. Yet, in spite of the ongoing flux that people undergo during their lives, they still sense that underneath the changing surface of their lives, they are essentially one and the same person. In the Western tradition, this self-sameness and unity was attributed to having a soul. Who one was, was essentially one's soul. At birth (or conception) one's soul entered one's emerging body and remained connected to the body until the body perished. Then the self-same soul continued to exist after the death of the body. Thus, personal identity was bestowed at birth and lasted for eternity. For some theological positions, a person's lifetime actions and/or faith was judged and on the basis of this judgment, one's soul went to heaven or hell where it remained for eternity or until the second coming.

The idea that one's personal identity was situated in one's soul (or in one's soul-like mind) was sustained after the advent of the scientific investigation of nature by the modernist proposition that there were two kinds of reality. There was a spiritual (or mental) reality, which had no extension in space, and a physical reality, which had spatial extension. One's soul, the seat of one's personal identity, had the spiritual kind of reality, and, thus, was not susceptible to the laws that governed nature. The things in the world, including one's own and other's bodies, had the physical kind of reality and could be investigated with scientific procedures. In this model, the idea of soul was joined with idea of mind and gained the property of knower. Thus, who one truly is, has homunculus-like characteristics of that aspect of personhood that knows.

In the last decades of the 20th century, the dualist view of modernist philosophy was overturned and philosophy was secularized. The notion of mind was naturalized and its modernist connection with soul was abandoned. With the overturning of dualism, the notion that one's personal identity was identified with one's soul was no longer philosophically supportable. The notion of a homunculus-like knower was rejected and the very idea of a personal self or identity was questioned. Instead, the new postmodern philosophy advocated that the idea of self had no actual referent; that is, there was no real self and no real center of personal identity. It proposed that the idea of a personal self was an artifact of a subject-verb language grammar.

The narrative approach to personal identity occurs within the context of the postmodern rejection of the idea that personal identity is linked to a person's unchanging soul-like mind. However, the narrative approach takes seriously people's experience of having a self-identity. It retains the postmodern position that understanding (including self-understanding and personal identity) is affected by the language in which it is articulated. The narrative approach holds that people construct and recognize their identity through the narrative or storied form of understanding.

This chapter begins with sections on the idea of personal identity and on the narrative form of expression. After that is a section outlining two opposing positions about the connection between narrative form and life experience. The final and major section of the chapter describes Paul Ricoeur's "middle way" in which the oppositions are integrated into a substantially deepened understanding of the role of narrative in the process of personal identity formation.

NARRATIVE AND PERSONAL IDENTITY

Bruner proposed that people primarily understand and make sense of their experience in two different cognitive operations. One operation, which he called *paradigmatic* cognition, gives meaning by identifying things and incidents as instances of a particular category. Paradigmatic knowing operates by determining what kind of thing something is. The second operation, which he called *narrative* cognition, gives meaning by relating actions or occurrences to an outcome. Narrative knowing operates by linking or configuring a series of events on the basis of their facilitation or prevention of the achievement of a goal.

Paradigmatic answers to the question "Who am I?" are given by identifying oneself as an instance of a conceptual category; for example, "I am a male," "I am a college professor," "I am a citizen of the United States." These kinds of answers about one's identity are often asked for on college admission and job application forms, but the self-descriptions they offer are thin and lack the richness and complexity of the person we experience ourselves to be. We are active agents who have engaged in actions that were expected to accomplish goals. Some of what we hoped to accomplish we have achieved, whereas other hopes have not been realized. The description of who one is needs to display the rich and complex unfolding of one's life process over time. Simple paradigmatic categorization of the category memberships into which one fits, although helpful in certain settings, is too limiting to capture the development and movement through the manifold episodes that make up one's life.

Narrative is the form of cognition that links one's life episodes into a whole and thereby gives one's identity a unity and self-sameness through time. When we want someone to know who we really are, we tell them our life story. The notion that our personal identities are maintained as life-stories has been the focus of much contemporary scholarship. For example, Hermans' *Self-Narratives* (1995), Kerby's *Narrative and the Self* (1991), McAdams' *A Life-Story Model of Identity* (1985) and *Stories We Live By* (1993), Randall's *The Stories We Are* (1995), and my *Narrative and Self-Concept* (1991) have addressed the function of self-stories in establishing personal identity. The relation of self-story to identity has also appeared in recent psychotherapeutic literature. In the psychoanalytic literature Spence (1984) and Shafer (1992) have proposed that therapy consists of engaging clients in the development of life-stories that characterize themselves as unified and whole selves. White and Epston (1990) have proposed an approach to therapy that they call *narrative therapy*. In their approach clients are viewed as the protagonists in their own life-stories and the therapeutic process involves assisting clients to re-vision their self-story as one in which they are active agents rather than passive victims (Parry & Doan, 1994).

Narrative cognition is articulated in the linguistic form of telling and writing stories. In the narrative literature, the term *narrative* is used to refer both to the cognitive operations involved in narrative understanding and to the storied texts in which it is expressed. Narrative is a type of thought and type of discourse in which multiple actions, happenings, and events are synthesized into a temporal unity or story. The understanding produced in narrative discourse reflects people's lives as lived and, thus, can elicit emotional responses. Hearing or reading a story can produce feelings that relate to the life events depicted in the text.

"People do not deal with the world event by event or with text sentence by sentence. They frame events and sentences in larger structures" (Bruner, 1990, p. 64). The operation that transforms the many incidents into a single story is emplotment. Emplotment relates the elements of a story to a result by noting their contributions to achieving or failing to achieve an outcome. A plot organizes into a totality various story components. The elements a plot gathers together are "unintended circumstances, discoveries, those who perform actions and those who suffer them, chance or planned encounters, interactions between actors ranging from conflict to collaboration, means that are well or poorly adjusted to ends, and finally unintended results" (Ricoeur, 1991, p. 21).

Plot is the narrative structure through which people understand and describe the relationship among the events and choices of their lives. Plots function to compose or configure events into a story by: a) delimiting a temporal range that marks the beginning and end of the story, b) providing criteria for the selection of events to be included in the story, c) temporally ordering events into an unfolding movement culminating in a conclusion, and d) clarifying or making explicit the meaning events have as contributors to the story as a unified whole.

Plots mark off a segment of time in which events are linked together as contributors to a particular outcome. The segment of time can range from the boundless (the story of God's creation of the universe), to centuries (the story of the settlement of the United States), to life times (biographies), to daily or hourly episodes (the story of going shopping). In each case the plot establishes the beginning and end of the storied segment, thereby creating the temporal boundaries for the narrative Gestalt. Plots also function to select from the myriad of happenings those that are direct contributors to the terminal situation of the story (Carr, 1986). For example, if the plot of the story concerns a person's winning a game, those events and actions pertinent to the winning are selected for inclusion in the highlighted figure of the story. Other events, such as the clothes worn, the day on which the game was played, the eating of breakfast, and so forth, because they are not central to the plot, are included simply as background.

The subject matter of stories is human action. Stories are concerned with human attempts to progress to a solution, clarification, or unraveling of an incomplete situation. "Other things exist in time, but only humans possess the capacity to perceive the connectedness of life and to seek its coherence" (Vanhoozer, 1991, p. 43). Stories are linguistic expressions of this uniquely human experience of the connectedness of life (Ricoeur, 1992). The ground of storied expressions is the phenomenon of individual protagonists engaged in an ordered transformation from an initial situation to a terminal situation. The capacity to understand stories derives from the correlation between the unfolding of a story and the temporal character of human experience and the human pre-understanding of human action (Ricoeur, 1984). Although the protagonists of stories can be expanded by analogizing to institutions, organizations, or groups of people and by anthropomorphizing to animals (as in fairy tales), these story forms retain the primary character of an imitation of personal action (Aristotle, 1954).

Mandler (1984) writes that a fully developed narrative accounting begins with a setting in which a narrator introduces the characters, the location, and the time in which the story takes place. After the setting has been established, the story proceeds with one or more episodes, each of which has a beginning and a development. In the episode, the protagonist, reacting to the beginning events, sets a direction and outlines a path to achieve an outcome. Each episode includes the outcome of the attempts to reach the goal and assumes that the attempts are understood as the causes that bring about the outcome. When the outcome has been given, the episode ends, and the ending links the episode to the whole story. After the whole series of episodes has been presented, the narrative includes an ending portion that coalesces the episodes into one story.

Storied narratives are ubiquitous in people's lives. In everyday conversation people tell stories about their own and others' life episodes and they listen to similar stories told by other conversational partners. People are also engaged with stories when they view television, motion pictures, and dramas and when they read novels and histories. Among the many stories that people tell and hear, there is a distinct type of story—the story about one's own life, that is, the self-story. Self-stories differ from the ordinary stories people tell about themselves in that the subject matter of self-stories is their whole life time, rather than a time-limited life episode (i.e., stories about a difficult drive to work, about attending a baseball game, or about a recent vacation trip). The genre of the self-story is a type of autobiography; however, it differs from autobiographies crafted for public consumption in that the function of self-stories is to provide an answer to the question "Who am I?" McAdams (1993) describes the self-story as "a special kind of story that each of us naturally constructs to bring together different parts of ourselves and our lives into a purposeful and convincing whole" (p. 12). Randall (1995) says that people have an autobiographical imperative or push to consider the story of their particular self in their search for identity.

The scholar who has pursued the relation of narrative and personal identity in greatest depth is Paul Ricoeur, and it is his work that is the focus of this chapter. Ricoeur first addressed narrative identity in the *Conclusion* of the third volume of *Time and Narrative* (Ricoeur, 1985). He returned to this theme in chapters written for Wood's *On Paul Ricoeur* (Wood, 1991) and in his *Oneself As Another* (Ricoeur, 1992). Ricoeur argues that narrative integrates life events and actions into a unified whole, that it captures the temporal nature of human existence, and that it overcomes the disjunction between the experience of being the same person throughout one's life and the experience of changing through life experience. The problem that Ricoeur says was "absolutely central" to him was the relation between [narrative] art and life (in Carr, Taylor & Ricoeur, 1991). That is, is life as lived structured narratively or does narrative impose a foreign structure on life? If, as McIntosh states "unconscious thought [life as lived] has a distinctive and coherent structure of its own ... which stands in sharp contrast to the structure and character that language brings to thought" (1995), what relationship holds between identity described in narrative discourse and identity as felt in life as lived? The basic theme of this chapter is Ricoeur's attempt to solve the riddle of the disparity between life and narrative discourse as the source of personal identity. Are we the conceptualized and languaged presentation of our selves or are we the nonlanguaged felt meaning of who we are?

NARRATIVE AND LIFE

The linguistic turn in philosophy and its evolution into post-structuralism and social constructionism has served to make the relation between the self as lived and the self as described narrative problematic. The concern of these two groups is not if the contents of life-narratives are accurate representations of the person's life they are describing. That is, are the facts of the story true; did the father molest the daughter or not? Rather, the concern is if the structure of narrative discourse matches the structure of life as lived. Chatman (1978) points out that narrative structure is itself semiotic-that is, it "communicates meaning in its own right, over and above the paraphraseable contents of its story" (p. 23). Narrative structure imparts meaning because it transforms individual events and actions into a connected whole.

Two opposite positions exist regarding whether or not life itself is structured in a narrative manner. One group of narrative theorists holds that life structure and narrative structure are discontinuous; the other group holds that they are continuous. The problematic represented by these two groups is the focus of Ricoeur's efforts. Before moving to Ricoeur's attempted solution, I draw out the problematic in more detail.

Life versus Narrative

Although most narrative theorists do not go so far as the social constructionists and deny the existence of a self, many do accept a position influenced by the poststructuralist understanding that language is severed from an extralinguistic reality and that our languaged constructions do not correspond to objects to which they ostensibly refer. The position of these theorists has been termed by Carr (1991) as the standard view of narrative.

Their view is that the literary form of narrative, with its linkage of life events and actions as contributors to a final outcome, is an imposed structure and is not descriptive of life as lived. Life consists of a mere sequence of events in which one thing simply follows after the other; it is not the connected unity that narrative depicts. Narrated life stories are distortions, not descriptions, of life as lived.

Leading narrative theorists who hold that there is a discontinuity between life-stories and life as lived are: (a) Kermode (1967), who in his *The Sense of an Ending* wrote: "In 'making sense' of the world we ... feel a need ... to experience that concordance of beginning, middle and end which is the essence of our explanatory fictions" (pp. 35–36). But he says that the coherent properties of the story should not be ascribed to the real. (b) Chatman (1978) in *Story and Discourse* said that the unified temporality of the beginning-middle-end emplotment "apply to the narrative, to story-events as imitated, rather than to real actions themselves, simply because such terms are meaningless in the real world" (p. 47). (c) Mink's (1979) often quoted aphorism reads: "Stories are not lived but told. Life has no beginnings, middles, or ends" (pp. 557–558). And, (d) White in a chapter titled "The Value of Narrativity in the Representation of Reality" (1981) asked rhetorically, "What wish is enacted, what desire is gratified, by the fantasy that real events are properly represented when they can be shown to display the formal coherency of a story" (p. 4)? "Does the world really present itself to perception in the form of well made stories ...? Or does it present itself more in the way that the annals and chronicles suggest, either as a mere sequence without beginning or end or as sequences of beginnings that only terminate and never conclude" (p. 23)?

Carr, in *Time, Narrative, and History* (1986), identified Ricoeur with the standard view; and in a later work (1991) acknowledged that although Ricoeur "does not pose the 'art vs life' question in quite explicit terms as I [Carr] have" (p. 167), in the end, he "courts the same consequence" (p. 173) as those holding the standard view. As I show later, I disagree with Carr's assessment of Ricoeur's position and see Ricoeur as creatively bridging the differences between life and its narrative description.

Life as Narrative

Other narrative theorists oppose the standard view's position that there is a noncoherence between narrative structure and life structure. They hold that life itself is structured narratively. Carr (1991) holds the life as narrative position. He recognizes that narrative structure constructs through the device of emplotment a synthesis of diverse life elements. Narrative emplotment effects a "synthesis of the heterogeneous" (p. 172) in three ways: (a) it unites a series of actions or events into a larger unity; (b) it brings together goals, means, interactions, circumstances, unexpected results, and so on; and (c) it "unites the levels of temporality by surmounting the merely sequential with the configural" (p. 172). But Carr asks, "Is life not, itself, already precisely a synthesis of the heterogeneous?" (p. 172). In life we unite events together when we engage in complex and long term efforts; we bring together goals and means with plans, and we experience time (as Husserl has shown), not as mere sequence, but as essentially configural. Narrative discourse is a mirroring of the sort of activity of which life consists. Life is not chaotic whereas narratives are well formed, nor is life confused whereas narratives are orderly. Life, too, is well formed and orderly. Carr states that he has been "urging that narration is not only a mode of discourse but more essentially a mode, perhaps *the* mode of life" (p. 173).

MacIntyre (1981) is another advocate of the notion that life as lived essentially manifests a narrative form. He says, "We all live out narratives in our lives and … we understand our own lives in terms of the narrative that we live out" (p. 212). For MacIntyre, narratives are inextricable from life as lived. Hardy (1968) also holds the view that life is lived in narrative form. "We dream in narrative, day-dream in narrative, remember, anticipate, hope and love by narrative" (p. 5). The life as narrative position holds that life is innately structured narratively. Narrative structuring is not a format learned from our culture and then used to construct a coherent identity. As an illustration of this point, Bruner (1990) in *Acts of Meaning* writes: "We have an 'innate' and primitive predisposition to narrative organization that allows us quickly and easily to comprehend and use it" (p. 80). There is a prelinguistic readiness for narrative that is triggered by the acts and expressions of others, and "narrative structure is even inherent in the praxis of social interaction before it achieves linguistic expression" (p. 77).

RICOEUR'S MOVE THROUGH THE DICHOTOMY

Is there a way to move through the two positions regarding the correlation of the meaning inherent in narrative structure and the meaning inherent in life as it is lived-through? The narrative versus life position is that there is no correlation—narrative structuration imparts a coherence and temporal unity to events although unreflective lived life itself is discordant and consists of disconnected episodes following one after another. The life as narrative position is the idea that life as lived is directly and literally structured as a narrative discourse. I believe that the most thorough attempt to move through this dichotomy has been undertaken by Ricoeur. He was unwilling to accept that either position was completely correct or completely in error. I describe his strategy in some detail because I think his approach may be transferable to resolving other impasses in understanding the relation between language and lived life.

Ricoeur's strategy is derived from his continuing interest in the negotiation between "living experience and [languaged] conceptualization" (1995b, p. 123). He accepts the idea that there is a realm of human life that is outside language to which language can refer; this acceptance differentiates him from the poststructuralists. Ricoeur, however, also accepts the notion that the structure and conceptual network of a language does not literally produce a mirrored description of the realm of human life. Because direct discourse and lived life are made up of dissimilar structures and elements, Ricoeur turned to language's capacity to be used artistically and figuratively to reveal structures which would have remained unrecognized without art (Carr et al., 1991). Ricoeur, before his investigation of narrative identity, had rejected Husserl's assumption that reflection on one's own consciousness was cognitively privileged. In his explorations in *The Symbolism of Evil* (1969) and *Freud and Philosophy* (1970), he came to appreciate the limits of literal language to penetrate life's experiences. This appreciation led him to advocate the necessity of interpreting texts if one were to gain access to their references about human experience.

His interest in the symbolic meaning of language resulted in more intense study of figural, as distinct from literal, language usage. He investigated two artistic language innovations—metaphor and narrative—that produce meaning-effects that reveal aspects of life, covered over in the literal use of language. In *The Rule of Metaphor* (Ricoeur, 1977), he described how, through the use of metaphor, new meaning is produced by the resistance of words in their ordinary use and in their incompatibility at the level of the literal interpretation of a sentence. In *Time and Narrative* (Ricoeur, 1984–1989), he described how narrative similarly reveals new meaning by means of the plot. In both metaphor and narrative, "The new thing—the as yet unsaid, the unwritten-springs up in language. Here a living metaphor, that is a new pertinence in the predication, there a feigned plot, that is a new congruence in the organization of the events" (1984, p. ix). Thus, through imaginative use of language a new species of meaning is created in spite of the resistance of current categorizations and structures of language. Metaphor operates at the level of sentences, whereas narrative operates as the level of discourse. As Ricoeur stated: "Whereas metaphorical redescription reigns in the field of sensory, emotional, aesthetic, and axiological values, ... [the] function of plots takes place by preference in the field of action and of its temporal values" (p. xi).

Ricoeur proposed that although language neither describes reality nor is severed from reality, it does serve to redescribe reality. In his "Intellectual Autobiography" (Ricoeur, 1995a), he remembers having raised the question "Was the distinction between sense and reference still valid in the case of metaphorical statements" and "Could one say of metaphor that it uncovered aspects, dimensions of the real world that direct discourse left hidden"

(p. 28)? And he reached the conclusion that: "It is the language freest of all prosaic constraints ... that is most available to express the secret of things" (p. 28).

For Ricoeur, the art of narrative discourse provides a clearing for the appearance of life as lived; however, the meaning produced by the structure of the narrative text is not a replica of human existence as it is lived. To clarify the dynamic relation that holds between life as lived and life as emplotted in narrative, Ricoeur sought to untangle the notion of mimesis or imitation, which Aristotle had represented as the essential characteristic of narrative. Ricoeur recognized three processes in which selfhood is imitated (mimesis): (a) the process in which one's originary or pre-linguistic feeling of selfhood is sensed—$mimesis_1$ (b) the process in which one's selfhood is articulated in a narrative composition—$mimesis_2$, and (c) the process in which one's selfhood is transformed by integrating one's articulated understanding of who one is with the felt sense of who one is—$mimesis_3$. Ricoeur understands that narrative mimesis or imitation of life is an unfolding process that moves through these three senses of mimesis. The answer to who one is (i.e., one's personal identity) does not appear immediately out of the words of the story of one's life, but only becomes apparent as one circles through the three senses of emplotment. The understanding that narrative gives of the self is derived through circling through the mimetic parts to whole self and from whole to the parts; that is, the personal identity derives from a kind of understanding described by the phrase *hermeneutic circle*. Understanding the self as a whole is dependent on understanding the three senses of mimesis and the understanding of the mimesis comes from knowledge of the whole. The three senses of narrative mimesis are not separate parts that are synthesized into a story; rather they are three perspectives on a unified figure. In this they resemble the changing appearances of the single drawing of a Necker cube. The remainder of the chapter addresses the three appearances of the narrative self that come into view as one examines one's self-story. I employ Ricoeur's nomenclature—$mimesis_1$, $mimesis_2$, and $mimesis_3$—to designate the three senses of narrative imitation of life.

Mimesis$_1$

$Mimesis_1$ is the felt sense we have of who we are that underlies the articulated narrative compositions we tell about ourselves. Although the felt sense is not languaged, it does have sufficient content to inform and guide the stories ($mimesis_2$) we construct about our personal identity. $Mimesis_1$ is the sense we have of our lives as they are lived. Life as lived is not experienced as having the same level of coherence that is described in the stories we tell about it. In our everyday, unreflective activity, we do not experience our actions and life events as fully integrated parts of a plot; but neither are they experienced as mere disconnected fragments following one after another.

Ricoeur holds that the primordial experiences we have about ourselves, although not in narrative form, do have a "prenarrative quality." For him, the prenarrative characteristic of lived-through experience is derived from an inherent understanding that people have that human actions differ in kind from physical movements. Ricoeur uses the term *prenarrative* because, although recognition that actions are carried out to accomplish intended outcomes is a necessary element for constructing a narrative, it is not sufficient. In addition to recognizing the purposeful character of actions, narrative composition requires the configurative force of an articulated plot in order to give unity to multiple and diverse life actions and incidents. Thus, life as lived is felt as inchoate or incipient narratives; it appears as unfinished and "constitutes a demand for narrative" (1984, p. 74). Our prefigured felt life experiences call for a reflective review that can consider the intended effects of our actions as well as the unintended effects (which we could not have been aware of at the time of the act). The reflective review integrates the prenarrative understandings we had at the time of the happenings with understandings that we now have from the perspective of hindsight.

Ricoeur (1991) defines the operation of emplotment as "a synthesis of heterogeneous elements" (p. 21). He holds that the narrative structure is the appropriate mode of discourse most suited to portraying personal identity because our pre-expressed, prelanguaged, preconfigured experience is an unfinished identity and calls out for completion through narrative configuration. He believes that our prelanguaged experience of ourselves has a quasinarrative structure in that it has already organized experience as purposeful actions and temporally related.

Although the articulated narration of what we have been and seek to be adds the unifying structure that displays one's identity through time as the self-same person, the narrative self does not display all that is felt about who we are. Merleau-Ponty (1945/1962) points to an awareness of one's self that stands behind the languaged descriptions about it. "Behind the spoken *cogito*, the one which is converted into discourse and into essential truth, there lies a tacit *cogito*, myself experienced by myself .... The tacit *cogito*, the presence of oneself to oneself ... is anterior to any philosophy" (p. 403). In addition to our languaged awareness of ourselves, there is a tacit, nonlanguaged awareness of self. Life as lived is "never completely comprehensible, [and] what I understand never quite tallies with my living experiences, in short, I am never quite at one with myself" (p. 347).

McIntosh, in his *Self, Person, World* (McIntosh, 1995) offers a description of the tacit and nonlanguaged awareness we have of ourselves. Using Stern's (1985) investigations of the ways a maturing child develops struc-

tural strategies for organizing experience, McIntosh argues that development is cumulative. Organizing schemes developed at various phases in life
are not replaced by later ones, but they remain active in the present. This
description of adult life differs from that assumed by Piaget and Kohlberg
who hold that when people become adults they discard the structure strategies developed in earlier stages of life. For example, Piaget's adults who
have achieved the level of formal operational intelligence no longer experiences the world as they did during their stage of sensori-motor intelligence.
For McIntosh, however, adults retain the multiple structural strategies they
have employed during the various periods of their development. Thus,
adults do not simply structure their experience of themselves and the world
in a single, fully mature mode, but, rather in many discordant modes.

Stern (1985) reports that there is sufficient research about the first two
months of life to call into question Freud's belief that the infant does not differentiate him or herself from others. The experience of preverbal infants
is not an undifferentiated buzz, but one in which the "yoking of diverse experiences is accompanied by distinct subjective experiences" (p. 60). Stern
holds that infants develop multiple senses of their self as they organize their
experiences of interaction with others and the world (pp. 37–68). He has
identified four senses of self which, although appearing at different periods
of ontogenetic development, remain part of our adult repertoire of self understanding. The four senses are of: (a) an emergent self, which forms from
birth to age two months; (b) a core self, which forms between the ages of two
and six months; (c) a subjective self, which forms between seven to fifteen
months; and, (d) a verbal self, which forms with the acquisition of language.
As noted before, "These senses of self are not viewed as successive phases
that replace one another. Once formed, each sense of self remains fully
functioning and active throughout life. All continue to grow and coexist"
(Stern, 1985, p. 11). The three earliest senses of self appear before the acquisition of language and continue to function in their original preverbal
forms and as unarticulated, direct experiences throughout one's life-time.

1. The emergent sense of self. The first sense of self derives from the
   infant's experience of its own body: its coherence, actions, inner
   feeling states, and the memory of all these. (See Bauer, 1996 for a
   more recent investigation of memory in infants.) The processes involved in the formation of the sense of an emergent self are:
   amodal perception, physiognomic perception, and the perception
   of vitality affects (e.g., notice of change in the rate of movement,
   change in intensity of sound, or changes in feelings of hunger).
   "The global subjective world of emerging organization is and remains the fundamental domain of human subjectivity. It operates
   out of awareness as the experiential matrix from which thoughts

and perceived forms and identifiable acts and verbalized feeling will later arise" (Stern, 1985, p. 67).

2. The core self. Stern reports that a shift occurs in infants at the age of two to three months in which they appear to move to an integrated sense of themselves "as distinct and coherent bodies, with control over their own actions, ownership of their own affectivity, a sense of continuity, and a sense of other people as distinct and separate interactants" (1985, p. 69). These characteristics constitute a second development in the infant's sense of self. Stern refers to this new sense of self as the sense of a core self. The sense of the core self is composed of four self-experiences: (a) the sense of self-agency—the infant can direct his or her actions (the arm moves when the infant wants it to); (b) the sense of self-coherence—the infant recognizes him or herself as a nonfragmented, physical whole with boundaries; (c) the sense of self-affectivity—the infant experiences patterned inner qualities of feelings, and (d) self-history—the infant has the sense of enduring and a sense of continuity with his or her own past.

3. The subjective self. The third sense of self occurs when an infant discovers that he or she has a mind and that others have minds as well. This realization occurs between the seventh and ninth month of life and leads to the sense of a subjective self. The infant gains awareness that what is going on in his or her mind may be similar enough to what is going on in others' minds that communication (without words) can take place.

4. The verbal self. With the advent of language use during the second year of life, a new layer is added to the child's sense of self. Acquisition of language profoundly changes the contents of experience. Unlike the previous layers of the sense of self, the sense of a verbal self does not derive from the senses that come before it. Where the preverbal world of the infant consists wholly of materially existing objects and their actions and interactions, with language comes a huge expansion of the categorical understanding of the world. Before language, infants categorize on the basis of bundles or syndromes of features (primarily the physical features of objects). Categories are conceptualized as prototypes and objects are recognized on the basis of the resemblance to these prototypes. With language the categorization prevalent in the infant's culture is acquired. Languaged category systems are culturally contingent and, "in our culture, more or less at odds with what is innate" (McIntosh, 1995, p. 61). The relativism of the languaged world stands in contrast to the cross-cultural uniformity of the preverbal worlds we inhabit. Experiences and the senses of self that arise in

the domains of emergent, core, and subjective relatedness, and
which continue irrespective of language, "can be embraced only
very partially in the domain of verbal relatedness" (Stern, 1985, pp.
162–163). The sensual, sensory richness of preverbal experience is
sacrificed in the packaging of experience into language.

In McIntosh's and Stern's depiction, beneath our adult articulated self
identity are the three felt, but nonlanguaged, senses of self. Although these
senses of self are subject to modification and evolution as maturation proceeds, in their fundamental aspects they endure throughout our lives as the
foundations on which our full sense of personal identity rests. These nonlanguaged senses are not lesser aspects of our identity but are an integral
and vital part of who we are.

Simms, in her 1993 article in *The Humanistic Psychologist*, sees a convergence between Stern's descriptions of the infant's experience of the world
and Merleau-Ponty's conception of the lived world and of incarnate subjectivity. Simms notes that "both Merleau Ponty and Stern see the emergence
of the symbolic capacity of the self in the second year of the infant's life as a
rift that alienates the lived experience from the symbolized experience" (p.
39). The nonlanguaged senses of self are embodied senses. Merleau-Ponty
locates the primal source of our understanding in our body's perceptual involvement in the world. The perceptual world is not posited by a poststruc-
tural language system but is the product of one's bodily presence in the
world. Merleau-Ponty calls for our return from the empiricists' and ratio-
nalists' abstracted depictions of the real to the origins of the appearance of
the world to us "at the very center of our experience; we must describe the
emergence of being and we must understand how, paradoxically, there is
for us an in-itself" (1945/1962, p. 71). "We must return to the *cogito* in search
of a more fundamental *Logos* than that of objective thought, one which endows the latter with its relative validity, and at the same time assigns to it its
place" (p. 365). To know who we are means taking into account more than
our objective notions about our identity; it requires being in touch with the
felt meanings accompanying our fundamental perceptual experiences.

In her concluding paragraph, Simms (1993) links Stern and Merleau-Ponty
through their summons to enlarge the personal identify beyond that which can
be displayed through linguistically provided categories by including the preverbal senses of the self.

For both authors … language can still reach toward a self that experiences
the world fully. Stern's insistence that the preverbal senses of the self still co-
exist with the verbal self in the adult, and Merleau-Ponty's insistence that
language itself is rooted in the gestures of the body—both call us to conceive
of a primordial, interpersonal and meaningful relationship with the world

that grounds our adult conceptions in an innocent and direct engagement of body and world." (p. 39)

Stern's and Merleau-Ponty's descriptions of the felt sense of self that underlay and inform our articulated self-stories extend Ricoeur's account of the prenarrative felt self (mimesis$_1$). Stern's (1985) review of the research literature on early childhood shows that the prelanguaged senses of the self are less discordant and more structured than Ricoeur thought. The aspect of discordance in the pre-narrative experience that Ricoeur addressed is the temporal discontinuity among life's action events. The co-existence of four differently structured senses of the self by Stern adds another aspect of discordance. Thus, the unifying function of narrative configuration is called on to connect the actions and happenings of our lives and to integrate the various nonlinguistic senses of self.

Mimesis$_2$

Mimesis$_2$ refers to the configured self-story. Narrative plots imitate life as lived by configuring actions and felt sense into meaningful wholes and thereby unveil an order and coherence that was not previously experienced. Merleau-Ponty writes that we are not "a succession of 'psychic' acts ... but one single experience inseparable from itself, one single 'living cohesion'" (1945/1962, p. 407). Narrative structuring (mimesis$_2$) serves to accomplish the move from the disjunctive felt senses of self in life as lived (mimesis$_1$) to a unified identity that is inherent, but not yet accomplished, in our pre-narrative existence.

The construction of a narrative self-story consists of more than simply gathering together the discordant elements present in mimesis$_1$ and laying them out in chronological order. Language brings its own categories and structures through which it organizes the differently structured prenarrative world. The story transforms the prenarrative experience through the generative power of emplotment structure. However, the relationship between the prenarrative mimesis$_1$ and the narrated mimesis$_2$ is one of mutual influence. The configured story affects the nonlanguaged understandings of the self as well as being affected by them. The self-story also serves to enhance the presence of weak or forgotten elements of the prenarrative world. By being configured the senses of the self are themselves reshaped and absent relationships among the senses are established and stabilized. Perhaps, most importantly, narrative configuration introduces history into one's personal identity. "[I understand my past] by following it up with a future which will be seen after the event as foreshadowed by it, thus introducing historicity into my life" (Merleau-Ponty, 1945/1962, p. 346).

Ricoeur proposed that life as lived "is no more than a biological phenomenon as long as it has not been interpreted" (1991, p. 28). Mimesis$_2$ is the interpretation and understanding of life as lived as it takes on the form of emplotment. The plots of our personal identity remain attached to our reformed and stabilized prenarrative senses of self. The continued presence of these senses serve as correctives or guides to the reflectively produced story. Not just any telling can authentically integrate the prenarrative into an acceptable account. The "felt meanings" of prenarrative living serve to identify phrases and plots which more closely conform to the non-languaged pre-understandings of personal actions (Gendlin, 1991).

The nonlanguaged senses of self can not be translated transparently into languaged personal narrative. In their telling or writing, the senses of self undergo a transformation. There are significant differences between the identity story as it is lived and the story as it is told. In order for experiential meaning to be expressed in language, it has to be converted into literary form and, thus, comply with the requirements of a language's grammatical structure and sign system (Gendlin, 1991). Told stories are also affected by the audience to whom they are communicated, whether it is research interviewers or an anticipated reader of one's autobiography. When told stories are produced as part of a conversation or interview, they are shaped by the questions and responses of the person to whom they are told. The resulting story is no longer the exclusive product of the teller alone, but can be said to be co-authored (McLaughlin & Tierney, 1993) by both the teller and the listening partner.

As a retrospective process of attributing meaning to one's life events and actions, narrative is more than a simple recounting of one's life activities as they were experienced; they are newly created configurations. Several elements of narrative construction produce stories that are not simple journal-like reproductions of life as it was lived: These elements are: (a) memory as reconstruction of past events, (b) the smoothing processes of Gestalt-type configuration, and (c) the use of culturally available plots.

1. Memory as reconstruction. Narrative knowledge is not a simple recall of the past. Narrative construction is a retrospective, interpretive composition that displays past events in the light of current understanding and present evaluation of their significance. The retrospective nature of narrative knowing and human understanding has been noted by Gadamer (1981), who wrote: "All beginnings lie in darkness, and what is more, they can be illuminated only in the light of what came later and from the perspective of what followed" (p. 140). While referring to the original past life events, narrative transforms them by ordering them into a coherent part-whole plot structure. Thus, narrated descriptions of life episodes are not mirrored reflections of what occurred; rather, they

are interpretations of life in which past events and happenings are understood as meaningful from the current perspective of their emplotted contribution to an outcome.

In personal stories, narrative structuring draws experiential traces from memory. Memory is not a container of taped replays of life events. Recollection is a partial reconstruction of the past that attends to and connects memory traces according to the press of present needs and interpretations (Casey, 1987). Narrative structuring operates dialectically with memory to recreate past occurrences in light of the function of emplotment, which is to produce a coherent story that leads to denouement and closure. Thus, the recollected images that make up the retrospective story are not simple replications of the actual events as they originally occurred. Told stories are missing aspects of our senses of self that we cannot recall or can not bring into awareness. We do not have conscious access to all the nuances of the various senses of self that have served, out of awareness, to guide and evaluate our actions. Ricoeur's (1992) position has been that because the fullness of people's preconfigured senses of self are not directly accessible to them through (phenomenological) reflection, their nonlanguaged sources of self identity need to be approached indirectly through the interpretation of expressions and actions.

2. Narrative smoothing. Life as lived is more diverse and disjointed than the stories we tell about ourselves. Our daily lives consist of eating and sleeping, going to and from work, and running errands. Narratives are not simply running descriptions or videotapes that include descriptions of every moment of time covered by a storied episode. Narrative structuring highlights and marks off from the flow of one's mundane daily tasks the happenings, thoughts, and actions that are needed to comprehend the way in which the storied episode unfolded. In life we are engaged in many projects at once, not all of which interlock into a single, unified episode. An event may be extraneous and irrelevant to one episode, but important for understanding another. A narrative production, in contrast to life as lived, usually concerns a single major plot, incorporating only the subplots and events that contribute to that plot and selecting out all irrelevant happenings (Carr, 1986). In configuring a story of a life episode, narratives often omit details and condense parts ("flattening"), elaborate and exaggerate other parts ("sharpening"), and make parts more compact and consistent ("rationalization") to produce a coherent and understandable explanation (Cortazzi, 1993). Narrative, like the visual Gestalt process, draws out from a background those elements which compose the patterned figure or plot that is the focus of attention. Additionally, narrative operates according to the principle of closure in which the process of "smoothing"

leads to perceiving incomplete figures as wholes (Glass, Holyoak, & Santa, 1979).

3. Culturally available plots. Meaning-giving interpretative plots are adapted from the repertoire of stories made available in one's culture. Although a chosen plot needs to resonate with the prenarrative experiences on which it is based, it also functions dialectically to select for the told story those events and actions that were significant contributors to the story's resolution (Polkinghorne, 1991). The creative and constructive character of narrative composition allows for different stories about the same past events. The interpretive point of view that informed the first narrative retrospection can change over time and in different settings. The evaluation of the outcome and the significance of an element's contribution to the completion of an episode may lead to differences from one narrative articulation to another of the same happenings and actions. Thus what is known narratively about a life episode from the perspective of the accumulated experience of old age may differ from the narrative knowing of the episode developed in midlife.

Narrativization functions not only to construct an identity of who I have been, but also to plan who I will be. People construct imagined hypothetical stories as a means to plan their future actions or to anticipate possible future actions of others. They can play out various stories in their imagination to produce "what if" scenarios. These imagined stories draw analogically from a person's prior collection of storied understandings. Recalled connections among actions and outcomes are used to plan future action episodes (McGuire, 1990).

The purpose of narrative configuration in the production of personal identity is to create excess meaning beyond the felt experiences of self through the process of figuration. Self-narratives are not chronicles or dairies of our lived-through lives. They are formed to produce meaningful answers to the questions "Who am I" and "What is my life about?" Without their retrospective perspective, selective, and culturally located properties, they would resemble flat home videos instead of being the source of personal identity.

Mimesis$_3$

In mimesis$_3$, the textual interpretation of one's personal identity produced in mimesis$_2$ is taken up by the person whose life is the subject of the story. The story not only reveals the temporal coherence of the person's actions, but also transforms the meaning of those actions as lived. The text of mimesis$_2$ serves to amplify life as lived by bringing to languaged awareness meanings that had not been explicated before. The prefiguration of life as lived, having been configured by narrative emplotment, becomes the source of refigured personal action. The third mimesis is our reception of the self-story generated in mimesis$_2$. Receiving our self narrative involves incorporating into our operating personal identity the understanding uncovered and created in the configural construction of the story. Implied in the newly developed self-story is an expanded and amended identity of who we are in the midst of becoming. The articulated self-story of mimesis$_2$ is a reconfigured identity of who we have become and who we are to be. Gadamer explains mimesis$_3$ as the "application" of one's articulated identity, and Ricoeur defines it as the "appropriation" of one's storied identity. By confronting the newly told story about ourselves, we re-evaluate our lives, gaining sensitivity to the meaning of our temporality and to the limits and potentials of our actions. By incorporating the narratized story into our selfhood, our actions become informed by the understanding of who we are as portrayed in the newly told story.

Ricoeur proposed that narrative establishes personal identity through the unfolding of the three mimeses. However, he maintains that the process of personal identity does not stop once we have moved through the three phases. Mimesis$_3$, once incorporated into our identity, returns us to the prereflective existence of mimesis$_1$. By appropriating the articulated identity into one's self, a person's new prereflective actions of mimesis$_1$ are changed. These changes provoke the necessity for a new articulation (mimesis$_2$) of who we are, and this new articulation becomes appropriated again in subsequent actions. The circular process continues throughout our life. We do not establish our personal identity once and then live with it the rest of our lives. Personal identity is not something discovered once and for all but is a continuous process of creation throughout one's life. Who we are is not a permanent thing that we are; rather we are a process of becoming.

Because of the temporal dimension of human existence, life-stories are eroded as we are confronted with physiological and cognitive changes and challenged by modifications in social demands made on us as we pass through different developmental markers. The passage of time erodes a person's narratively constructed identity (Ricoeur, 1991) making it necessary to re-construct it time after time. McAdams (1993) has traced the course of construction, erosion, and reconstruction throughout life's developmental stages (Erikson, 1959). McAdams (1993) divides the development of personal identity into three eras—the prenarrative, the narrative, and the postnarrative. The prenarrative era, which is the period of infancy through early adolescence, is a time in which materials are gathered for the self-stories one will construct during the narrative period. Although children in the prenarrative era are not yet engaged in the construction of unifying self-identity stories, their experiences have an effect on the production of their later identity stories. Experiences of the first two years of life leave one with "a set of unconscious and nonverbal 'attitudes' about self, other, and world (McAdams, 1993, p. 47). These attitudes concern the trustworthiness of the human and physical environment and its responsiveness to one's needs. The attitudes developed during these years can show up in later self-stories as a tone of hopelessness and mistrust or a tone of hopefulness and trust. The narrative era extends from the time in adolescence when a young adult begins to construct operational self-stories and continues through adulthood during which the self-stories are refined and reconstructed. McAdams' third era, the postnarrative era, does not occur in all lives. It corresponds to Erikson's mature stage in which the developmental task is to establish the integrity of one's life. In this third era, one's life can be looked at as something that is approaching culmination and the life-story is a nearly completed tale. During this era, the life story about what one has become can be accepted (integrity) or rejected (despair), but can no longer be substantially altered.

Narrative theory of personal identity understands human existence as a becoming. We are activities; that is, verbs, not noun-like substances. Because narrative is the cognitive process that displays temporal unfolding, it produces the kind of understanding that matches the kind of becoming that characterizes human existence. For Ricoeur, the stories of our personal identity are neither an innately, prereflective production nor a culturally imposed story on what is essentially a fragmented, one thing after another, existence. The content of which our articulated self-stories are composed is our active embodied engagement with others, the world, and our selves. This activity is itself informed by our articulated self-stories. Before we have learned to speak we have developed several senses of ourselves. Ricoeur has spelled out a theory of how personal identity arises out of our life as lived into the form of an emplotted story, which, in turn, transforms our life as lived. The construction and re-construction of personal identity occurs throughout our lives. Our personal identity is the ever-evolving descriptions of our movement through life. It is our struggle to continue to understand who we have been and what we can become.

REFERENCES

Aristotle (1954). Rhetoric. In W. Rhys Roberts (Trans.), *Rhetoric*. New York: Modern Library.

Bauer, P. J. (1996). What do infants recall of their lives? Memory for specific events by one-to two-year olds. *American Psychologist, 51*(1), 29–41.

Bruner, J. (1986). *Actual minds, possible worlds*. Cambridge, MA: Harvard University Press.

Bruner, J. (1990). *Acts of meaning*. Cambridge, MA: Harvard University Press.

Carr, D. (1986). *Time, narrative, and history*. Bloomington: University of Indiana Press.

Carr, D., Taylor, C., & Ricoeur, P. (1991). Discussion: Ricoeur on narrative. In D. Wood (Ed.), *On Paul Ricoeur: Narrative and interpretation* (pp. 160–187). London: Routledge.

Casey, E. S. (1987). *Remembering: A phenomenological study.* Bloomington: Indiana University Press.

Chatman, S. (1978). *Story and discourse: Narrative structure in fiction and film.* Ithaca, NY: Cornell University Press.

Cortazzi, M. (1993). *Narrative analysis.* London: Falmer.

Erikson, E. H. (1959). *Identity and the life cycle* (Vol. 1). New York: International Universities Press.

Gadamer, H.-G. (1981). *Reason in the age of science* (F. G. Lawrence, Trans.). Cambridge, MA: MIT Press.

Gendlin, E. T. (1991). Thinking beyond patterns: Body, Language, and situations. In B. den Ouden & M. Moen (Eds.), *The presence of feeling in thought* (pp. 22–151). New York: Peter Lang.

Glass, A. L., Holyoak, K. J., & Santa, J. L. (1979). *Cognition.* Reading, MA: Addison-Wesley.

Hardy, B. (1968). Toward a poetics of fiction: An approach through narrative. *Novel, (2)*1.

Hermans, H. J. M., & Hermans-Jansen, E. (1995). *Self-narratives: The construction of meaning in psychotherapy.* New York: Guilford.

Kerby, A. P. (1991). *Narrative and the self.* Bloomington: Indiana University Press.

Kermode, F. (1967). *The sense of an ending: Studies in the theory of fiction.* New York: Oxford University Press.

MacIntyre, A. (1981). *After virtue: A study in moral theory.* Notre Dame, IN: University of Notre Dame Press.

Mandler, J. M. (1984). *Stories, scripts, and scenes: Aspects of a schema theory.* Hillsdale, NJ: Lawrence Erlbaum Associates.

McAdams, D. P. (1985). A life-story model of identity. In E. Hogan & W. Jones (Eds.), *Perspectives in personality.* New York: Plenum.

McAdams, D. P. (1993). *The stories we live by: Personal myths and the making of the self.* New York: William Morrow.

McGuire, M. (1990). The rhetoric of narrative: A hermeneutic, critical theory. In B. K. Britton & A. D. Pellegrini (Eds.), *Narrative thought and narrative language* (pp. 219–236). Hillsdale, NJ: Lawrence Erlbaum Associates.

McIntosh, D. (1995). *Self, person, world.* Evanston, IL: Northwestern University Press.

McLaughlin, D., & Tierney, W. G. (Eds.). (1993). *Naming silenced lives: Personal narratives and the process of educational change.* New York: Routledge.

Merleau-Ponty, M. (1962). *Phenomenology of perception* (C. Smith, Trans.). New York: Humanities. (Originally published 1945)

Mink, L. O. (1979). History and fiction as modes of comprehension. *New Literary History, 1,* 541–58.

Parry, A., & Doan, R. E. (1994). *Story re-visions: Narrative therapy in the postmodern world.* New York: Guilford.

Polkinghorne, D. E. (1991). Narrative and self-concept. *Journal of Narrative and Life History, 1*(2 & 3), 135–153.

Randall, W. L. (1995). *The stories we are: An essay on self-creation.* Toronto: University of Toronto Press.

Ricoeur, P. (1969). *The symbolism of evil* (E. Buchanan, Trans.). Evanston, IL: Northwestern University Press.

Ricoeur, P. (1970). *Freud and philosophy* (D. Savage, Trans.). New Haven, CT: Yale University Press.

Ricoeur, P. (1977). *The rule of metaphor: Multidisciplinary studies of the creation of meaning in language* (R. Czerny, Trans.). Toronto: University of Toronto Press.

Ricoeur, P. (1984). *Time and narrative* (Vol. 1). (K. McLaughlin & D. Pellauer, Trans.). Chicago: University of Chicago Press.

Ricoeur, P. (1984–1989). *Time and narrative* (Vols. 1–3). (K. McLaughlin & D. Pellauer, Trans.). Chicago: University of Chicago Press.

Ricoeur, P. (1985). *Time and narrative* (Vol. 3). (K. McLaughlin & D. Pellauer, Trans.). Chicago: University of Chicago Press.

Ricoeur, P. (1991). Life in quest of narrative. In D. Wood (Ed.), *On Paul Ricoeur: Narrative and interpretation* (pp. 20–33). London: Routledge.

Ricoeur, P. (1992). *Oneself as another* (K. Blarney, Trans.). Chicago: Chicago University Press.

Ricoeur, P. (1995a). Intellectual autobiography. In L. E. Hahn (Ed.), *The philosophy of Paul Ricoeur* (pp. 3–53). La Salle, IL: Open Court.

Ricoeur, P. (1995b). Reply to David Pellauer. In L. E. Hahn (Ed.), *The philosophy of Paul Ricoeur* (pp. 123–125). La Salle, IL: Open Court.

Schafer, R. (1992). *Retelling a life: Narration and dialogue in psychoanalysis.* New York: Basic.

Simms, E.-M. (1993). The infant's experience of the world: Stern, Merleau-Ponty and the phenomenology of the preverbal self. *The Humanistic Psychologist, 21*(1), 26–40.

Spence, D. P. (1984). *Narrative truth and historical truth.* New York: Norton.

Stern, D. N. (1985). *The interpersonal world of the infant: A view from psychoanalysis and developmental psychology.* New York: Basic Books.

Vanhoozer, K. J. (1991). Philosophical antecedents to Ricoeur's time and narrative. In D. Wood (Ed.), *On Paul Ricoeur: Narrative and interpretation* (pp. 34–54). London: Routledge.

White, H. (1981). The value of narrativity in the representation of reality. In W. J. T. Mitchell (Ed.), *On narrative* (pp. 1–23). Chicago: University of Chicago Press.

White, M., & Epston, D. (1990). *Narrative means to therapeutic ends.* New York: W. W. Norton.

Wood, D. (Ed.). (1991). *On Paul Ricoeur: Narrative and interpretation.* New York: Routledge.

Chapter 3

The Promise and Limitations of the Moral Self Construct

Larry Nucci
University of Illinois at Chicago

"I think I am a moral man." California Representative Gary Condit responding to questions regarding his relations with a congressional intern.

Accounting for moral agency has proven to be a complex and difficult problem for moral psychology. How is it that we move from knowing right from wrong to acting in relation to that moral understanding? Are differences in the tendencies to engage in moral action a function of differences in kinds of people, or differences in kinds of knowledge that people have? Can we even successfully pose such a dichotomy? What I hope to accomplish within this chapter is to examine recent attempts to resolve these questions through work that is being done on what is referred to as the "moral self." My aim is to explore whether the constructs of moral self and moral identity have utility, or whether in fact such constructs are redundant with a structuralist moral psychology, or even reductionist and mechanistic. Some of what I have to say here is inconsistent with what I have written on this same topic in a recently published book (Nucci, 2001). This inconsistency in my own writing reflects the struggle to avoid the dualism that results from the disjunction of moral motivation from moral judgment (a disjunction that dates back at least to Aristotle). What I argue here is that some forms of what is being argued for with respect to the moral self instantiate such dualism, and are thereby inconsistent with moral psychol-

49

ogy. In particular, I want to argue against the notion that it is the goal of maintaining self-consistency that motivates individuals to act morally (Bergman, 2002; Blasi, 1993).

This is not to say that there are not important connections between one's personal identity and moral conduct. These connections, however, would appear to be reciprocal, arising out the interplay between one's moral judgments and the construction of the self within a particular lifeworld. As such, one can speculate on the relations that might exist between a person's moral understandings, and their qualities as a person, and the ways in which such qualities might enter into contextualized moral actions. As the philosopher William Frankena (1963) puts it, the morality of principles and the morality "of doing and being" (p. 53) are complementary aspects of the same morality such that for every principle there is a corresponding disposition or tendency to act in accordance with it. What needs to be added to Frankena's formulation is that the employment of moral principles is itself a function of contextualized decision-making colored by the ways in which particular persons relate themselves to given situations. Thus the notion of "moral self" cannot be easily divorced from the ways in which individuals construe themselves more generally within their particular lifeworlds. What this also implies, and what I argue in this chapter, is that our theory of moral decision-making must make room for such contextual factors if it is to accurately capture the ways in which individuals with particular life histories, worldviews, and personal identities weigh moral and nonmoral factors in generating particular courses of action.

The effort to define the moral self, and related work on moral identity has been offered as a counterpoint to more traditional conceptions of moral agency framed in terms of personal character and moral virtue. This structuralist alternative to these traditional approaches has its roots in Kohlberg's (Kohlberg & Turiel, 1971) devastating critique of traditional character education, and his subsequent account of moral development. Therefore, to get us started, let's look at the notions of moral virtue and character, and the response to virtue theory offered by Kohlberg's structuralist moral theory.

ARISTOTLE AND VIRTUE

Socrates, we are told, held the view that, "nobody does wrong willingly: we choose the lesser good only as a result of ignorance" (Nussbaum, 1986, p. 240). Aristotle, in contrast, rejected this view as simply inconsistent with the phenomena (Nussbaum, 1986). On Aristotle's account, good and right action are not simply a question of epistemology, but result from being a particular kind of person for whom virtuous conduct is part and parcel of the person's very being. Essentially all contemporary western virtue theories are grounded in Aristotle's viewpoint. Aristotle's approach to ethics begins not with the question of what it means to act morally, but with the more general question, "What does it mean to lead a good life?" Aristotle held that all things in nature are always moving toward a flourishing of their own nature. That is to say, that all living things have a telos. Trees grow up to be grown up trees. The business of leading a good life is to move toward the human telos and to achieve eudaimonia or a flourishing (Nussbaum, 1997). With respect to ethics, the process of flourishing entails the gradual development of virtues, or personal characteristics that will support ethical conduct. In youth, this process involves the building up of habits that in time translate into ways of being that constitute virtuous conduct.

Because Aristotle wrote so long ago, and because most of his surviving works are in the form of lecture notes, rather than the equivalents of articles or books, his ideas have become a sort of Rorschach of the given time period (Nussbaum, 1986). Aristotle's notion of habit, and his emphasis on the phenomenological, have led to an assimilation of his positions to logical positivism and behaviorist theories of learning and development. His notion of human flourishing has been adopted by utilitarians as being in support of the pursuit of happiness, and an ethics based on outcomes. Modern translators of his work, such as Nussbaum, have taken issue with these various assimilations. On Nussbaum's reading, the child according to Aristotle, is not simply a creature who is causally affected and manipulated, but an active, cognitive being that responds selectively, and whose actions are explained by his or her own view of things. Thus, Aristotle's approach to habit formation has more in common with such notions as the construction of cognitive schemata than it does with behaviorist notions of association. This nonbehaviorist view of habituation allows for Aristotle to propose a developmental progression in which such habits become subsumed within reasoned judgment. In terms of ethics, the core or master virtue is justice, around which the other virtues serve supporting roles.

The development of the virtuous person, then, involves the cultivation of the right set of habits, ethical values, and a conception of the good human life as the harmonious pursuit of these. Such a person will be "concerned about friendship, justice, courage, moderation and generosity; his desires will be formed in accordance with these concerns; and he will derive from this internalized conception of value many ongoing guidelines for action, pointers as to what to look for in a particular situation" (Nussbaum, 1986, p. 306). Because Aristotle perceived these values and commitments to be trans-situational, he took them to be what the person is in and of himself.

KOHLBERG'S CRITIQUE OF VIRTUE THEORY, AND RESPONSE

Kohlberg's (Kohlberg & Turiel, 1971) critique of virtue theory was not aimed directly at Aristotle, but at American traditional character education. The traditional view combined elements of Aristotle's conception of virtue with behaviorist and social learning theory conceptions of socialization. Kohlberg's critique responded to both elements of traditional character education on four main points.

First, Kohlberg established that the definition of what counts as a virtue varies as a function of cultural and historical setting. A humorous updating of this critique has been offered by Daniel Lapsley (1996) who compared the checklist of virtues from his own elementary school report card, against the list of 23 virtues to be used as core values in character education classes, that had been compiled in 1988 by The Panel on Moral Education of the American Association for Curriculum Development (ASCD). The only virtue that overlapped between the two lists was "courtesy." Additionally, the list compiled by the ASCD panel left out 9 of the 11 values in "The Children's Morality Code," an earlier effort to guide teachers similar to the ASCD list published in 1929 by W. J. Hutchins.

The second issue raised by Kohlberg was the empirical evidence provided by Hartshorne and May's (1929) research in the late 1920s and early 1930s challenging the assumption that there were such things as character traits. This carefully done series of studies demonstrated convincingly that whether or not a person engaged in a particular form of conduct presumed to be consistent or inconsistent with a particular character trait or virtue depended on the context. Faced with the evidence from their series of studies, Hartshorne and May were left to conclude that there was no such thing as character. For example, they concluded there were no people with the character trait of honesty. People were honest in some situations, and dishonest in others. These findings of Hartshorne and May were subsequently buttressed by the research conducted in the second half of the century on the related notion of personality traits (Mischel, 1973; Ross & Nisbett, 1991; Sarbin & Allen, 1968). The results of these studies led researchers to conclude that people cannot be accurately be described in terms of stable and general personality traits, because people tend to exhibit different and seemingly contradictory aspects of themselves in different contexts. In place of trait theories, contemporary personality psychologists tend to view personality as something one *does* in particular settings, rather than as something one *has* independent of context (Mischel, 1990; Ross & Nisbett, 1991).

Kohlberg's third point builds from these conclusions about personality and virtue. The application of virtues always occurs in context, thus requiring an application of judgment not only as to which virtue is applicable, but often to determine which of two or more competing virtues should hold

sway. Actually, this contextual aspect of the application of virtue was anticipated by Aristotle who saw the application of virtue as entailing the use of
practical wisdom. Kohlberg's insight into this issue was to recognize that
moral virtue essentially reduces itself to the structures of reasoning that
people employ to resolve moral situations.

Kohlberg's final point is that moral reason does not emerge spontane-
ously as a result of environmentally evoked hard wired modules or Platonic
forms, nor is the capacity for moral reasoning the result of the gradual
building up of habits, but rather the construction and reconstruction of
forms of understanding that emerge through processes of cognitive equilibration as outlined within Piaget's (1932) genetic epistemology.

Kohlberg's alternative to the morality of personal virtue is his six stage
theory of moral development. The brilliance of Kohlberg's theory is that it
offers simultaneous resolution to nearly every conundrum faced by moral
psychology. Kohlberg's structuralist theory accounts for the contextual
variation in people's morality through the application of moral reasoning.
Moral maturity is understood as the progressive development of more morally adequate forms of moral judgment. The invariance of personal virtue is
replaced by the contextual invariance of cognitive structure, and the telos of
eudaimonia or human flourishing is replaced by the telos of equilibration.
This is not to say that Kohlberg was opposed to the notion of the development of personal goals and projects as a part of self-actualization. It was that
Kohlberg did not see how one could define that aspect of personal development in any but the most individual of ways, and that such aspects of personal growth were not in and of themselves aspects of morality. In essence
Kohlberg agreed with the philosopher William Frankena's distinction between leading the "good life" in the Aristotelian sense of flourishing, and
leading a life that is good in an objectively moral sense. In what is one of the
most important of his works, Kohlberg (1971) argued in his "Is to ought"
paper that the process of equilibration of structures of moral thought
moves inevitably toward a philosophically defensible moral ought. In this,
Kohlberg was in agreement with the notion that there is but one moral virtue, and that is the virtue of justice. My reading of Kohlberg's early work is
that he viewed the progression toward stage six as culminating in structures
of thought that produce decisions that are morally binding on people.
Thus, he ends up in alignment with Socrates view that to know the good is to
do the good.

INCONSISTENCIES, CONTRADICTIONS AND HETEROGENEITY

Unfortunately, Kohlberg's theory does not fit all of the relevant phenomena. Kohlberg (1984) acknowledged early on that there were certain minor
contradictions with his theory regarding the binding nature of stage six. He

mentions in some of his early work the well-known contradiction between the principled moral positions of Thomas Jefferson, and his relationship with his slave, Sally Hemmings. Kohlberg explained this contradiction as evidence that persons knowing what is morally right may not have the will to act on that knowledge if they are under great social pressure. Kohlberg saw this as particularly the case when a person takes a moral stand at variance with generally held social convention. Kohlberg (1969) dealt with this type of contradiction by invoking the construct of "ego strength"—a psychological notion quite divergent from his structuralism.

The problem of social pressure came up again in the results of Milgram studies on authority and social conformity when it was found that a portion of subjects judged to be stage six moral reasoners were nonetheless willing to go along with social authority and continued to shock the supposed "learner" in the study to the point where the shocks caused great pain and discomfort and posed physical danger to the person supposedly receiving the shocks (see Kohlberg, 1969). This study is often cited as evidence (e.g., Kohlberg, 1984) that moral development is associated with moral behavior because proportionately more post-conventional reasoners resisted the authority than did subjects with lower stages of moral judgment. However, the fact that any post-conventional reasoners went along with the authority would seem to be a problem for the theory. Moreover, the fact that a considerable number of people at lower developmental stages resisted the authority, suggested that personal features other than moral stage may have been involved in guiding people's behavior.

An early comprehensive review (Blasi, 1983) of available research concluded that there was a general trend for moral behavior to be associated with developmental stage; that in fact, people at higher stages of development were less likely to engage in various forms of moral misconduct than were people at lower stages. This was particularly the case if one looked at forms of behavior that had moral consequences for the welfare of others. Nonetheless, the power of the association was far less than perfect, and suggested that other factors beyond moral judgment, as assessed by Kohlberg's stages, were involved in generating moral actions.

These results led some followers of Kohlberg to generate multifactor models of moral reasoning (Gerson & Damon, 1978; Rest, 1983). With some variation in the exact number of steps, a distinction is drawn in these models between the deontic evaluation of the morally right thing to do, and evaluation of whether or the moral judgment, once made, poses a responsibility for action on the person. In these formulations, then, Kohlberg stage accounts for the judgment of moral right and wrong, whereas some other factor accounts for the actual judgment that one is personally responsible to act in a manner consistent with that deontic moral judgment.

MORAL SELF/IDENTITY

In contrast with these multiprocess models are efforts to fill in the perceived missing step between moral judgment and action by bringing in the moral self, and more particularly the notion of moral identity. The first and perhaps most comprehensive of these approaches (Blasi, 1984) built from Erikson's work on identity formation, but was most heavily influenced by Loevenger's theory of ego development. Loevinger's theory can be read as providing for a compatible bridge to Kohlberg in being constructivist and transformational, rather than logical positivist and behavioral. Employing Loevinger as a starting point, Blasi began to look at the possibility that the link between moral judgment and action lies in the degree to which morality and moral concerns were integrated into the person's sense of self. The basic idea here is that from moral identity derives a psychological need to make one's actions consistent with one's ideals. Thus, in Blasi's (1993) words, "self-consistency is the motivational spring of moral action" (p. 99). More recently, Clark Power (Power & Khmelkov, 1998) redefined character in a similar vein as the specifically moral dimensions of self. Like Blasi, Power stated that the motive for moral action is not simply the direct result of knowing "the good", but from the desire to act in ways that are consistent with one's own sense of self as a moral being. As Power put it, "Individuals may undertake a particular course of action, even at some cost, because they want to become or remain a certain kind of person" (p. 5). In contrast with the traditional character construct, the approach taken by Blasi, and joined now by many others (Bergman, 2002; Colby & Damon, 1992; Hart & Fegley, 1995; Keller & Edelstein, 1993; Noam, 1993) "does not attempt to replace moral ideas with a set of non cognitive personality characteristics: it sees personal identity as operating jointly with reason and truth in providing motives for action" (Blasi, 1993, p. 99). Thus, one's moral "character" is not something divorced from moral cognition, and the complexity that it entails.

General Issues in the Construction of Self

Although the notion of the moral self has its roots in Eriksonian psychology and Loevenger's theory of ego development, theories of moral identity are not constrained by these associations. If we look more broadly at cognitive accounts of self, we see that the construction of personal identity is itself multifaceted, incorporating values and social roles from a number of contexts. Research on the development of children's conceptions of self (Damon & Hart, 1988; Harter, 1983) provides evidence that with age, children construct increasingly differentiated notions of themselves as actors within different contexts. These differentiated constructs emerge as a result of children's efforts to interpret their differential competence, and involve-

ment in various areas of activity (academic, making friends) and a corresponding tendency with age to assign meaning to those levels of
competence and commitment. Harter (1983) has suggested that development of self-concepts may very well entail a reiterative process whereby a
child's initial attempts to construct an integrated notion of self (e.g., in
terms of characteristic behaviors) is followed by a period of differentiation
(e.g., good at some things, bad at others). These differentiated general descriptions are then incorporated within a higher level of integration (e.g.,
general traits), which are then subsequently differentiated. This process
eventuates at the most advanced levels of development in a conceptualization of self in multidimensional and contextual terms (Broughton, 1978;
Chandler, Lalonde, & Sokol, 2003; Damon & Hart, 1988).

The inherent complexity of self-definition has its counterpart in efforts
at self-evaluation. Current evidence supports the proposition that we construct both a general sense of self-worth, and domain-specific evaluations of
our own competence (Byrne, 1984; Harter, 1985, 1986; Rosenberg, 1965).
This in turn suggests that it is possible for us to have a positive view of ourselves, while still having a sense that we are not very good in a particular
area of performance. In other words, it may be that we can feel good about
ourselves if those areas of performance in which we are not so great, are not
terribly important to who we are. Research examining how children apply
their sense of self to academic performance provides empirical evidence
that this is indeed the case. There is little evidence to suggest that students'
views of themselves in terms of academic capabilities (academic self-esteem) are necessarily tied to students' general sense of self-worth (Harter,
1983; Marsh, Smith & Barnes, 1985). For students for whom school matters, performance in school has a relation to the students' self-esteem. For
those for whom school matters little, their academic performance has little
relationship to their more general sense of self-esteem.

The question for the present discussion is whether something like this
can be operating with respect to morality. If we move from the area of aca-
demics back to the issue of the moral self, one can see both parallels and differences. One significant difference is that people are not as free to discount
their moral selves as they are to discount other aspects of their personal en-
deavors such as their performance in mathematics, or on the dance floor
(Power & Khmelkov, 1998). This is because morality is inherent in human
interaction, and engages us in binding "objective" ways. Perhaps, however,
the objective or binding nature of morality may be overstated as a basis for
presuming its centrality in the construction of personal identity. Whether
one attends to the moral implications of events may be more compelling
than whether one develops skill as a dancer, but it may not attain the same
degree of salience or centrality for everyone. There is no prima facie reason
to assume that the basic process of constructing the moral aspect of self is

fundamentally different from the construction of other aspects of personal identity. Thus we should expect interpersonal variations in the connection between self and morality.

This assumption of interpersonal variation in moral identity has not been extensively researched. However, some recent work (Blasi, 1993) has provided evidence that some individuals let moral notions penetrate to the essence and core of what and who they are, whereas others construct their central defining features of self in other ways. This is not to say that morality is somehow absent from many people, but rather that the moral aspects of self may be subjectively experienced in different ways. Blasi puts it this way,

> several individuals may see morality as essential to their sense of self, of who they are. For some of them, however, moral ideals and demands happen to be there, a given nature over which they feel little control. In this case moral ideals exist next to other characteristics, all equally important because they are there. Others instead relate to their moral ideals as being personally chosen over other ideals or demands, sense their fragility, and feel responsible to protect them and thus to protect their sense of self. (1993, pg. 103)

Morality and the Self

This variability in the centrality of morality within one's personal identity is of interest for the present discussion only if there is also evidence that it matters for moral action, and that it serves as a bridge between moral judgment and behavior. Here, one can raise some interesting questions. Setting aside the small fraction of individuals who are sociopaths, people generally attend to moral social interactions and have common views of prima facie moral obligations (Turiel, 1998). Thus, it is hard to imagine how morality does not comprise an important aspect of the sense of self of most people. Of course, one can argue that people vary in their sense of what it means to be moral in a given context, and in this sense display individual differences in how they engage the world as moral beings. But that is different from suggesting that morality is somehow nearer and dearer to some people than to others.

Let's consider some cases for sake of argument. Is it the case that people who engage in voluntarism and community service are more committed to morality than William Ayers and his wife, Bernadine Dorn, when as leaders of the Weathermen, they planned violent actions against the United States during the Vietnam war period? Or, did they read the situation they faced differently, and out of a sense of morality engage in violent actions (Ayers, 2001)? Are those of us who engage in research less morally committed than our colleagues who directly serve the public through their training of teachers or physicians? Was Martin Luther King's philandering indicative of his

moral character, or should we assume that his moral identity is better captured by his work on civil rights? Which is the true Dr. King, or did he have
dual moral identities? Do we know whether or not Congressman Gary
Condit is a moral man as he claims?

The research evidence around this issue is less than compelling. What is
usually presented as evidence regarding the centrality of morality to individuals' personal identity is some association between personal definition,
and prosocial conduct. Hart and Fegley (1995), for example, studied the
moral identities of a group of inner city adolescents who exhibited a high
degree of community service voluntarism, and care for others. These adolescents were identified by community leaders, teachers, and churches as
youth who had done such things as organize youth groups, and work in
homeless shelters. They and a comparison group of adolescents from the
same community were asked to generate a list of all of the important characteristics that they could think of that described themselves as they are in the
present, the person they were in the past, the person they dreaded becoming, and they kind of person they would ideally like to become. What Hart
and Fegley (1995) assumed was that persons whose actual selves incorporate a subset of their ideal selves will be more driven to realize the goals of
the ideal self, than persons whose ideal self and actual self are unrelated.
What they discovered in their study was in line with that hypothesis. Two
thirds of the adolescents high on voluntarism and care, and less than a third
of the comparison adolescents exhibited overlap between the characteristics of their actual and ideal selves. Moreover, there was very little correlation between these adolescents' moral stage, as measured within the
Kohlberg framework, and their involvement in community service.

A second, widely cited illustration of the connection between moral self
and conduct is Colby and Damon's (1992) study of moral exemplars as recounted in their book "Some do care." What they report are a series of biographical sketches that purport to demonstrate that the decision to become
active in community service, or civil rights activities are linked to the ways in
which these individuals constructed their own personal identities. As with
the Hart and Fegley (1995) study, Colby and Damon report that their morally exemplary people ranged widely in their Kohlbergian stage of moral
development from lower conventional stages to post-conventional.

These two studies, and other similar ones lead one to the conclusion that
moral development seems to matter little when it comes to moral action,
and that what does matter are the qualities of the person. But there are several problems with such a conclusion. First, it is not clear that the actions described constitute moral conduct. If, for example, I volunteer to work in a
soup kitchen because it will increase my chances of getting into my college
of choice, is my voluntarism moral? If I volunteer because it will make me
feel good about myself, rather than because I feel compelled to volunteer in

order to alleviate the suffering of others, is my action moral? Without knowing why I volunteered, one cannot know to what extent I either did or did
not engage in moral deliberation. This holds both for those who volunteer
as well as those who do not. After all, one third of the volunteers in Hart and
Fegley's study, did *not* display an integration between their ideal and actual
selves, and one third of the subjects who did not volunteer, *did* display this
sort of overlap between their actual and ideal self descriptions. Finally, it is
worth noting that the kinds of self-descriptions generated by adolescents in
this sort of study are very general in nature. These global self-descriptions
can hardly reflect an individual's goals within specific contexts.

Second, one can come to moral conclusions at any Kohlbergian stage
of moral development. Colby and Damon recognize this, but do not provide convincing evidence whether there is or is not a linkage between the
moral decisions of the person's they studied, their self-definitions, and
their actions.

The only work (Blasi & Glodis, 1995) that has tried to systematically explore the relationship between moral identity and motivation for moral
action resulted in findings and interpretations much more nuanced than
that reported in most other research. These researchers examined
whether people who define morality as a central part of their personal
identity experience a sense of "personal betrayal" when they act in opposition to those moral values. They hypothesized that such a sense of personal betrayal would be more evident in person's whose sense of identity
stemmed from their own active efforts at becoming the person they were,
than among persons whose identity emerged from a relatively passive, unreflective acceptance of themselves. In their study, they asked 30 women
to indicate an ideal that they considered to be very important to their
sense of self, one that she cared deeply about, and to which she was deeply
committed. Among the ideals listed were: friendship, caring for others,
morality and justice, self-reliance, and improving one's mind and knowledge. Six to ten weeks later, each of the women was presented with a story
in which a fictional character chooses a course of action advantageous fi-
nancially and career-wise, but which compromised her ideals. The compromised ideal in each case was the one listed by the subject as a central
value in her earlier interview.

What Blasi and Glodis (1995) found was that some of their subjects
tended not to see the situation as relevant to their ideals. Instead they focused on the pragmatic consequences of the decision presented in the scenario, and expressed feelings of satisfaction with the protagonist's
pragmatic choice. Others, on the other hand, saw the situation as entailing a
serious contradiction of their ideals, and expressed such feelings as shame,
guilt and depression over the protagonist's choice to violate those ideals.
The feelings expressed by subjects in the study were a function of whether

their own sense of identity was one for which they were actively involved. Subjects whose ideals were not experienced as passively received from outside influences, but rather as central concerns to be pursued were those who reported the most distress in response to the scenario entailing a contradiction or betrayal of those ideals.

Now it is important to note that in discussing their findings, Blasi and Glodis avoid claiming that it is essential for a person to have constructed a moral identity of this sort in order for someone to act in morally consonant ways. They recognize that morality may be viewed as important for other reasons, such as social approval, or simply out of concerns for the objective consequences of actions. The latter, of course, is a way of saying that individuals might act morally simply for moral reasons. They also suggest that such intense personal involvement may not be implicated in many day-to-day moral interactions that don't entail dilemmas pitting one's pragmatic self interests against the needs of someone else. The authors suggest that one's personal identity may only become at stake in cases requiring substantial subordination of other motives. Of course, whether one views such situations as placing the self at risk, are a function of whether morality exists as an ideal central to one's self definition. Blasi (1993) asserts that moral and other ideals are chosen as core values because they are understood to be important. As Blasi puts it, "to some extent personality is shaped by what one knows to be worthy of education and commitment" (p. 119).

This work is provocative in that it may be seen as linking Aristotelian notions of eudaimonia (self-flourishing) to the work that has been done on moral cognition. It also implies that constructivist assumptions of how one generates moral knowledge are also important to the active construction of the moral self, and consequent moral responsibility, and character. But all of this work on the moral self and moral identity leaves open a set of important interrelated and as yet unanswered issues:

- *Self consistency as reductionism*. Each of the moral-self theories maintain that the core motivation for moral action among adolescents and adults is the desire to maintain consistency between one's moral actions and one's moral identity. This claim is reductionist and mechanistic by reducing all complex contextualized moral judgments to the simple evaluation of whether the action is or is not consistent with one's sense of self.
- *Self-consistency as ethical egoism*. This explanation of moral action reduces questions of morality from questions about one's obligations to others through judgments of fairness and human welfare to judgments of whether or not the actor will "feel right" about him or herself. There are, of course, behavioral psychologists who believe that such positive and negative consequences are at the core of all

human motivation. From such a psychological premise, however, all morality is addressed through instrumentalism, and ethical egoism. I doubt that to have been the goal of moral-self theorists, particularly since their work is based on the neo-Kantian framework of Kohlberg's (1971) moral psychology. This apparent instrumentalism has not, however, been addressed in their writings.

- The philosopher William Frankena (1963) avoids this problem by arguing that just because one might feel good as a result of having done something moral is not of consequence as long as one intended to do the action because it was judged to be the right thing to do. In Frankena's rendering, however, self-consistency is ruled out as a primary motive. A moral-self theory can be invoked in this situation, but only in a structural sense that a given person, being who they are will likely read a given situation in a particular way, and being who they are, act in accordance with their judgment, and as a consequence feel good about themselves. In this reading, however, self-consistency is the result of a concordant moral decision and subsequent action, rather than a motive for action.

- One can take this recovery of theory a step further and argue that a subjective sense of moral inconsistency may be felt as a "betrayal of self" after-the-fact, and result in feelings of guilt and the desire to self-improve. This is similar to arguments offered by philosophers such as Rorty (1973) who suggest that reflection on and owning up to one's past is essential to the notion of moral responsibility. As Chandler et al. (2003) vividly put it, without such a backward accounting of one's self, "Judgment day would simply go out of business." (p. 13). This suggests, however, that self-consistency is not a guide to moral action, but rather an affective component of the process of moral equilibration and development.

- *Lack of developmental continuity from childhood to adolescence.* Perhaps the biggest gap in theory is the paucity of explanatory connection between children's morality, and the period in early adolescence where the construction of moral identity is presumed to exert its influence on moral responsibility. Sources as diverse as Freud, Piaget, and the Catholic Church place the age at which children become capable of assuming moral responsibility at about 6 to 8 years at which time children's moral judgments become regulated by conceptions of just reciprocity (Turiel & Davidson, 1986). This is well before the age at which moral identity can be invoked as an explanation for moral motivation. In a recent review, Bergman (2002) offered hints at the elements of a more complete developmental model in his discussion of Damon's (1984) early work on the relations between moral development and self-understanding, but does not make full use of the insights that are offered. This is because, Bergman, like the other theorists he reviewed, are all handcuffed by their commitment to Kohlberg's stages of moral development as *the* account of moral growth. Thus, Bergman is quite taken with the notion of A and B moral reasoning types without recognizing that this post-hoc attempt to save the Kohlberg enterprise is simply a special case better understood within theories of moral and social growth that disaggregate moral and nonmoral social judgments throughout development (Turiel, 1998). These more recent moral theories allow for the prospect that we may prioritize moral over nonmoral concerns throughout the lifespan, and not simply at advanced stages of moral development. Children, then, are to be seen as capable moral beings, and the construction of moral identity—the generation of moral dispositions in concert with one's moral concepts—may be viewed as more continuous than current formulations allow. Of course these newer moral theories also admit of greater intra-individual contextual, and inter-individual cultural variation than does Kohlberg's global theory in the ways in which people interpret their social worlds, and generate moral actions.

TOWARD A CONTEXTUALIST STRUCTURAL THEORY OF MORAL COGNITION

What I want to propose is that the shortcomings of present efforts to integrate some account of personal agency, and perhaps self and identity with moral judgment can be overcome if we let go of Kohlberg's (1984) account of moral development, and move toward a more contextualized structuralism, and a more contextualized view of moral identity. Kohlberg's resolution of the shortcomings of classical views of character formation, bound up all forms of judgments of social right and wrong within a single developmental system which moved progressively to a point where morality triumphs over convention, personal interest, and pragmatics. What we have come to realize is that what Kohlberg treated as a single structural system was in fact several systems, or domains of social judgment, of which morality was one (Turiel, 1978, 1983, 1998). We now have extensive evidence that concepts of morality center around issues of fairness and human welfare, and that they emerge as distinct from conceptions of societal convention at very early ages (Smetana, 1989). Moreover, both morality and convention are distinct from a third conceptual framework concerning issue of personal prerogative and privacy (Nucci, 1996). Each of these domains: morality, societal convention, and the personal undergoes structural developmental changes with age. Each, however, is a distinct conceptual framework with an independent developmental course and sequence.

We now know that Kohlberg's formulation of moral development captured typical age-related coordinations of moral and nonmoral concerns for children and early adolescents, and for adults within modern cultures. What he failed to recognize is that people's moral judgments could be employed in simple situations in the absence of recourse to other social concepts, and that contextualized social judgments by people at all ages, including childhood could be dominated by moral considerations or by nonmoral ones. In other words, understanding moral decision-making requires a much richer appreciation of how moral and nonmoral social factors are evaluated in context.

An example of the utility of this approach for understanding the relations between moral reasoning and behavior is provided by Smetana's (1982) research on pregnant women's reasoning about abortion. What she found was that women's judgments about abortion depended on their treatment of the issue as a matter of personal choice and privacy, or a moral issue involving the life of another person. Most of the women who chose to have an abortion also viewed the issue as a matter of privacy and personal choice. For these women their reasoning about abortion was uncorrelated with their reasoning as assessed with a Kohlberg interview. Conversely, most of the women who treated abortion as a moral issue went to term with their pregnancies. Their reasoning about abortion was assessed to be the same as the level of moral judgment they displayed in a standard Kohlberg assessment of moral development. Smetana also looked at the women's religious affiliation. She found that Catholicism among her subjects was associated with the tendency to go to term with a pregnancy. However, this aspect of personal identity and religious values was mediated through the treatment of abortion as a personal or moral issue. It was the latter set of choices, and not religious affiliation that predicted the woman's decisions regarding abortion.

Thus, the reading of an issue as falling within in the moral domain, appears to be the critical variable in predicting the force of moral judgments upon moral actions. The salience of morality varies across social situations, and the assessment of salience is indeed the wildcard in this formulation. To some extent, it is established by the "objective" situation. Usually what people mean by context is this external configuration of elements. But, context is also internal and is affected by the relative point in development the person has reached within each conceptual system, the person's informational assumptions, the person's position within the social hierarchy, his or her social roles, and a series of idiosyncratic elements such as the person's mood, whether or not he or she had a good night's sleep, just had a fight with one's spouse, and so forth. In the case of Smetana's (1982) Catholic subjects, the context framing their reading of abortion included their identification as members of the Catholic Church. A similar mechanism may well have been at work for many of the exemplars cited by Colby and Damon (1992) who connected up their moral engagement in particular situations with their own religious or spiritual commitments.

Some recent work by Turiel (2002) and Wainryb (Wainryb & Turiel, 1994) nicely illustrates how where one sits in the social hierarchy also affects how one reads the morality of social practices. In most of the world's cultures, men sit in positions of relative power in their relations with women. Men, for example, are accorded more decision-making authority over everyday decisions. Men tend to view these privileges as rights, and expect obedience from their wives and daughters as a matter of duty. That is to say, that men are inured to the apparent inequities involved, and prioritize the nonmoral conventional elements of their cultural practices as more salient in the interpretation of the social situation. Women in these situations, tend to see the same "objective" facts quite differently. They are more likely than the men to see the inequities inherent in the social practices and to prioritize morality over social convention.

That social roles blind us to the "objectively" moral elements of the context is neither a new idea (see Sarbin & Allen, 1968 for an early discussion), nor recent phenomenon. Nicholas II, last of the Russian tsars as described by John Lawrence (1993) in his history of Russia,

> conceived it to be his duty and his fate to carry on his shoulders the whole burden of the Russian aristocracy. His duty to his family, to his country, to God were indistinguishable to him. He felt bound unconditionally to his office and by his coronation oath to preserve Russia holy and Orthodox under his absolute rule while he lived, and to hand undiminished powers to his son when he died. To limit his own powers by the acceptance of basic laws that even the tsar must not break, to accept the merest shadow of a constitution or even to appoint a prime minister would be an offense against God and against his own son even more than a political imprudence. (p. 210)

Talk about moral identity! I leave it to you, the reader, to decide whether or not poor Tsar Nicholas was a person of character.

And we can take this a bit further. All of us lead lives that are multifaceted. We are parents, spouses, children, teachers, researchers, scholars of different sorts. Some of us are community volunteers; some are not. Each of these role relationships places different demands on us that have different mixtures of moral and nonmoral elements. The self-same person, to use Michael Chandler's (ref. this volume) phrase, can appear to employ morality in inconsistent ways across these contexts. This was the very essence of Hartshorne and May's (1928, 1929, 1930) discoveries. And, what are we to make of this? Does our moral identity shift with each context? Or, is it the case that as the self-same person it is the salience of morality that shifts with the context?

At this point, one can imagine a rising chorus of concern that a contextualist structural account of moral development and moral reasoning is relativistic. Indeed, it is in the sense that an honest moral psychology does not presume that morality is always prior to nonmoral concerns. However, it is not relativist in its view of the moral, nor in its assumptions about the directionality of individual or social practices when moral concerns are taken into account.

Let us take the case of the hierarchical status of women as a case in point. The moral arguments of the women reported in the research just mentioned (Turiel, 2002) were not made on the basis of consensual agreement. They were based on nonrelativist moral arguments of inequities, harm, and injustices. Those men open to hear the arguments of women would not be persuaded simply by the fact that many of the women seem to agree on a particular point, but by the nonarbitrary and nonrelativist force of morality itself.

MORAL PRIORITY AND IDENTITY

The question for moral psychology is how to account for when individuals prioritize morality, and when they don't. Given that morality operates independently of our other social cognitive systems (Turiel, 1983, 1998), we can expect morality to guide our actions at any point in development. This is why correlations between moral stage and behavior are often so meaningless. More recent work on moral cognition unfortunately undoes Kohlberg's (1984) unified moral stage telos. However, this more recent work (Turiel, 2002) opens up a second possibility that moral reflection is a capacity available in different forms at all points in development, and that people at all points in their social growth can evaluate social situations from a moral point of view. This is not to say that the moral reflections of a typical 4 year old are the same as those of a typical adult. But, that the capacity to attend to and prioritize the moral is available at all ages.

This opens an interesting possibility for the role of self and identity in the construction of one's morality. It has to do with the very nature of moral openness. Whether we are born male or female, tsar or serf will affect our reading of the moral meaning of situations. Within those broad social categories and social roles we also operate as individuals. We are capable of independently assessing the moral meaning of practices and social events. Just as these larger external forces shape our view of things, so also do our own individual biases, opinions, and interests alter our orientation toward the morality of social situations. Who we are as individuals, and not simply "where we sit" in relation to the social system affects the way in which we read the salience of the moral elements of situations. It is this reading of the moral weighting of the situation that impacts moral action. In this way, we can argue that identity affects our moral actions. Of course, we can and do make decisions in context that we come to regret. We may even engage in actions that shake our belief in ourselves as moral actors. But this can only come after the fact, and does not constitute "moral" motivation. Blasi's (1993) work speaks directly to this point when he notes that this sort of moral identity crisis is rare.

If self and identity are a matter of connecting up who we were, with who we are, and who we are becoming, then the possibility exists that we can construct notions of ourselves that allow us to be more or less open to changes in our moral orientation—both in a developmental sense—and in terms of the ways in which we frame or attend to the moral and nonmoral elements of given situations.

The current infatuation with moral identity as a core aspect of moral functioning overlooks the prospect that an overly tight linkage between morality and self can actually be dysfunctional. It is possible that we can so define ourselves in terms of morality, that rather than becoming moral exemplars, we actually freeze our morality in dysfunctional ways. We have already considered the case of Tsar Nicholas as an example of someone whose sense of himself so tied him to a conventional moral system that he was unable to respond to the moral contradictions inherent in his own position. But, it can work the other way as well. One can become so focused on a sense of moral outrage and so identified with a moral cause as to become a one-dimensional moral zealot such as the anti-abortion extremists, or the animal rights zealots who in their sense of moral purpose engage in acts of violence in the name of morality. Consider the following description of Nicoli Lenin by a former Marxist, Berdyaev:

> Lenin's revolutionary principles had a moral source; he could not endure injustice, oppression, and exploitation, but he became so obsessed with maximalist revolutionary idea, that in the end he lost the immediate sense of difference between good and evil; he lost the direct relationship to living people; he permitted fraud, deceit, violence, cruelty. He was not a vicious man, he was not even particularly ambitious or a great lover of power, but the sole obsession of a single idea led to a dreadful narrowing of thought and to a moral transformation which permitted entirely immoral methods in carrying on the conflict. (Lawrence, 1993, p. 206)

If instead of adopting a static moral identity, we remain open to the ways in which we attend to moral components of social life, then the possibility exists that we will be open to moral disequilibration. In essence, we can be more or less open to moral self-improvement—not only in the sense of development, but in the ways in which we frame the moral meaning of social events or relationships. When we change those ways in which we orient toward the social world, we change a part of who we are. The direction of change will generally be toward the moral. This was at the heart of Kohlberg's (1971) bold philosophical claims in his "Is to Ought" paper. Moral directionality is not developmentally deterministic as described by Kohlberg (1984), nor simply a function of Western liberalism (Shweder, 1982). It results from the fact that the dialectic between moral concerns for fairness and harm to person's, and nonmoral considerations such as social hierarchy is not an arbitrary one—so long as we are open to hearing the moral voice in the dialogue. When this occurs we are simultaneously altering how we think morally, and the person in and of himself. They are complementary aspects of one and the same thing. And, perhaps, this is how best to think of moral teleology, and the notion of moral flourishing.

The primary contribution of the work done on the moral self is that it provides a coherent basis from which to consider the interface between the development of the moral agent and the construction of moral and social understandings. This approach "does not attempt to replace moral ideas with a set of non-cognitive personality characteristics: it sees personal identity as operating jointly with reason and truth in providing motives for action" (Blasi, 1993, p. 99). Thus, such research and theory has made an important substantive contribution to public discourse at a time when notions of moral agency are being overwhelmed by the rhetoric of character formation and indoctrinative forms of socialization. If the reach of such theorists has exceeded their grasp, it is because they have not fully appreciated the multifaceted aspects of moral judgments in context (Turiel, 1998), nor sufficiently allowed for the heterogeneity that exists within a given person's self-system. For research on this issue to move forward, and the promise of conceptual models about the moral self to be realized, research on this issue will need to get beyond biographical studies of more and less moral people, or assessments of the correspondence of general ideal and "actual' personal values to microgenetic studies of the ways in which people's judgments and actions in context reciprocally foster the development of moral agency. As Frankena (1963) put it, and as the evidence indicates, moral principles, and doing and being are two sides of the same morality.

REFERENCES

Ayers, W. (2001). *Fugitive days: A memoir.* New York: Beacon Press.

Bergman, R. (2002). Why be moral? A conceptual model from developmental psychology. *Human Development, 45*, 104–124.

Blasi, G. (1983). Moral cognition and moral action: A theoretical perspective. *Developmental Review, 3*, 178–210.

Blasi, G. (1984). Moral identity: Its role in moral functioning. In J. Gewirtz, & W. Kurtines (Eds.), *Morality, moral behavior, and moral development* (pp. 128–139). New York: Wiley.

Blasi, G. (1993). The development of identity: Some implications for moral functioning. In G. Noam & T. Wren (Eds.), *The moral self* (pp. 99–122). Cambridge, MA: MIT Press.

Blasi, G., & Glodis, K. (1995). The development of identity: A critical analysis from the perspective of the self as subject. *Developmental Review, 15*, 404–433.

Broughton, J. (1978). The development of concepts of self, mind, reality, and knowledge. In W. Damon (Ed.), *Social cognition*. San Francisco: Jossey-Bass.

Byrne, B. (1984). The general/academic self-concept nomological network: A review of construct validation research. *Review of Educational Research, 54*, 427–456.

Chandler, M., Lalonde, C., & Sokol, B. (2003). Personal persistence, identity development, and suicide: A study of native and non-native North American adolescents. *Monographs for the Society for Research in Child Development, 68*, 1–130.

Colby, A., & Damon, W. (1992). *Some do care: Contemporary lives of moral commitment.* New York: Free Press.

Damon, W. (1984). Self-understanding and moral development in childhood and adolescence. In J. Gewirtz & W. Kurtines (Eds.), *Morality, moral behavior, and moral development*. New York: Wiley.

Damon, W., & Hart, W. (1988). *Self understanding in childhood and adolescence.* Cambridge, MA: Cambridge University Press.

Frankena, W. K. (1963). *Ethics.* Englewood Cliffs, NJ: Prentice-Hall.

Gerson, R., & Damon, W. (1978). Moral understanding and children's conduct. In W. Damon (Ed.), *Moral development* (pp. 41–60). San Francisco: Jossey-Bass.

Hart, D., & Fegley, S. (1995). Prosocial behavior and caring in adolescence: Relations to self-understanding and social judgment. *Child Development, 66*, 1346–1359.

Harter, S. (1983). Developmental perspectives on the self-system. In P. H. Mussen (Ed.), *Handbook of child psychology. Vol. IV: Socialization, personality, and social development* (pp. 275–285). New York: Wiley.

Harter, S. (1985). *The self-perception profile for children: Revision of the perceived competence scale for children.* Unpublished manuscript, University of Denver.

Hartshorne, H., & May, M. A. (1928) *Studies in the nature of character. Vol. 1: Studies in deceit.* New York: Macmillan.

Hartshorne, H., & May, M. A. (1929). *Studies in the nature of character. Vol. 2: Studies in service and self control.* New York: Macmillan.

Hartshorne, H., & May, M. A. (1930). *Studies in the nature of character. Vol. 3: Studies in organization of character.* New York: Macmillan.

I think I am a moral man. (2001, September 3). *Newsweek (perspectives)*, p. 17.

Hutchins, W. J. (1929). The children's morality code. *Journal of the National Education Association, 13*, 292.

Keller, M., & Edelstein, M. (1993). The development of the moral self from childhood to adolescence. In G. Naom & T. Wren (Eds.), *The moral self* (pp. 310–336). Cambridge, MA: MIT Press.

Kohlberg, L. (1969). Stage and sequence: The cognitive developmental approach to socialization. In D. A. Goslin (Ed.), *Handbook of socialization theory and research* (pp. 347–380). Chicago: Rand McNally.

Kohlberg, L. (1971). From is to ought: How to commit the naturalistic fallacy and get away with it in the study of moral development. In T. Michel (Ed.), *Cognitive development and epistemology* (pp. 151–235). Cambridge MA: Harvard University Press.

Kohlberg, L. (1984). *Essays on moral development. Vol 2: The psychology of moral development*. San Francisco: Harper and Row.

Kohlberg, L., & Turiel, E. (1971). Moral development and moral education. In G. Lesser (Ed.), *Psychology and educational practice*. Chicago: Scott Foresman.

Lapsley, D. (1996). *Moral psychology*. Boulder, CO: Westview.

Lawrence, J. (1993). *A history of Russia* (7th rev. ed.). New York: Penguin Books.

Marsh, H. W., Smith, I. D., & Barnes, J. (1985). Multidimensional self-concepts: Relation with sex and academic achievement. *Journal of Educational Psychology, 77,* 581–596.

Mischel, W. (1973). Toward a cognitive social-learning reconceptualization of personality. *Psychological Review, 80,* 250–283.

Mischel, W. (1990). Personality dispositions revisited and revised: A view after three decades. In L. A. Pervin (Ed.). *Handbook of personality theory and research* (pp. 11–134). New York: Guilford.

Noam, G. (1993). "Normative vulnerabilities" of self and their transformations in moral action. In G. Noam (Eds.), *The moral self* (pp. 209–238). Cambridge, MA: MIT Press.

Nucci, L. (1996). Morality and the personal sphere of actions. In E. Reed, E. Turiel, & T. Brown (Eds.), *Values and knowledge* (pp. 41–60). Hillsdale, NJ: Lawrence Erlbaum Associates.

Nucci. L. (2001). *Education in the moral domain*. Cambridge, UK: Cambridge University Press.

Nucci, L. (2002). Because it is the right thing to do. *Human Development, 45,* 125–129.

Nussbaum, M. (1986). *The fragility of goodness*. Cambridge, UK: Cambridge University Press.

Nussbaum, M. (1997). *Great philosophers: Martha Nussbaum on Aristotle*. BBC Education and Training, Jill Dawson (producer). Princeton, NJ: Films for Humanities & Sciences.

Piaget, J. (1932). *The moral judgment of the child*. New York: Free Press.

Power, C., & Khmelkov, V. T. (1998). *Character development and self-esteem: Psychological foundations and educational implications*. Unpublished manuscript Liberal Studies, University of Notre Dame.

Rest, J. (1983). Morality. In P. Mussen (Ed.), *Handbook of child psychology: Vol. 3. Cognitive development* (4th ed.; J. Flavel & E. Markman, Vol. Eds., pp 556–628). New York: Wiley.

Rorty, R. (1973). The transformation of persons. *Philosophy, 48,* 261–275.

Rosenberg, M. (1965). *Society and the adolescent self-image*. Princeton, NJ: Princeton University Press.

Ross, L., & Nisbett, R. M. (1991). *The person and the situation: Perspectives on social psychology*. Philadelphia, PA: Temple University Press.

Sarbin, T., & Allen, V. L. (1968). Role theory. In G. Lindsey & E. Aronson (Eds.), *Handboook of social psychology Vol. 2*. Boston, MA: Addison Wesley.

Shweder, L. (1982). Liberalism as destiny. A review of Lawrence Kohlberg's Essay's on moral development, Volume I: The philosophy of moral development. *Contemporary Psychology,* 421–424.

Smetana, J. (1982). *Concepts of self and morality: Women's reasoning about abortion.* New York: Praeger.

Smetana, J. (1989). Toddler's social interactions in the context of moral and conventional transgressions in the home. *Developmental Psychology, 25,* 499–508.

Turiel, E. (1978). The development of concepts of social structure: social convention. In J. Glick & K. A. Clarke-Stewart (Eds.), *The development of social understanding.* New York: Gardner Press.

Turiel, E. (1983). *The development of social knowledge: Morality and convention.* Cambridge UK: Cambridge University Press.

Turiel, E. (1998). The development of morality. In W. Damon (Ed.), *Handbook of child psychology: Vol. 3. Social, emotional, and personality development* (5th ed.; N. Eisenberg, Vol. Ed., pp. 863–932). New York: Academic Press.

Turiel, E. (2002). *The culture of morality.* Cambridge: UK, Cambridge University Press.

Turiel, E., & Davidson, P. (1986). Heterogeneity, inconsistency, and asynchrony in the development of cognitive structures. In I. Levin (Ed.), *Stage and structure: Reopening the debate.* NJ: Ablex.

Wainryb, C. & Turiel, E. (1994). Dominance, subordination, and concepts of personal entitlements in cultural contexts. *Child Development, 65,* 1701–1722.

Part II

SELF AND MIND

Chapter 4

Unity and Modularity in the Mind and the Self: Towards a General Theory

Andreas Demetriou
University of Cyprus

Intelligence, mind, personality, and self are complementary aspects of the same entity: The person in its interaction with the physical, the social, and the symbolic world. Obviously, this is a generally accepted truism. Intelligence refers to the abilities underlying knowledge acquisition, understanding, and learning that aim to continuously keep the person able to cope with the changing demands of the world. *Mind* refers to exactly the same processes, although the emphasis shifts from the relationships of the person with the environment to the relationships of the person with himself or herself or others as thinking agents. That is, it refers to self-awareness about thinking, understanding, and learning. *Personality* refers to dispositions to relate with the world and interact with it in particular ways. Thus, one might say that personality sets the frames in which intelligence and mind are put in use. The *self* refers to all of these dimensions together as they are experienced, sensed, understood, and defined by each individual to produce this individual's personal identity. Despite their complementarity, these aspects of the person have been studied separately in psychology and the theories formulated about each of them are conceptually and epistemologically very different. As a result, the common ground and the dynamic relationships between the dimensions represented by these theories are not clearly illuminated.

73

This chapter summarizes a series of studies designed to contribute to the formation of an overarching model that would restore in theory the unity of intelligence, mind, self, and personality that exists in reality. Specifically, the chapter attempts to answer questions such as the following: What is exactly involved in self-awareness and self-representation? In other words, what from the various intellectual functions and processes and the personality dispositions and tendencies underlying one's interaction with the world is projected on the level of one's self-construct? How do the products of self-awareness interrelate to produce an integrated self-system, which includes the domains of cognition and personality? That is, how is it possible that persons have a strong sense of unity and identity while they are very differentiated and diversified in their abilities, characteristics, and tendencies? What does it change with development in these dimensions and their self-representation? How is the sense of unity so strongly preserved in development despite the fact that abilities, processes, and characteristics change extensively as a result of development?

Each of the various dominant traditions of psychology have focused on some of these questions and provided answers that are useful for the formation of an integrated model that would generate coherent and integrated answers to them. However, this model does not exist at present and thus none of the extant traditions of psychology have tried to answer these questions as such. Thus, in this introduction, we first summarize the answers given by the various traditions. Noting the similarities and differences between these answers provides the basis of the common model that can then be tested empirically.

ARCHITECTURES OF THE MIND, PERSONALITY, AND SELF

The Organization of the Mind

Psychometric (Carroll, 1993; Jensen, 1998; Thurstone, 1938) and other (Gardner, 1983; Sternberg, 1985) theories of intelligence have provided models specifying the dimensions and abilities underlying human intelligence and their interrelations. Theories of intellectual development, such as the classical theory of Piaget (1970) or the neo-Piagetian theories proposed later (Case, 1992; Fischer, 1980; Halford, 1993; Pascual-Leone, 1988) have attempted to describe the nature and inter-patterning of cognitive processes underlying intelligence from birth to maturity. All of these theories are somehow related to, and, to the one extend or the other, have influenced our model about the developing mind to be discussed next. However, this presentation focuses only on our model because of space limitations. The reader who is interested in a discussion of the relationships of this model to other theories is referred to other sources (Demetriou, 1998, 2000; Demetriou,

Efklides, & Platsidou, 1993; Demetriou & Kazi, 2001; Demetriou, Kazi, & Georgiou, 1999; Demetriou & Raftopoulos, 1999; Demetriou, Raftopoulos, & Kargopoulos, 1999). Figure 4.1 presents a graphical representation of this model.According to this model, the mind includes two levels of knowing, one oriented to the environment and another oriented to the self. That is, the first level includes representational and understanding processes and functions that specialize on the representation and understanding of information coming from the environment. The second level includes functions and processes oriented to monitoring, representing, understanding, and regulating the environment-oriented functions and processes. Optimum or intelligent performance at any time depends on the interaction between the two levels because efficient problem-solving or decision-making requires the application of environment-oriented functions and processes under the guidance of representations held about them at the level of self-oriented processes. This interaction ensures individual flexibility that cannot be present in an organism that is fully under the control of the environment. The interaction of the two levels occurs under the constraints that stem from the biological condition of the individual at any given point in his life. These constraints may be viewed as an additional "contentless" level in the architecture of the mind that involves processes and functions which operate as the interface between the two knowing levels previously mentioned.

The environment-oriented level of the mind.   The environment-oriented knowing level includes systems that specialize on the representation and processing of different types of relations in the environment. Our research has identified and delineated the following seven environment-oriented specialized capacity systems (SCS):

1. The *categorical* deals with similarity-difference relations and it underlies the construction and use of concepts about the world.
2. The *quantitative* deals with quantitative variations and relations and it underlies all aspects of mathematics that humans produce and use.
3. The *causal* deals with cause-effect relations and it underlies the actions that humans do to decipher causal relations and the explanatory models that they build to explain the dynamic aspects of the world.
4. The *spatial* deals with orientation in space and the imaginal representation of the environment.
5. The *propositional* deals with the integration of information that flows in verbal interactions and in the evaluation of the validity and invalidity of information that is provided in these interactions.
6. The *pictographic* underlies the representation of the environment or of thoughts themselves through the production of drawings or any other kind of signs.

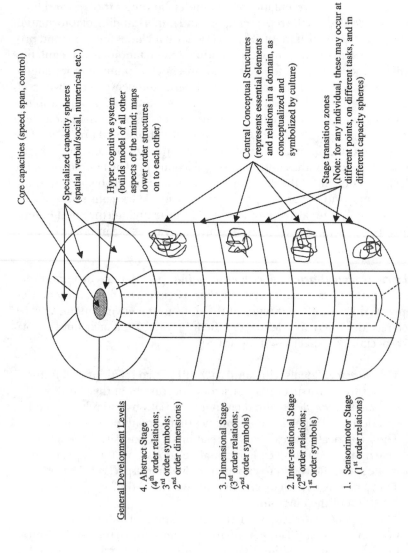

Core capacities (speed, span, control)

Specialized capacity spheres
(spatial, verbal/social, numerical, etc.)

Hyper cognitive system
(builds model of all other
aspects of the mind; maps
lower order structures
on to each other)

Central Conceptual Structures
(represents essential elements
and relations in a domain, as
conceptualized and
symbolized by culture)

Stage transition zones
(Note: for any individual, these may occur at
different points, on different tasks, and in
different capacity spheres)

General Development Levels

4. Abstract Stage
(4th order relations;
3rd order symbols;
2nd order dimensions)

3. Dimensional Stage
(3rd order relations;
2nd order symbols)

2. Inter-relational Stage
(2nd order relations;
1st order symbols)

1. Sensorimotor Stage
(1st order relations)

FIG. 4.1.   The general model of the architecture of the developing mind.   *Note.*   Based on Fig. 13 in Demetriou, Efklides, & Platsidou (1993).

7. The *social* system deals with the relations between individuals

We have proposed that the development and functioning of these structures is governed by three principles, namely the principles of *domain-specificity*, *procedural-computational specificity*, and *symbolic bias or specificity*. That is, each of them (a) specializes on the representation and processing of different types of relations or objects in the environment; (b) it involves different types of mental operations and processes which honor the peculiarities of the domain concerned; (c) finally, it makes use of symbolic systems, such as mental images, numerical and mathematical notations, or language, which are conducive to the efficient representation and processing of the domain concerned. Because of these structural differences, the environment-oriented systems can function *and* develop in relative autonomy of each other. (Demetriou & Efklides, 1985, 1989; Demetriou et al., 1993; Kargopoulos & Demetriou, 1998; Shayer, Demetriou, & Pervez, 1988).

The self-oriented level of the mind. Obviously, problem-solving creatures other than humans, such as animals and computers, may possess SCS-like systems governed by these three principles. However, possession of SCS-like systems is not sufficient to credit these creatures with mind. For this to be possible a fourth principle should hold. This is *the principle of self-mapping*. This principle states that mind is possible only if cognitive experiences, which differ between each other in regard to domain-specificity, procedural-computational specificity, and symbolic bias, are felt or cognized by the problem-solver as distinct of each other. Otherwise, they have to be felt or cognized as functionally similar or equivalent.

Thus, the self-oriented level involves processes and functions that guide the monitoring, understanding, and regulation of the processes and functions residing at the other two cognitive levels. The input to this level is information arising from the functioning of the environment-oriented systems under the current processing constraints (sensations, feelings, and conceptions caused by mental activity). This input is organized into the maps or models of mental functions and the self to be described next.

We used the term *hypercognitive* to denote this hierarchical relation between this and the other two levels of the mind. The term *hypercognitive* is used rather than the term *metacognitive* because it is a broader and more accurate description of the level of mind that is responsible for self-monitoring, self-representation, and self-control. In Greek, the adverb *hyper* means "higher than" or "on top of" or "going beyond" and when added to the word *cognitive* indicates the supervising and coordinating functions of the hypercognitive system (Demetriou, 1998, 2000; Demetriou, et al., 1993). The adverb *meta* means "coming after"; thus, our proposed term is more accurate than the term *metacognitive* because it refers to more of the functions associated with this level of mind. That is, it can denote an autonomous level of the architecture of the mind that exists from the beginning and that operates on the other levels rather than as a by-product of their functioning. In fact, metacognition is only one of the functions of the hypercognitive system.

We have shown that the hypercognitive level involves active self-knowing processes and self-descriptions and concepts. We used the terms *working* and *long-term hypercognition* to refer to these two types of processes, respectively. Working hypercognition involves on-line self-monitoring, self-recording, self-evaluation, and self-regulation processes and skills that enable the individual to activate efficiently and accurately her various systems, cognitive, emotional, or other, according to the requirements of the moment. Thus, working hypercognition controls the use of current processing potentials. The functioning of working hypercognition produces knowledge about the mind and the self that is organized into three interrelated systems of concepts or models. These three systems constitute long-term hypercognition.

Specifically, hypercognition includes, first, a general model of the mind which reflects the abilities and processes involved in the other two levels of the mind. The so called theory of mind that has been intensively studied in the last 15 years belong to this system of self-knowledge. Second, it also involves prescriptions and strategies about the efficient use of the abilities and processes involved in the other levels of the mind. Together, the hypercognitive map of mental abilities and the prescriptions and strategies about their use constitute the individual's conception about intelligence and its use. Finally, it involves a cognitive self-image. That is, it involves the representations that persons hold about their own condition in regard to different mental functions, abilities, strategies, and skills (Demetriou et al., 1993).

The level of processing potentials. Processing potentials are defined in terms of three parameters: *speed of processing*, *control of processing*, and *storage*. Speed of processing refers to the maximum speed at which a given mental act may be efficiently executed. Control of processing refers to the processes that identify and register goal-relevant information and block out dominant or appealing but actually irrelevant information. Storage refers to the processes that enable a person to hold information in an active state while integrating it with other information until the current problem is solved. Thus, these functions determine the system's efficiency in selecting and executing the mental acts relevant to the current goal of processing. Thus, this level is close to the psychometric conception of general intelligence (Demetriou, 2001; Demetriou et al., 1993).

The Organization of Personality

Personality seems to be organized in a way which appears formally equivalent to the hierarchical organization of the mind as previously presented. That is, it may also be analyzed as a three-level hierarchy, involving a level of general temperamental constrains, a level of distinct personality dimensions or dispositions, and a level of self-representations and self-concepts about the other two levels.

Specifically, temperament is considered as the substrate on which personality and the self are constructed. According to Kagan (1994), *temperament* refers to regulation of arousal states, ease and intensity of arousal in reaction to stimulation, and general tendencies to receive and react to stimulation in particular ways. Examples of temperamental dispositions include irritability, mood, motor activity, sociability, attentiveness, adaptability, approach to or avoidance of novelty. These dispositions are considered to be inherited to a considerable degree. These early tendencies and dispositions are gradually shaped, during development, into the more stable dimensions of personality and style that characterize the individual from childhood onward. Temperament may be regarded as the personality equivalent of processing potentials just discussed.

The currently dominant view is that personality can be described in reference to five dimensions, the so called Big Five factors of personality, namely, *extraversion, agreeableness, conscientiousness, neuroticism*, and *openness to experience*. Extraverts are sociable, active, self-confident, and uninhibited. Introverts, on the other hand, are withdrawn, shy, and inhibited. Agreeable individuals are generous, warm, kind, and forgiving, whereas individuals low in agreeableness are suspicious, impatient, argumentative, and aggressive. Conscientious individuals are organized, ambitious, determined, reliable, and responsible. Individuals low in conscientiousness are distractible, lazy, careless, and impulsive. Individuals high in neuroticism are nervous, anxious, tense, and self-centered. Individuals low in neuroticism are confident, clear-thinking, alert, and content. Finally, individuals who are open to experience are curious and with wide interests, inventive, original, and artistic. Individuals who are not open to experience are conservative, cautious, and mild. The Big Five dimensions may be regarded as the personality equivalents of the SCSs (Costa & McCrae, 1997).

Finally, there are the self-systems that translate these Big Five dimensions into self-concepts and self-descriptions that help the persons to guide and monitor their behavior in the actual environment, frequently in spite of the tendencies arising from these dimensions (Graziano, Jensen-Campbell, & Finch, 1997). For example, this level includes the various dimensions of self-esteem, such as global, social and academic self-esteem. Thus, the self-systems, corresponding to our hypercognitive level of the mind, translate the personality dispositions into particular modes of understanding and action.

The Organization of the Self

Interestingly, the analysis of the self is very similar to the analysis of the mind and personality as just proposed. According to the classical theory of James (1892), the self involves two hierarchical levels, the "I-self" and the "Me-self." The I-self is the knower, and as such includes all self-observation and self-recording processes that generate the knowledge that persons have about the bodily, the social, and the mental aspects of themselves. This knowledge is the Me-self.

James's distinction between a knowing (the I-self) and a known self (the Me-self) is present in modern theories of the self. For example, in Markus's model (Markus & Wurf, 1987) the working self-concept is differentiated from the collection of self-representations possessed by the individual. The working self-concept involves all presently accessible self-representations and it is directly involved in the formation and control of behavior at both the intra- and the inter-personal level. Therefore, in this model, the working self-concept assumes the functions of the Jamesian I-self or our working hypercognition, which generates self-descriptions that belong to the Jamesian Me-self or long-term hypercognition.

Empirical research suggests that the self-construct is indeed hierarchically organized. This research suggests there is a general self-concept at the apex, a number of major domains at a middle level (i.e., the self-concept about the academic, the social, the emotional, and the physical domain) and a number of more specific domains within each of these major domains (i.e., maths and science in the academic domain or physical ability and physical appearance in the physical domain). Moreover, each of these domains includes a descriptive part that specifies what an individual can and cannot do and an evaluative part that specifies how important the individuals are for the possibilities and impossibilities for each of the domains. Thus, there is global domain-specific self-worth or self-esteem (see Bracken, 1996; Harter, 1999; Hattie, 1992).

DEVELOPMENTAL DYNAMICS

All of the functions, processes, skills, dispositions, and characteristics included in the various levels and systems of the mind as specified in the model above undergo extensive changes from birth to maturity. Different scholars and traditions have focused on different components of this model and attempted to describe and explain their development. Space limitations do not allow us to elaborate on the development of the various systems. Reference can only be made to findings regarding changes in the relationships between the self-oriented and the other levels of the mind, because these are related to the studies presented here.

There is general agreement that, with development, the self-system changes in regard to several dimensions. That is, with age self-representations involve more dimensions that are better integrated into increasingly more complex structures. Thus, emphasis gradually moves from concrete self-descriptions to more abstract trait- and characteristic-like self-definitions. Moreover, self-representations become more accurate in regard to the actual characteristics and abilities to which they refer (Demetriou, 2000; Harter, 1999).

Finally, self-regulation becomes increasingly more focused, refined, efficient, and strategic. That is, the individual gradually acquires command of his or her information processing capabilities and temperamental dispositions. Practically, this implies that cognitive capabilities and personality dispositions come under increasing a priori control of the person's long-term hypercognitive maps and self-definitions. In Freud's terms mind and personality come under ego control (Demetriou, 2000; Demetriou & Kazi, 2001; Flavell, Green, & Flavell, 1995).

For many scholars, development is synergetic and dynamic. That is, it occurs when there is a shift in the interrelationships between different dimensions or systems of the person (Case et al., 1996; Demetriou & Raftopoulos, 1999; van Geert, 1994). Until now, many scholars have proposed models that capture the development in each of the main realms that concern us here, that is mind, personality, and self. However, there have been very few and sketchy attempts to study and model changes in the relationships between these three realms. Some of our studies, which are directly concerned with this question, are summarized next.

DYNAMIC RELATIONSHIPS BETWEEN THE LEVELS OF MIND, PERSONALITY, AND SELF

Structural Relationships

A large study, which is fully presented in Demetriou & Kazi (2001), aimed to highlight self-awareness in regard to cognitive abilities, personality, and thinking styles and possible changes in self-awareness during growth. This study involved 840 individuals about equally drawn from 10 to 15 years of age were. These individuals were examined by the following five types of tasks or questionnaires.

First, a set of tasks addressed seven domains of thought. Six of these domains correspond to the environment-oriented systems specified by our theory. Specifically, a set of mathematical analogies and algebraic reasoning tasks addressed the quantitative system. A set of hypothesis testing and design of experiments tasks addressed the causal system. A set of tasks requiring to understand social intentions and dialectical thinking addressed the social thought system. A set of mental rotation and image manipulation tasks addressed the spatial system. A set of drawing tasks addressed the pictographic system. Finally, to address creativity, we used a set of tasks requiring the production of new ideas and symbols about the situation described.

Second, there was an inventory examining how participants represent themselves in regard to various processes involved in each of the cognitive domains represented in the task battery previously mentioned. Statements about *quantitative thought* referred to the subject's facility in solving mathematical problems or applying mathematical knowledge to everyday problems (e.g., "I immediately solve everyday problems involving numbers"). Statements about *causal thought* referred to the ability to formulate hypothesis, to design experiments, or to construct models that would accommodate experimental findings (e.g., "To find out which of my guesses is correct, I proceed to methodically consider each time only the things my guess proposes"). Statements about *spatial thought* referred to visual memory (e.g., "I retain a very clear picture of things") and facility in thinking in images ("When I have to arrange things in a certain space, I first visualize what it will be like if I place them in certain way and then I arrange them in fact"). The statements about drawing referred to ability to draw a man, a landscape, and a map (e.g., "I can draw a person very accurately"; " I can paint a building as if it were a photograph"). Finally, the statements about social thought referred to the facility in understanding other's thoughts and feelings (e.g., "I understand easily the intentions of others before they express them").

Third, there was an inventory addressed to various social and personality characteristics, such as ambition and ideal self ("I am an ambitious person", "I want to be the center of attention"), impulsivity ("I do the first thing that comes to my mind"), systematicity ("I set the order in which I will deal with various things depending on their importance"), and self-control ("I know to control my feelings"). Also this inventory addressed general cognitive characteristics, such as learning ("I retain a lot of elements of what I hear") and reasoning ability ("I like drawing logical conclusions, which can be justified by the data I have").

Fourth, there was an inventory addressed to different styles of activity and thought that are associated with different kinds of occupation. That is, activities, which require *originality* ("I like working on problems for which there are no pre-prepared solutions"), an *executive style*, which requires following rules ("When solving a problem, I prefer to follow existing rules"), or a *judgmental or evaluative style*, which requires evaluating other people ("I like to judge others' choices"). This inventory was based on Sternberg's (1988; Ferrari & Sternberg, 1998) theory of self-government.

The evidence generated by this study was first examined with the aim to highlight the nature and organization of self-awareness in regard to all of the processes involved. Specifically, a series of confirmatory factor analysis and structural equation models is congruent with the assumption of two knowing levels, one oriented to the environment and another to the self and that the second accurately represents the condition and organization of the first. One of these models is shown in Fig. 4.2. It can be seen in this model that for each ability-specific factor that was abstracted from performance there is a corresponding factor that reflects the organization of abilities at the level of self-representation. Moreover, there is a second order general factor related to all of the domain-specific performance factors. This factor is directly related with self-representation of logicality. Thus, it is clear that the hypercognitive system involves specialized representations about each of the domain-specific cognitive modules and also self-representations about general cognitive abilities that represent the persons general sense of cognitive efficacy. These representations play a pivotal role in the organization of the self-system because they influence directly both the state of the domain-specific representations of the cognitive modules and also the various dimensions of personality and thinking style.

Regarding the organization of personality and the self, there were two layers of factors. One of them, which is more basic, included factors standing for three pivotal dimensions of the self, namely ideal self, impulsivity, which reflects a primary disposition of temperament, and systematicity, which is the other pole of this disposition to act. Interestingly, the impulsivity factor was closely and negatively related to the general cognitive ability factor, but was not related to either of the two cognitive self-image factors. However, ideal self and systematicity were related to the two general cognitive self-representation factors.

The three personality factors do function as the interface between cognitive self-representation and thinking styles. It can be seen that the factor standing for the ideal self exhibited the strongest effect on three of the four thinking styles factors. This suggests that the dimension represented by this factor is as important in the formation of a person's choices as the logical reasoning and discourse factor is in the organization of the more cognitive aspects of one's self-image. Expectedly, the factor representing the executive style was more closely related with systematicity than with the two other factors representing personality characteristics. The factor representing originality was related highly with the factor standing for ideal self, but was not related to systematicity and it was negatively related to impulsivity. The factor

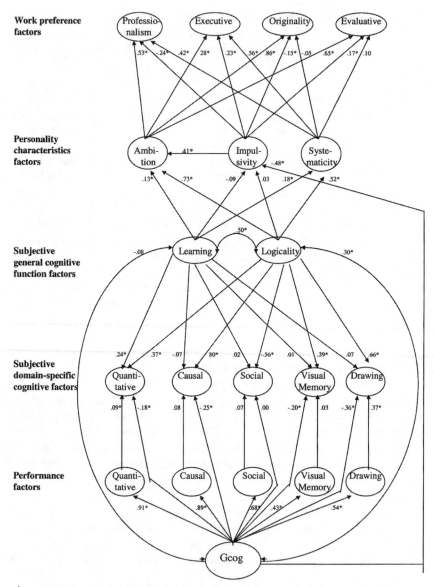

Work preference factors

Professionalism · Executive · Originality · Evaluative

.53* · .24* · .42* · 28* · .23* · .56* · .86* · -.15* · -.05 · .65* · .17* · .10

Personality characteristics factors

Ambition · .41* · Impulsivity · Systematicity

.13* · .73* · -.09 · .03 · .18* · .52*

-.48*

Subjective general cognitive function factors

-.08 · Learning · .50* · Logicality · .30*

Subjective domain-specific cognitive factors

.24* · .37* · -.07 · 80* · .02 · -.56* · .01 · .39* · .07 · .66*

Quantitative · Causal · Social · Visual Memory · Drawing

.09* · -.18* · .08 · -.25* · .07 · .00 · -.20* · .03 · -.36* · .37*

Performance factors

Quantitative · Causal · Social · Visual Memory · Drawing

.91* · .89* · .68* · .43* · .54*

Gcog

x^2(614)=1274.580, p=.001, CFI=.937, GFI=.920, AGFI=.903, SRMR=.048, RMSEA=.003

FIG. 4.2. The final model of the dynamic relationships between modules across the different levels of the mental architecture.

84

representing a judgmental style was related highly with ambition, much lower but positively with impulsivity, and to a very low degree with systematicity. It seems, therefore, that nonimpulsive individuals with high ambitions are oriented to activities requiring originality; impulsive and ambitious tend toward evaluative activities; impulsive and systematic individuals orient themselves to the rule-abiding activities.

Developmental Relationships

Then the evidence produced by this study focused on the developmental aspects of our questions. Testing for age differences in mental architecture by means of multiple groups confirmatory factor analysis indicated that the mental architecture is stable throughout adolescence. That is, the same constructs were found for all three measures (performance, self-awareness of performance, and thinking styles) across all age groups included in the study. However, there was one very interesting difference between these age groups. Specifically, the correlation between the construct representing the environment-oriented level of the mind and the construct representing the self-oriented level of the mind was very low at the age of 11 years, but increased systematically and became strong at the age of 15 years. That is, the correlation between these two higher order factors was .05, .11, .20, .45, and .60 at the age of 11, 12, 13, 14, and 15 years, respectively. This finding suggests that many of the changes traditionally associated with the transition from childhood to adolescence may primarily affect the communication between the two knowing levels of the mental architecture, rather than the modules and actual processes at each level. Thus, self-monitoring and self-representation at the environment-oriented level become increasingly accurate and detailed (Demetriou & Kazi, 2001).

Individual Differences

It is well known that there are stable individual differences in persons' attitudes to self-evaluation and self-representation. For example, there are persons who are systematically lenient whereas others are systematically strict in the evaluation of their own performance. How can one reconcile this common knowledge with the findings just presented that indicated that self-representations do reflect accurately the actual organization of cognitive abilities?

To answer this question, we ran a longitudinal study. In this study, which is fully presented in Demetriou and Kazi (2001), we retained for further testing subjects who varied systematically in their accuracy and attitude to self-evaluation. That is, based on the combination of the performance attained on the cognitive tasks and their self-evaluation of this performance we formulated the following four groups of subjects: (1) low performance-low success evaluation, (2) low performance-high success evaluation, (3) high performance-low success evaluation, and (4) high performance-high success evaluation. Persons in group 1 (low-accurates) and 4 (high-accurates) are accurate in their self-evaluation, because their evaluations are consistent with their performance. Persons in group 2 and 3 are not accurate. That is, persons in group 2 (law inaccurates) are lenient whereas persons in group 3 (high inaccurates) are strict to themselves. These subjects were tested on all of the tasks and batteries just described once a year for 3 consecutive years.

In accord with expectation, the performance of all four person groups improved systematically across all three testing waves and age groups in all systems. In fact, the lower the initial performance, the higher the improvement from the one testing wave to the next. Did self-evaluation also change? Figure 4.3 illustrates the answer to this question. On the one hand, it is clear that self-evaluations do improve from the one testing wave to the next across all four person groups—more notably so for low accurate and high inaccurate persons. On the other hand, the relative differences between the four groups persist across all three testing waves across all age groups.

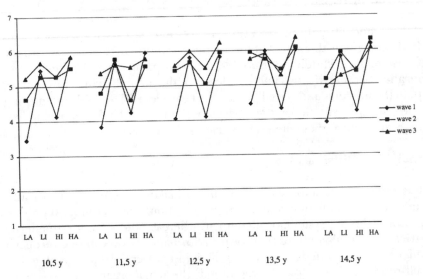

FIG. 4.3. Post-performance success evaluation averaged across SCSs as a function of age, person category, and testing wave. From "Mind, Self, and Personality: Dynamic Interactions From Late Childhood to Early Adulthood," in A. Demetriou & S. Kazi, *Unity and Modularity in the Mind and the Self: Studies on the Relationships between Self-awareness, Personality, and Intellectual Development from Childhood to Adolescence,* 2001, London: Routledge. Copyright © 2001 by Routledge. Reprinted with permission.

These findings suggest that self-evaluation and self-representation remain generally consistent in time. That is, persons tend to be accurate, lenient, or strict to the output of their cognitive functioning and other dispositions. This implies the operation of a kind of internal monitor that adjusts evaluations and representations in regard to particular behaviors or events to stay consistent with one's self-definitions despite variations caused by changes in the environment or in the developmental status of the cognitive abilities and tendencies themselves. This monitor seems to be "driven" by a factor that may be termed *personal constant*. That is, the individual adopts a particular attitude to his or her performance and ability, which is consistently applied across different domains. This constant is used to adjust any signals regarding his or her functioning to a level that is personally characteristic. If properly quantified, this constant may be regarded as the quantitative expression of self-efficacy or global self-worth.

This personal constant undergoes major redefinitions or rescalings at crucial points in development when cognitive possibilities are transformed. For instance, it is a common finding that during the transition from childhood to adolescence self-evaluations first decrease as compared to self-evaluations produced in late childhood and they are then restored to previous levels. After this change, self-evaluations are much more accurate than before (Harter, 1999). Moreover, we observed this phenomenon to be associated with any major cognitive reorganization throughout adolescence and early adulthood. This indicates that after each major cognitive change the criteria for self-evaluation are transformed to accommodate the new cognitive characteristics and possibilities (Demetriou & Kazi, 2001).

These interpretations bear an important implication in regard to the fact that the hypercognitive maps of all persons may accurately represent the architecture of their mind and self and still be accurate or inaccurate in regard to the evaluation of personal performance and behavior. That is, on the one hand, the accuracy of the hypercognitive maps refers to relative differences between cognitive and personality functions and abilities *within* persons. The personal constant, on the other hand, is consistently applied across the board of cognitive and personality functions and abilities thereby explaining differences in self-evaluation and self-representation *between* persons. Thus, assuming this constant can explain why both types of differences are generally stable. That is, relative differences between abilities and tendencies within persons and relative differences in self-evaluation and self-representation across persons vis-à-vis each of the abilities and tendencies. In other words, it explains why hypercognition can simultaneously preserve an accurate structure of cognitive processes in the mental maps it constructs and also involve a strong personal element in terms of how these processes are effected (or are thought to be effected) in the real world.

Obviously, the operation of this constant bears some important practical implications, because it may influence how the individual uses his or her cognitive and self-awareness skills and resources. That is, it may affect such functions as persistence toward the attainment of mental and other goals, or sensitivity to feedback. For example, persons who are low in ability but who think highly of themselves may not work as hard as needed to achieve certain goals or they may ignore signs of failure because they consider themselves sufficiently successful. On the other hand, persons who are high in ability but negative in their self-evaluations, may transmit an image that underscores their true potentialities and capabilities; in turn, this may cause their exclusion from the distribution of otherwise available resources. In other words, the self-awareness moderation mechanism becomes a factor of personal development in two distinct but interrelated respects: as a moderator of one's self-actualization of potentials and as a moderator of others' attitudes to any self-actualization endeavor.

FAMILIES OF MIND: RELATIONSHIPS BETWEEN SELF-REPRESENTATIONS AND PARENTS' REPRESENTATIONS

The evidence presented so far was limited to the individual. However, individuals do not develop alone but in groups with other individuals. In fact, many argue that the mind in general and the self-system in particular may primarily be a social rather than an individual construction (Bogdan, 2000; Rogoff, 1990; Wertsch, 1991). Therefore, examining the relationships between the representations that person hold about each other is necessary if we are to understand how social interactions help shape and are shaped by minds and selves. In the sake of this aim, we ran a series of studies that examined the representations that parents and children have about each other. Specifically, these studies aimed to answer the following two questions: (1) How do the children's actual cognitive abilities and self-representations about them relate to their parents' respective representations? (2) How aware children are of their parents' representations about them and how aware parents are of their children's self-representations.

If the architecture proposed by our theory is a strong characteristic of the human mind, we should expect that it would also structure the intersubjective space of mutual representations. That is, the systems and dimensions previously specified must be present in both the self-representations and the representations that different persons hold about each other. This would imply that the architecture of mind proposed by our theory is a common language that may be used by individuals to negotiate their views and beliefs about each other.

To answer these questions, we examined the parents of about one third of participants involved in the first study. Specifically, both of the parents were first presented samples of the cognitive tasks solved by the children and they were asked to indicate (on a 7-point scale) their evaluation of their child's ability to solve each of the tasks. These evaluations can be compared with children's corresponding actual performance and self-representations and also with the parents' representations as evoked by the cognitive abilities inventories previously described. Moreover, to examine the parents' representations about the various children's characteristics involved in the study, all self-representation inventories (i.e., the inventory addressed to cognitive abilities, general personal strategies and characteristics, and thinking and activity styles) were restated to refer to the children. The parents were asked to state (using the same 7-point scale) how much each of the items applies to their own child. Finally, both children and parents were examined on the reflected appraisals inventory. Specifically, children were asked to answer all of inventories from the perspective of each of their parents (i.e., answer how you think your mother and father each answered about you). Parents were asked to respond from their child's perspective (i.e., answer how you think your child answered about him or herself). Thus, this inventory, together with the other inventories, can show how family members represent themselves, each other, and each other's representations about themselves.

A first picture of the relationships between the various aspects of self-representations and reciprocal representations are shown in Table 4.1. This table shows the correlations between children's self-representations, their reflected appraisals about the representations they believe that their parents have about them and parents' representations and reflected appraisals.

The first conclusion is concerned with the relations between self-image and public image. It can be seen that the correlations between the various dimensions of self-image and the children's reflected appraisals of their parents' representations were significant in most of the cases. This suggests that these two images are related. At the same time, it needs to be noted that the size of these correlations varied across domains and persons. It can be seen that children's self-representations are closer to representations they think their parents have about them when they refer to domains transparent to awareness, such as quantitative or imaginal thought rather than in regard to domains opaque to awareness, such as social and causal thought. Moreover, children think that their mother's representations about them are more similar to their own self-representations than their father's corresponding representations for all dimensions. It needs to be stressed, however, that although related, self-image and public image are clearly distinct. This is strongly suggested by the fact that the correlations between the child's reflected appraisals ascribed to each of the two parents were always considerably higher that the correlations between the various self-image dimensions and the corresponding reflected appraisals.

TABLE 4.1

Correlations Between Self-Representations, Mother's Representations About the Child, and Reflected Appraisals Representations Across Different Dimensions

		1	*2*	*3*	*4*	*5*
1	Child's self image					
	Quantitative					
	Social					
	Imaginal					
	Ambition					
	Impulsivity					
	Originality					
2	Child's reflected appraisal for the mother					
	Quantitative	.61				
	Social	.42				
	Imaginal	.54				
	Ambition	.56				
	Impulsivity	.36				
	Originality	.47				
3	Child's reflected appraisal for the father					
	Quantitative	.54	.68			
	Social	.30	.76			
	Imaginal	.47	.74			
	Ambition	.47	.82			
	Impulsivity	.37	.87			
	Originality	.49	.74			
4	Mother's image of the child					
	Quantitative	.41	.36	.32		
	Social	.20	.01	.06		
	Imaginal	.17	.23	.37		
	Ambition	.17	.15	.05		
	Impulsivity	.18	.32	.37		
	Originality	.06	.05	.06		
5	Mother's reflected appraisal for the child					
	Quantitative	.52	.40	.33	.77	
	Social	.14	.05	.06	.57	
	Imaginal	.13	.20	.24	.52	
	Ambition	.18	.18	.14	.83	
	Impulsivity	.18	.27	.35	.53	
	Originality	.07	.00	.12	.59	

Note. Quantitative thought is regarded as transparent to awareness and social thought is regarded as opaque to awareness. Ambition seems to fall in-between (N=95).

Second, attention is also drawn to the very high correlations between the children's reflected appraisals for their mother and their father. This finding clearly implies that children believe that they have a "public image," which is transmitted to their parents. Thus, they think that their two parents' images of them are very similar to each other.

Finally, the last row of Table 6.1 presents information about the relationships between parents' reflected appraisals of the children self-representations and the children's self-representations of themselves. It is highly interesting to note that the correlations between the mother's representations of the child and her reflected appraisals of the child's self-representations are impressively high—even higher than the correlation between the child's self-representations and the child's representations of her mother's representations. This indicates that in the mother's mind her actual opinion of the child and what she believes that the child thinks of himself are less differentiated than the child's self-representations and the representations that she believes her mother holds.

A series of models were fitted to examine the structural relationships between the various dimensions of ability and representation in the child and the two parents. Only one of these models is presented here because of space limitations. This model is shown in Fig. 4.4. This model included only three of the various cognitive abilities examined in the study, that is, quantitative thought, social thought, and drawing.

It can be seen that this model involved three SCS-specific factors representing children's performance on the tasks addressed to the three SCSs already mentioned, three SCS-specific factors representing children's self-representations about these SCSs, and, finally, two sets of three SCS-specific factors representing the two parents' representations about these three SCSs. The three factors in each of the four sets were regressed on a second-order factor.

Moreover, the following structural relations were build into the model. First, each of the child's three self-representations factors were regressed on (a) the residual of the corresponding SCS-specific factor representing actual performance and, (b) the corresponding SCS-specific factor of the mother. Second, all three factors of the mother and the father were regressed on the child's general cognitive ability factor. Moreover, each of these SCS-specific factors of the mother was regressed on the corresponding SCS-specific performance factor of the child. Third, each of the three factors of the father was also regressed on the corresponding factor for the mother. Finally, the three second-order factors (i.e., the child's general self-representation factor and the two general factors of the parents) were allowed to correlate.

The fit of this model to the data was excellent (see Fig. 4.4). Thus, it can be concluded, first, that all cognitive domains are present in performance,

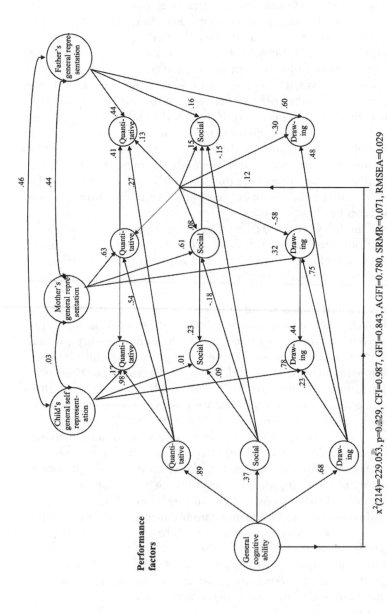

FIG. 4.4. The model of the interrelationships between children's abilities and self-representations and parents' representations of children's abilities. From "Mind, Self, and Personality: Dynamic Interactions From Late Childhood to Early Adulthood," in A. Demetriou & S. Kazi, *Unity and Modularity in the Mind and the Self: Studies on the Relationships between Self-awareness, Personality, and Intellectual Development from Childhood to Adolescence*, 2001, London: Routledge. Copyright © 2001 by Routledge. Reprinted with permission.

$x^2(214)=229.053$, p=0.229, CFI=0.987, GFI=0.843, AGFI=0.780, SRMR=0.071, RMSEA=0.029

in self-representation, and in other persons' representations of other persons. The second conclusion is equally interesting. That is, the mother does influence the formation of the child's self-representations and the father's representations of the child. It can be seen that the mother's representations about the child are based on two complementary sources. That is, the child's general cognitive ability itself and the domains that are transparent to evaluation and monitoring. This indicates that the mother is sensitive to the child's general efficiency as a problem solver as reflected in the child's speed, accuracy, and general strategies. It may also indicate, however, that the mother somehow averages over different activities so that the child's strengths and weaknesses are pulled together into a general representation for the child. At the same time, some domains, that are transparent to awareness, such as mathematics or drawing, are reflected directly and clearly in the mother's system of representations about the child. Then the mother's representations influence both, the self-representations of the child herself and the father. It can be seen that the child's self-representations in some domains are influenced by the mother's corresponding representations as much or more than they are influenced by the actual state of the corresponding domains.

Do the same relationships hold for the realm of personality? The model shown in Fig. 4.5 is relevant to this question. It can be seen that this model involved the factors of ambition, impulsivity, and systematicity for each of the three persons examined, that is the child and the two parents. According to the structural assumptions built into this model, each of the three factors standing for the mothers' representations about the child was regressed on the corresponding factor standing for children's self-representations. Moreover, each of the three factors standing for the fathers' representations was regressed on the corresponding factor of the mother. Thus, in line with the model involving the cognitive domains, the mother was again found to play a pivotal role in the family system of representations about the child. However, in the present case, it was the mothers' representations that were formed on the basis of the corresponding personality dimensions of the child rather than vice-versa.

The findings of this study suggest strongly that, as expected, that the dimensions described by this theory are present in both the individual's self-representations and the others' representations about the individual. This indicates that the structures described by this theory are not just latent constructs underlying individual behavior. They also organize the representations that individuals hold about themselves and each other. Because of this very fact, these structures have a shared or an interpersonal dimension that enables the persons to formulate and negotiate the views and representations that they have about each other.

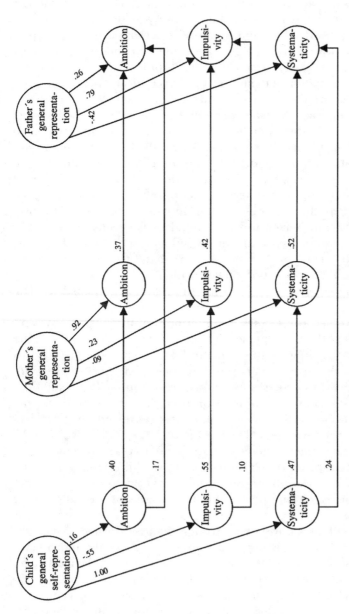

$x^2 (117)=109.435$, CFI=1.000, GFI=.894, AGFI=.846, SRMR=.080, RMSEA=.000.

FIG. 4.5.   Model of the interrelationships between children's and parents' representations of children's position on the dimensions of ambition, impulsivity, and systematicity. From "Mind, Self, and Personality: Dynamic Interactions From Late Childhood to Early Adulthood," in A. Demetriou & S. Kazi, *Unity and Modularity in the Mind and the Self: Studies on the Relationships between Self-awareness, Personality, and Intellectual Development from Childhood to Adolescence*, 2001, London: Routledge. Copyright © 2001 by Routledge. Reprinted with permission.

FROM PROCESSING SPEED TO COGNITIVE
SELF-REPRESENTATION AND SELF-EFFICACY

The previously mentioned studies showed that general cognitive ability is directly connected with one's self-representations of logicality and learning ability. However, in that study, general cognitive ability is an abstraction that came out from confirmatory factor analysis as a second-order factor. This second-order factor may represent a number of different processes and functions, such as general information processing potentials, self-monitoring and self-regulation skills and strategies or even general inferential processes. To disentangle these relationships a series of new studies was designed which aim to explore the relationships between each of the processes mentioned and the various dimensions of self-representation.

One of these studies, fully presented in Demetriou & Kazi (2001), aimed to explore in detail the relationships between the dimensions of processing efficiency, reasoning, and self-representation. Thus, this study examined 11-, 13-, and 15-year-old adolescents by a wide battery of tasks and inventories addressed to all of these processes. Specifically, processing efficiency was examined by a series of Stroop-like tasks. In these tasks, speed of processing is the time needed to read words denoting color names written in the same ink color (e.g., the word "red" written in red ink). Traditionally, the faster an individual can read these words, the more efficient his processing system is thought to be. Control of processing is usually tested under conditions that generate conflicting interpretations. In the Stroop phenomenon (Stroop, 1935), words denoting color are written with a different ink color (i.e., the word "red" written with blue ink), and the individual is asked to name the ink color as quickly as possible. These conditions are considered to test control of processing, because the subject is required to inhibit a dominant but irrelevant response (to read the word) in order to select and emit a weaker but relevant response (name the ink color) (Demetriou et al., 1993; Dempster & Brainerd, 1995).

To test the environment-oriented systems, the subjects were examined by a series of quantitative thought tasks, such as numerical analogies (e.g., 3 : 9 :: 6 : ?), verbal analogies (e.g., picture : painting :: word : ?; [paper, talk, literature], choose what is missing from the terms), propositional reasoning tasks (e.g., tasks addressed to transitivity), and spatial thought tasks, such as mental rotation.

To test the self-oriented level of the mind we used all of the inventories just described. Thus, we could specify the relationships between the various dimensions of self-representation and thinking style and the dimensions of processing potentials and the environment-oriented systems of the mind.

Based on a series of preliminary analysis, we selected participants who were very low or very high in speed of processing and analogical reasoning. Thus, we formed four groups of participants:

1. Slow processors and low reasoners.
2. Slow processors and high reasoners.
3. Fast processors and low reasoners.
4. Fast processors and high reasoners.

The self-image of these participants in regard to logical reasoning and learning ability was then examined. Figure 4.6 summarizes the principal findings. It can be seen that the faster in processing and the higher on the analogical reasoning tasks the participants were, the better they considered themselves to be in reasoning and learning ability. This finding suggests clearly that the hypercognitive system directly registers and represents the condition of the processing system and general inferential processes. Therefore, one might say that the famous construct of g of psychometric theories of intelligence (Jensen, 1998), on the one hand, and the recently revitalized constructs of global self-worth (Harter, 1999) and self efficacy (Bandura, 1989) of self and personality psychology, on the other hand, are directly connected so that the second closely monitors and reflects the condition of the first.

COGNITIVE DEVELOPMENT, SELF-REPRESENTATION, AND THE BIG FIVE FACTORS OF PERSONALITY

The studies presented so far focused on cognitive performance, self-representations about cognitive performance, thinking styles, and personality. However, personality was rather under-represented in these studies, because our tests did not address directly the dimensions of personality which are considered dominant by current personality theory (see Costa & McCrae, 1997; Graziano, Jensen-Campbell, & Finch, 1997). Moreover, our inventory of cognitive self-image did not address some important dimensions of the mind as specified by our theory. To remedy this limitation, a series of new studies were designed (see Demetriou & Kazi, 2001). One of the studies examined in detail the relationships between various dimensions of cognitive self-representation and thinking styles together with the so called "Big Five" factors of personality (i.e., extraversion, agreeableness, conscientiousness, neuroticism, and openness to experience). The main concern of the study was to specify how the Big Five factors interrelate with cognitive self-representation, on the one hand, and thinking styles, on the other hand. In the sake of this concern, we used three inventories.

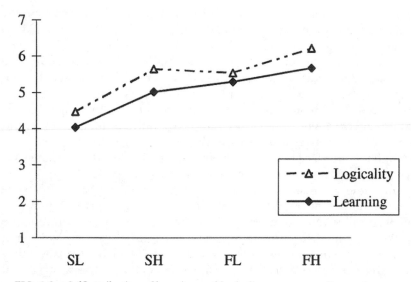

FIG. 4.6. Self-attribution of learning and logicality scores according to the combination of performance on the speed of processing and the verbal analogies tasks. From "Mind, Self, and Personality: Dynamic Interactions From Late Childhood to Early Adulthood," in A. Demetriou & S. Kazi, *Unity and Modularity in the Mind and the Self: Studies on the Relationships between Self-awareness, Personality, and Intellectual Development from Childhood to Adolescence,* 2001, London: Routledge. Copyright © 2001 by Routledge. Reprinted with permission.

Specifically, personality was addressed by the Greek version of an inventory addressed to the Big Five factors (Besevegis, Pavlopoulos, & Mourousaki, 1996). The inventory addressed to self-representation involved all of the dimensions included in the corresponding inventory used in the first study. In addition it involved a series of new items addressed to processes and functions which were not represented in the version used in the previous studies. That is, the new items addressed self-image in regard to various aspects of (a) speed of processing, (b) working memory, (c) self-monitoring and self-regulation, and (d) deductive and inductive reasoning. Thus, in its present version, the cognitive self-image inventory addressed most dimensions of each of the three levels of the mind, (i.e., the processing system, the environment-oriented systems, and the hypercognitive system). Thinking styles were addressed by a shortened version of the inventory used in the first of the studies described here. This study involved 20- to 22-year-old university students.

An exploratory factor analysis applied on all three inventories together showed that all dimensions of cognitive self-representation, personality, and thinking styles were present as very strong factors. To specify the exact nature of the relationships between the various kinds of factors, a complex structural equation model was built, which assumed that the various kinds of factors are organized in tiers. Figure 4.7 shows this model. It can be seen that the cognitive factors are located at the basis of this architecture. The personality factors are located in the middle. It may be noted here that locating the personality factors in the middle does not imply that they are considered as less basic than the cognitive factors in determining behavior. This architecture simply indicates that the cognitive factors exert their influences on derivative factors, such as thinking styles, or on actual behavior, through the interface of the personality factors. Finally, the thinking style factors, as derivatives, are located at the top.

The pattern of relationships is highly interesting. Specifically, it can be seen that four of the five dimensions of personality do intervene, in various combinations with each other, between the cognitive realm and thinking styles. It was found, for instance, that individuals who have a strong sense of cognitive efficiency are also open to experience. These individuals, if they are also emotionally stable, tend to think highly of themselves, as suggested by the rather strong relations between these two personality dimensions with the ideal self factor. In turn, thinking highly of oneself together with being open to experience orients one to activities that require originality. Those who think highly of themselves but are not open to experience tend to have a judicial style of thought, which orients them to activities requiring evaluation. Interestingly, a combination of emotional stability with extraversion seems to lead to impulsivity; impulsivity itself is negatively related to conscientiousness, which is, however, related to systematicity. In turn, systematic personalities tend to have an executive style, which leads them to activities with predefined rules. We believe that these findings are a first step in the direction of integrating the psychology of the mind with the psychology of personality. We elaborate more on this integration in the concluding section.

All of the measures generated by the study summarized represented self-representations or self-characterizations. Thus, it can show the relationships between the various dimensions of the self-oriented level of the mind and the self but it cannot highlight the relationships between the abilities residing at the environment-oriented level and the various dimensions of self-representation. This study is summarized next (Demetriou, Kyriakides, & Avraamidou, 2003).

This study included participants about equally drawn from each of the age groups 10 to 17. These participants were examined by a large task battery addressed to various components of each of five of the SCSs specified by our theory, namely the quantitative, the causal, the spatial, the qualitative, and the propositional. Moreover, the participants were examined by the cognitive self-representation inventory and the Big Five personality fac-

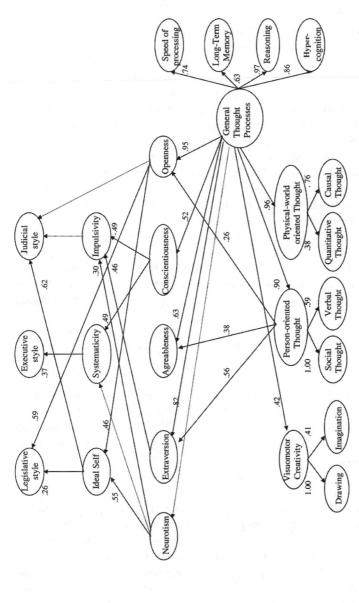

$x^2(859)=926.525$, p=.054, CFI=.981, GFI=.819, AGFI=.763, RMSEA=.023

FIG. 4.7. The model of the relations between cognitive self-image factors, personality factors, and thinking styles factors. From "Mind, Self, and Personality: Dynamic Interactions From Late Childhood to Early Adulthood," in A. Demetriou & S. Kazi, *Unity and Modularity in the Mind and the Self: Studies on the Relationships between Self-awareness, Personality, and Intellectual Development from Childhood to Adolescence*, 2001, London: Routledge. Copyright © 2001 by Routledge. Reprinted with permission.

tors inventory used in the study already described. Thus, this study provides the evidence needed to examine directly the relationships between the various SCSs, on the one hand, and cognitive self-representation and personality, on the other hand.

The model capturing the relationships between the various constructs is shown in Fig. 4.8. It can be seen that this model included the following constructs. First, there was a first-order factor for each of the five SCSs. These factors were regressed on a second-order factor, which stands for cognitive processes and abilities involved in the two domain-general levels of the mind, namely information processing and self-monitoring and self-regulation abilities. This factor overlaps but is not identical with psychometric g.

Second, there was also one first-order self-representation factor for each of the five SCSs and one self-representation factor for each of the three general cognitive abilities (processing speed, learning ability, and self-monitoring and self-regulation itself). Each of these factors was specified in reference to the corresponding set of self-attribution of ability scores. All eight self-representation factors were regressed on a second-order factor, which stands for the self-oriented or, in our terms, the hypercognitive level of the mind as such. This factor stands for both the individual's general cognitive self-worth and general attitudes to self-representation that are characteristic of each person. This second order factor was regressed on the second-order cognitive performance factor to specify the effects of actual performance on self-representation.

Third, there was a first-order factor for each of the five sets of the indicators representing each of the Big Five factors of personality. Each of these factors was regressed on both the general cognitive performance and the *residual* of the general cognitive self-presentation factor. This manipulation allows the specification of the relationships between each of the personality factors and both the cognitive and the hypercognitive level of the mind. That is, regressing the personality factors on both the general cognitive performance factor and the residual of the general self-representation factor enables one to capture what variance in each of the personality factors is accounted for by self-representation in addition to variance directly accounted for by cognitive performance itself.

It can be seen that the effects of the general cognitive performance factor on the personality factors were very weak in all cases. That is, these effects were circa .0 in the case of agreeableness, neuroticism, and extraversion. Expectedly, the effect of this factor on openness to experience, although rather low, was significant and positive (.19). Interestingly, the effect of cognitive performance on conscientiousness, although low, was significant and negative (–.11). In contrast to the generally low effects of the cognitive performance factor, the effects of the general self-representation factor on all but one of the personality factors were very substantial. That is, there was a

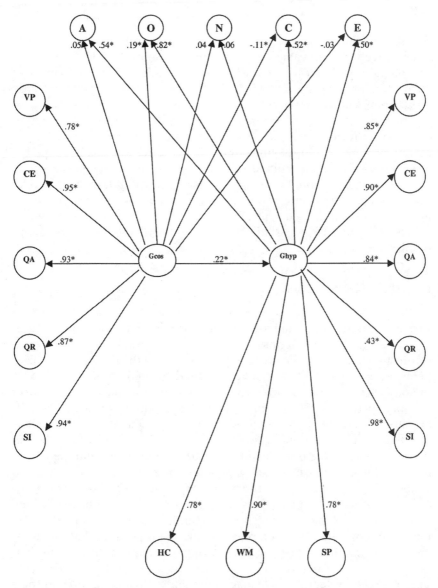

FIG. 4.8.   The model of the relationships between cognitive, hypercognitive, and personality factors; *Note 1.* X^2 (1187) = 2215.315, X^2/df = 1866, CFI = 910, GFI = 903, AGFI = 892, JRMR = .045, RMSEA = .032; *Note 2.* The symbols VP, CE, QA, QR, and SI stand for the verbal-propositional, the causal-experimental, the qualitative-analytic, the quantitative-relational, and the spatial- imaginal thought domains, respectively. The symbols HC, WM, and SP stand for hypercognition, working memory, and speed of processing, respectively. The symbols A, O, N, C, and E stand for agreeableness, openness to experience, neuroticism, conscientiousness, and extraversion, respectively. The symbols Gcog and Ghyper stand for the general cognitive performance and the general hypercognitive (self-representation) factor, respectively.

101

very strong effect of this factor on openness to experience (.82) and considerable effects on agreeableness (.54), conscientiousness (.52), and extraversion (.50). The effect on neuroticism was negligible (.06). This pattern of effects is almost identical to the pattern of our study summarized previously (Demetriou & Kazi, 2001).

Therefore, it is suggested that that personality is very weakly related to cognitive performance as such. However, it is closely related to self-representations about cognitive functioning. Therefore, the relationships between personality and cognitive functioning are indirect rather than direct and are mediated by the hypercognitive level of the mind. In fact, the relations between personality and self-representations about cognitive functioning were close enough to justify the claim that personality, as examined by self-report inventories, is, to a large extend, part of the general self-representation system.

CONCLUSIONS

Briefly, our theory postulates that the mind is a three-level hierarchical universe. Two of the levels in this universe involve knowing systems, one environment-oriented and the other self-oriented, and the third level involves general-purpose potentials that are activated as required by any system at the other levels. Furthermore, the environment-oriented level structures are constructionally, functionally, and developmentally distinct. The self-oriented level or, in our terms, the hypercognitive system, comprises maps of the environment-oriented systems, which are by and large accurate in their depiction of the organization and the relationships among environment oriented systems. These maps reflect the differential experiences generated by the activation of the various SCSs and are available whenever decisions related to course of action, covert or overt, must be made. The processing system is seen as a dynamic field that is always occupied by elements from the other two hierarchical levels, in proportions that vary from moment to moment. Specifically, the input to this system is environment-relevant information, skills, and processes, pertaining to an SCS (or something equivalent), and management and evaluation processes, pertaining to the hypercognitive system. These latter processes serve to orchestrate the processing of the former and evaluate the outcome of processing in relation to its goal. At the same time, however, orchestration and evaluation of processing is guided by both the dynamics underlying the organization of the environment-oriented systems and the already available hypercognitive maps of this organization. Moreover, the potentialities of the processing system constrain what problems can be solved, how they can be solved, and how they can be recorded.

However, the human mind is much more complex than simply cognitive abilities and processes, and their representation. That is, more dynamic dimensions, such as temperament and personality dispositions, and self-representations about other personality characteristics form the self-image as much as do the cognitive dimensions. These two types of dimensions (i.e., cognitive and personality dimensions) interact to shape the individual's preferred style of activities, which in turn can influence the choice of activities one would like to engage in.

One of the most interesting findings of the studies presented here relates to the dynamic organization of the self-image. The reader is reminded that all hierarchical models, as described in the first study, strongly indicated a unifying force pertaining to both the self-evaluation system and the self-attribution of abilities and characteristics system. In fact, we identified a kind of "personal constant", which moderates and adapts both on-line feedback generated at person-task encounters and also more general self-representations. Identification of this force lends support to the claim (e.g., Erikson, 1963; Freud, 1923; James, 1892; Harter, 1999; Pascual-Leone, 1983) that the human mind involves strong integrative functions which may underlie identity. An interesting conclusion is therefore suggested by the findings of the studies presented here. Specifically, the co-presence of this force with the domain-specific dimensions suggests that the mind is simultaneously both a modular and a transmodular system in both the cognitive and the social/personality systems.

The mind is modular at both the level of the environment-oriented cognitive processes and personality dispositions and the level of the self-representation of them. In fact, modularity at both levels is very strong for good reasons. It enables specialized and thus efficient interaction with the domain concerned. However, the mind is also unified or transmodular because the very ability to oversee, record, and differentiate the modules is by definition a transmodular function. Moreover, the personal constant identified here is a transmodular mechanism because it operates on all modules causing systematic adjustments at both the level of performance and subjectivity. This constant integrates influences from both general processing efficiency and temperamental dispositions. Thus, this constant represents processes that interconnect the person's mind and personality directly.

Therefore, humans have mind because there are environment-oriented systems and internal dispositions that they could be become mindful of. In evolution, mindfulness emerged as a result of humans first observing and manipulating each other and then as a result of self-observation, self-evaluation, and self-mapping (Bogdan, 2000). The self is the personalized aspect of this system and it may refer to cognitive abilities and processes (e.g., I am good in reasoning, learning, mathematics, drawing, social interaction, etc.) or to personality traits or dispositions (e.g., I enjoy being with people; I am stable; I am irritable, etc.). These traits and dispositions set the tone of each person's idiosyncratic functioning. At the same time, everything is embedded in a social context where minds, selves, and personalities interpret and interact with each other.

Development increases the intercoordination between the levels and dimensions of mind both within and across persons. The reader is reminded that there is a structural change in the relationship between the hyper-cognitive and the other levels of the mental architecture, which begins at the age of 11 to 12 years. It is widely accepted that at this age cognitive abilities are transformed extensively. We found here that at this age the personal constant is rescaled, obviously to tune the person's self-representations with his or her new realities. This interlevel tuning gets improved until the end of adolescence. In turn, this results in increasing communication between the environment-oriented and the self-oriented level of the mind. As a side-effect of this increasing communication, self-attribution of abilities and characteristics become more accurate with either age or improvement in cognitive performance. This implies that two major transitions in development, are related to the forces underlying the dynamic relationships between the environment-oriented and the self-oriented levels and systems of the architecture of the self rather than to forces concerned only with the relationships between environment-oriented mental operations.

TOWARDS AN OVERARCHING MODEL OF MIND, PERSONALITY, AND SELF

This analysis suggests that we can move in the direction of an overarching model that would capture the integrated functioning of the mind, personality, and the self. The model shown in Fig. 4.9 is an approximation to this ideal. It can be seen that we propose that the hierarchical levels of personality and the self-system correspond to the three hierarchical levels of mind depicted by our theory of the cognitive architecture. The model posits that the Big Five factors of personality correspond to the domain-specific systems that reside at the environment-oriented level of knowing. That is, the domain-specific systems of understanding channel the functioning of the mind and the Big Five factors channel patterns of action and relationships with the social and cultural environment (see Level I of the model shown in Fig. 4.9). In a similar vein, temperament is considered as the dynamic aspect of processing potentials. Thus, the processing potentials constrain the complexity and type of information that can be understood at a given age and temperament constrains how information is to initially be received and reacted to (see Level II of the model shown in Fig. 4.9). These constructs are controlled by the active processes of self-knowing implicated in James' I-self or Markus' working self-concept or by the monitoring and control

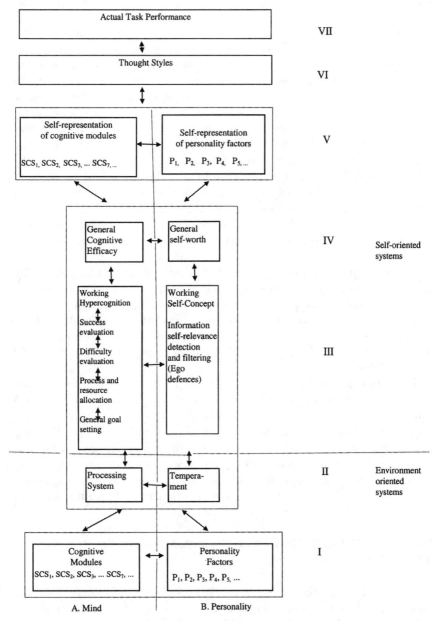

FIG. 4.9. The general model of the mind and personality. From "Mind, Self, and Personality: Dynamic Interactions From Late Childhood to Early Adulthood," in A. Demetriou & S. Kazi, *Unity and Modularity in the Mind and the Self: Studies on the Relationships between Self-awareness, Personality, and Intellectual Development from Childhood to Adolescence*, 2001, London: Routledge. Copyright © 2001 by Routledge. Reprinted with permission; *Note.* SCS stands for specialized structural system. P stands for personality factor.

processes involved in working hypercognition (see Level III of the model shown in Fig. 4.9). The functioning of these control processes generate feelings and representations of general cognitive efficiency or global self-worth and general self-esteem (see Level IV of the model shown in Fig. 4.9). In parallel to these general self-representations we have the more localized or specialized self-systems. These correspond to the various self-representations, which reside in the long-term hypercognitive maps of the organization of the mind (see Level V of the model shown in Fig. 4.9). Thus, the constructs at this level reflect how individuals register and represent themselves in regard to the various dimensions of understanding the world and the various dispositions of interacting with the world. Finally, thinking styles (see Level VI of the model shown in Fig. 4.9) and other context related systems (see Level VII of the model shown in Fig. 4.9) stand on their own as frames that shape perceived or actual adaptations to particular tasks or contexts.

As an integrated representation of the thinking and acting individual, this model captures both the dynamic (i.e., the motivational and emotional) and the meaning making (i.e., the representational) components of understanding, experience, and action. However, persons do not live alone. They live with other persons in groups and societies. Individuals exert influences on one another as they interact and negotiate their views about the world and one another.

It is reminded that our studies of the interactions between representations in the family suggest that the architecture previously described is intersubjective as much as it is intrasubjective. That is, others' representations of an individual are formed on the basis of his or her general efficiency in handling problems, his or her successes and failures in the various domains, and his or her dispositions and tendencies in the various personality dimensions and thinking styles. This finding suggests that this architecture frames both the individuals' subjective experiences and ensuing self-constructs and each others' descriptions and attributions.

DYNAMIC RELATIONSHIPS BETWEEN MIND, SELF, AND PERSONALITY

Recent research and theorizing on the relations between mind, personality, and self generate interesting ideas on how these aspects of the person may interact during development. Rothbart's theory of temperamental control (Rothbart & Bates, 1998) suggests how self-control may be related to the development of processing capacity. According to this theory, the ability to monitor and inhibit inappropriate impulses and tendencies depends on development of attentional networks, as these enable the individual to corepresent internal tendencies and external stimuli. This is so because to resist a temptation requires awareness and simultaneous representation of the two competing objects (the temptation, such as an immediately available and a more distant but more valued reward), the emotional- motivational consequences of each choice, and the mental or actual operations that can be used to direct attention and action from the lesser to the more important goal. Self-regulation will not be possible in these situations in as far as this complex of representations can not be held simultaneously in an active state. This occurs at the age of 5 years, that is, at the age at which delay of gratification was found to be possible. Therefore, the development of self-regulation seems to follow the development of both processing potentials and working hypercognition.

It needs to be noted that self-awareness itself is also directly involved in the formation of activity patterns associated with the functioning of personality. This is obvious in the relations between the development of self-understanding and self-regulation. The reader is reminded that preschool children cannot clearly recognize different mental processes and they do not comprehend that they can use one process in order to affect the functioning of another. Naturally, then, they do not use these processes as a means of self-regulation. With development in the understanding of the nature and functioning of these processes and in self-representation in regards to each of them, self-regulation of behavior and thought becomes increasingly more efficient (Demetriou, 2000).

The work of Kochanska and colleagues is also relevant to understanding how initial differences in processing and temperamental dispositions may evolve into distinct personality patterns (Kochanska, 1995, 1997; Kochanska, Coy, Tjebkes, Husarek, 1997). According to Kochanska et al. (1997), "early differences in inhibitory control forecast future personality development, and especially adult differences in conscientiousness or constraint, one of the Big Five" (p. 274). These findings are in line with an earlier longitudinal study conducted by Mischel and colleagues in the context of the delay of gratification paradigm. In a delay of gratification study, children are usually given two choices: a small reward that is immediately available or a large reward that requires a period of waiting. Waiting for the large reward is considered to indicate an ability to inhibit impulses and thus to signify self-control. In this study, parents of children involved in a delay of gratification study were asked in a follow-up study (10 years later) about the competencies and shortcomings of their children. The findings were very clear: children who were unable to delay gratification in the initial study were characterized as impatient adolescents, unable to postpone gratification. In contrast, those children able to delay gratification were characterized as adolescents who were academically more competent, more socially skilled, better able to cope with stress, more confident and self-reliant.

Moreover, these children obtained higher scores on the Scholastic Aptitude Test (Mischel, Shoda, & Peake, 1988). These findings on the relations between the development of self-control and personality fully concur with the model proposed here, which posits direct links between the processing system, self-representation of cognitive efficiency, and personality.

In conclusion, the main message of this chapter is rather simple. This is the combination of the principle of domain-specificity of the environment-oriented mental structures and dispositions with the principle of self-mapping underlying the operation of the hypercognitive system. This combination lays the ground for integrating the study of intelligence and cognitive functioning with the study of personality and self. According to this combination, there are environment-oriented systems which are modular and distinct by construction (the SCSs and the Big Five). These evolved to cope with different types of relations or demands in the physical and social environment. Together with these systems there is a self-oriented system which, once it was formed during evolution, observes, evaluates, and maps these modules. In doing so it produces self-concepts and self-definitions that reflect the differential condition of the modules and dispositions and it thus underlies one's sense of identity and self. All of these systems operate under the current constraints of the biological substrate of the organism which are themselves registered by the self-oriented system. Thus, all indexes of the unity of the person, such as general intelligence, global self-worth, self-efficacy, or self-esteem coexist with the multiplicity of the domain-specific self-concepts and self-images.

Development does not alter, by and large, the basic dimensions, foundational constructs, and levels involved in the architecture of the human mind and self. However, the exact possibilities, efficiency, and contents of all of these constructs and dimensions do change during development as a result of changes in the underlying biological constraints of the organism, its interaction with external agents, and the dynamic relationships between the constructs and dimensions themselves. In other words, the theory advanced here specifies the building blocks of intellectual ability, personality, and style of acting, which are brought to bear on the environment and it postulates that these blocks are also used in the incessant (re)construction of self-awareness. Self-awareness itself is, of course, always a powerful orienting force that directs the persons in their interactions with themselves, each other, and the world. Admittedly, we still have a long way to go before we chart all of the dynamic interactions involved in this universe, their states at different phases of life, and the mechanisms underlying their transformations and stability during the life-course.

REFERENCES

Bandura, A. (1989). Regulation of cognitive processes through perceived self-efficacy. *Developmental Psychology, 25*, 729–735.

Besevegis, E., Pavlopoulos, V., & Mourousaki, S. (1996). Children's personality characteristics as assessed by parents in natural language. *Psychology: The Journal of the Hellenic Psychological Society, 3*(2), 46–57.

Bogdan, R. J. (2000). *Minding minds.* Cambridge, MA: The MIT Press.

Bracken, B. (1996). Clinical applications of a context-dependent multi-dimensional model of self-concept. In B. A. Bracken (Ed.), *Handbook of self-concept.* New York: Wiley.

Carroll, J. B. (1993). *Human cognitive abilities: A survey of factor-analytic studies.* Cambridge, UK: Cambridge University Press.

Case, R. (1992). *The mind's staircase.* Hillsdale, NJ: Lawrence Erlbaum Associates.

Case, R., Okamoto, Y., Griffin, S., McKeough, A., Bleiker, C., Henderson, B., & Stephenson, K. M. (1996). The role of central conceptual structures in the development of children's thought. *Monographs of the Society for Research in Child Development, 61*(1–2, Serial No. 246).

Costa, P. T., Jr., & McCrae, R. R. (1997). Longitudinal stability of adult personality. In R. Hogan, J. Johnson & S. Briggs (Eds.), *Handbook of Personality Psychology* (pp. 269–290). San Diego, CA: Academic Press.

Demetriou, A. (1998). Nooplasis: 10 + 1 Postulates about the formation of mind. *Learning and Instruction: The Journal of the European Association for Research on Learning and Instruction, 8*, 271–287.

Demetriou, A. (2000). Organization and development of self-understanding and self-regulation. In M. Boekaerts, P. R. Pintrich, & M. Zeidner (Eds.), *Handbook of self-regulation* (pp. 209–251). New York: Academic Press.

Demetriou, A. (2001). Tracing psychology's invisible giant and its visible guards. In R. J. Sternberg & E. Grigorenko (Eds.), *The general factor of intelligence: How general is it?* (in press). Mahwah, NJ: Lawrence Erlbaum Associates.

Demetriou, A., & Efklides, A. (1985). Structure and sequence of formal and post-formal thought: General patterns and individual differences. *Child Development, 56*, 1062–1091

Demetriou A., & Efklides, A. (1989). The person's conception of the structures of developing intellect: Early adolescence to middle age. *Genetic, Social, and General Psychology Monographs, 115*, 371–423.

Demetriou, A., Efklides, A., & Platsidou, M. (1993) The architecture and dynamics of developing mind: Experiential structuralism as a frame for unifying cognitive developmental theories. *Monographs of the Society for Research in Child Development, 58*(5, Serial No. 234).

Demetriou, A., & Kazi, S. (2001). *Unity and modularity in the mind and the self: Studies on the relationships between self-awareness, personality, and intellectual development from childhood to adolescence.* London: Routledge.

Demetriou, A., Kyriakides, L., & Avraamidou, C. (2003). The missing link in the relationships between mind and personality. *Journal of Research in Personality, 37*, 547–581.

Demetriou, A., Kazi, S., & Georgiou, S. (1999). The emerging self: The convergence of mind, personality, and thinking styles. *Developmental Science, 2*, 387–422.

Demetriou, A., & Raftopoulos, A. (1999). Modeling the developing mind: From structure to change. *Developmental Review, 19*, 319–368.

Demetriou, A., Raftopoulos, A., & Kargopoulos, P. (1999). Interactions, computations, and experience: Interleaved Springboards of Cognitive Emergence, *Developmental Review, 19*, 389–414.

Dempster, F. N., & Brainerd, C. (1995) (Eds.). *Interference and inhibition in cognition.* New York: Academic Press.

Erikson, E. H. (1963). *Childhood and society.* New York: Norton.

Ferrari, M., & Sternberg, R. J. (1998). The development of mental abilities and styles. In D. Kuhn & R. Siegler (Vol. Eds.) & W. Damon (Series Ed.), *Handbook of child psychology: Vol. 2. Cognition, perception and language* (5th ed., pp. 899–946). New York: Wiley.

Fischer, K. W. (1980). A theory of cognitive development: The control and construction of hierarchies of skills. *Psychological Review, 87,* 477–531.

Flavell, J. H., Green, F. L., & Flavell, E. R. (1995). Young children's knowledge about thinking. *Monographs of the Society for Research in Child Development, 60*(1, Serial No. 243).

Freud, S. (1923). *The ego and the id.* New York: Norton.

Gardner, H. (1983). *Frames of mind: The theory of multiple intelligences.* New York: Basic Books.

Graziano, W. G., Jensen-Campbell, L. A., & Finch, J. F. (1997). The self as a mediator between personality and adjustment. *Journal of Personality and Social Psychology, 73*(2), 392–404.

Halford, G. (1993). *Children's understanding: The development of mental models.* Hillsdale, NJ: Lawrence Erlbaum Associates.

Harter, S. (1999). *The construction of the self.* New York: The Guilford Press.

Hattie, J. (1992). *Self-concept.* Hillsdale, NJ: Lawrence Erlbaum Associates.

James, W. (1892). *Psychology: The briefer course.* New York: Henry Holt.

Jensen, A. R. (1998). *The g factor: The science of mental ability.* New York: Praeger.

Kagan, J. (1994). On the nature of emotion. *Monographs of the Society for Research in Child Development, 59,* 7–24 (2–3, Serial No. 240).

Kargopoulos, P., & Demetriou, A. (1998). Logical and psychological partitioning of mind. Depicting the same map? *New Ideas in Psychology, 16,* 61–87.

Kochanska, G. (1995). Children's temperament, mothers' discipline, and security attachment: Multiple pathways to emerging internalization. *Child Development, 66,* 597–615.

Kochanska, G. (1997). Multiple pathways to conscience for children with different temperaments: From toddlerhood to age 5. *Developmental Psychology, 33,* 228–240.

Kochanska, G., Coy, K., Tjebkes, T. L., & Husarek, S. J. (1997). Individual differences in emotionality in infancy. *Child Development, 69,* 375–390.

Markus, H., & Wurf, E. (1987). The dynamic self-concept: A social psychological perspective. *Annual Review of Psychology, 38,* 299–337.

Mischel, W. Shoda, Y., & Peake, P. K. (1988). The nature of adolescent competencies predicted by preschool delay of gratification. *Personality and Social Psychology, 54,* 687–696.

Pascual-Leone, J. (1983). Growing into human maturity: Towards a metasubjective theory of adulthood stages. In P. B. Baltes & O. G. Brim (Eds.), *Life-span development and behavior, Vol. 5* (pp. 117–156). New York: Academic Press.

Pascual-Leone, J. (1988). Organismic processes for neo-Piagetian theories: A dialectical causal account of cognitive development. In A. Demetriou (Ed.), *The neo-Piagetian theories of cognitive development: Toward an integration* (pp. 25–64). Amsterdam: North-Holland.

Piaget, J. (1970). Piaget's theory. In P. Mussen (Ed.), *Carmichael's manual of child psychology, Vol. 1.* New York: Wiley.

Rogoff, B. (1990). *Apprenticeship in thinking: Cognitive development in social context.* New York: Oxford University Press.

Rothbart, M. K., & Bates, J. E. (1998). Temperament. In N. Eisenberg (Vol. Ed.) & W. Damon (Series Ed.), *Handbook of child psychology: Vol. 3. Social, emotional, and personality development* (5th ed., pp. 105–176). New York: Wiley.

Shayer, M., Demetriou, A., & Pervez, M. (1988). The structure and scaling of concrete operational thought: Three studies in four countries. *Genetic, Social, and General Psychology Monographs, 114,* 307–376.

Sternberg, R. J. (1985). *Beyond IQ: A triarchic theory of human intelligence.* New York: Cambridge University Press.

Sternberg, R. J. (1988). Mental self-government: A theory of intellectual styles and their development. *Human Development, 31,* 197–224.

Stroop, J. R. (1935). Studies of interference in serial verbal reactions. *Journal of Experimental Psychology, 18,* 643–662.

Thurstone, L. L. (1938). *Primary mental abilities.* Chicago: Chicago University Press.

van Geert, P. (1994). *Dynamic systems of development: Change between complexity and chaos.* New York: Harvester Wheatsheaf.

Wertsch, J. V. (1991). *Voices of the mind: A sociocultural approach to mediated action.* Cambridge, MA: Harvard University Press.

Chapter 5

Identity:
Does Thinking Make it So?

David M. Peterson
James E. Marcia
Jeremy I. M. Carpendale
Simon Fraser University

In this chapter we describe the theoretical placement of Erikson's (1959) identity concept and the identity statuses (Marcia, Waterman, Matteson, Archer, & Orlofsky, 1993), a paradigm designed to measure this construct. We review three studies, covering three different age groups, that link identity development with cognitive and epistemic development. Finally, we offer some thoughts on the importance of identity exploration.

The theoretical origins of Erik Erikson's psychosocial developmental approach, out of which the concept of identity has been drawn, lie in ego psychoanalytic thought. This psychodynamic approach, in contrast to classical analytic theory on one hand and object relational theory on the other, emphasizes the adaptation of the individual to the social context. Each of the psychodynamic approaches mentioned posits the development of a particular personality structure during a particular life cycle period. Classical analytic thought describes the *superego* as being formed during play age (5-7); object relational theory sees the *self* as being developed in early childhood (1-3); and ego psychoanalytic psychosocial developmental theory states that an *identity* is formed for the first time around late adolescence. Hence, each of these three psychodynamic approaches focuses on different personality structures formed during different ages.

We make the foregoing theoretical excursion because we want to place the concept of identity, at least as we think about it, in its proper context within the general realm of psychodynamic thought. In his psychosocial developmental theory Erikson has described eight life cycle stages, each with its own particular challenge and resulting ego strength. The developmental issue at late adolescence is the formation of an identity, which is both an experiential sense of oneself and a personality structure. Experientially, identity refers to feelings of both continuity and discontinuity with one's past that give meaningfulness to one's present and a direction to one's future. As a personality structure, an identity, similar to an individually constructed theory, affects how one perceives and understands one's world and how one acts within it. Although an identity is assumed to be formed for the first time around late adolescence, this is only the first identity construction. If the task is completed at that time, there is almost a guarantee that the individual will undergo successive identity reformulations throughout the life cycle, as that initial identity and subsequent identities become disequilibrated and an accommodative demand arises (Whitbourne, 1986)

In attempting to validate empirically Erikson's theory of identity, Marcia (1966) developed the four *identity statuses*, ways in which any late adolescent might be found to be dealing with the identity issue. These four identity positions are based upon the criteria of having undergone, or currently undergoing, a period of *exploration*, and making *commitments* in such important life areas as occupation, religious and political beliefs, and ideas and values about relationships. Identity *achievements* are persons who have undergone an exploratory period and are committed in the areas just mentioned. *Moratoriums* are individuals who are currently exploring issues and whose commitments are vague; they might be said to be in some sort of an *identity crisis*. *Foreclosures* are those who are committed, but who have undergone no exploratory period, usually having adopted others' directions for them as their own. Identity *diffusions* have undergone no real exploratory period and are not committed to any particular life directions. The identity statuses are traditionally determined by means of a semistructured interview and scoring manual. Research participants are asked, for example in the occupational area, about what their current occupational direction is, how they came to that, what their parents had in mind for them and what they think of the current plans, how their direction fits with their skills and perceived opportunities, and how willing they would be to give up their plans "if something better came along."

Cognitive variables have been important validating criteria from the inception of the identity statuses. One of the reasons why this area was considered important stems from the construct's origin in ego psychoanalytic theory. Ego processes are assumed to be either mechanisms of delay or products of delay (of impulse) (Rapaport, 1959). Thinking is primary in this realm. Hence, to the extent that a stage of ego growth (here, identity) has been accomplished, other ego functions, especially thinking, might be expected to be advanced. Of course, it makes sense the other way around, too: The more advanced cognitive processes are, the more likely one is to have negotiated successfully crises in ego growth—particularly identity. In any case, there should be correlations between identity and cognitive variables; and, indeed, there have been. Some of the cognitive variables we have found to be related to identity over the past 35 years are: performance on a concept attainment task under stressful conditions, formal operational thought (but only with social dilemmas), cognitive complexity, value orientations and reasoning systems, information processing orientations, decision-making styles, levels of both justice- and care-based moral reasoning, accuracy of recall of autobiographical memory, and levels of resolution of epistemic doubt (see Marcia et al., 1993; Marcia, 1994, 1999).

We shall now describe three recent studies relating identity development and cognitive development in three different age groups. The data from the first two studies have been reported elsewhere; the data from the third appears for the first time in this chapter. The first study, by MacKinnon and Marcia (2002), was conducted with mothers of young children (average age = 32), and looked at the interrelationship among three variables: identity status, attachment styles, and mothers' understanding of children's development. The measure of identity status was the standard interview modified for adults. (Recall that the identity formation process continues throughout the life span.) The attachment measure used was an extension of Main, Kaplan, and Cassidy's (1985) developed by Bartholomew and Horowitz (1991) and categorized participants into four attachment styles: Secure, Preoccupied, Dismissing, and Fearful. Cognitive sophistication was assessed by means of Sameroff and Feil's (1984) Concepts of Development Questionnaire. This measure is based on patterns of thought described in Piaget's stages of cognitive development and concerns parental understanding of children's development. Essentially, it describes parents' reasoning as either categorical or perspectivistic. Parents using categorical reasoning understand children in terms of their role names and they employ single explanations of behavior; for example, *either* environmental *or* constitutional. Parents employing perspectivistic modes of reasoning view children as having a psychological reality independent of role labels and their explanations of children's behavior are multifaceted.

We found expected relationships between attachment styles and identity statuses: Mothers higher in identity were generally more securely attached than mothers lower in identity development. But what is of most interest here are the findings for the cognitive variable. Overall, the identity achievement women had higher perspectivistic scores than women in the other identity statuses. However, the foreclosure women were split into two groups: Those who were high in cognitive sophistication were securely attached; whereas those who were low in cognitive sophistication were insecurely attached. Hence, there were about half of the foreclosure adult women who looked very much like identity achievement women on our experimental variables. This has led us to rethink the meaning of foreclosure for adult women. Firstly, there may be a type of foreclosure (securely attached, cognitively sophisticated) that is quite adaptive, at least for women in this age group. Secondly, if one assumes that attachment precedes identity, developmentally, then it might be the case that cognitive development is a kind of "protective factor" in identity development. Even if attachment is insecure, so long as cognitive development has proceeded well, it may be that chances for identity development are enhanced. This argument became even more compelling when we looked more closely at the insecurely attached identity achievement women. One hundred percent of these women (as contrasted with an average of about 30% for the rest of the sample) reported some form of childhood abuse, yet, perhaps because of their cognitive skills, they were able to optimally construct identities.

The second study we describe was conducted by Gary Saulnier (1998) with older men and women, average age = 72. He was interested primarily in the relationship between the resolution of Erikson's eighth psychosocial stage, Integrity-Despair, and cognitive performance. To measure *integrity*, he used an interview and scoring manual developed by Simon Hearn (1993) that locates participants in one of four integrity statuses. A relationship between integrity and identity in older persons had been found in a previous study (Hearn, Saulnier, Strayer, Glenham, Koopman, & Marcia, under revision). This link between integrity and identity lends some credence to the hypothesis that integrity may be identity writ large at the end of the life cycle. In any case, integrity, here, is taken as a kind of proxy for identity in describing the study's findings. Three measures of cognition were given to participants in Saulnier's study: tolerance for ambiguity (Budner, 1962), the Social Paradigm Belief Inventory developed by Kramer (1983), and Gibbs, Bassinger, and Fuller's (1992) measure of Kohlbergian moral reasoning. Similar to the cognitive sophistication measure used in the previous study with mothers, the social belief measure is based on "post-formal" reasoning, and locates participants as being primarily *relativistic-dialectical* (i.e., synthetic) reasoners or *formistic-mechanistic* (i.e., absolute) reasoners. Findings from this study once again confirmed a relationship between identity and cognitive development. Tolerance for ambiguity was positively related to integratedness. Also, the integrated status had more dialectical reasoners than did the other statuses, among whom formistic-mechanistic reasoning predominated. And, finally, integrated persons were most numerous at the highest levels of sociomoral reasoning. Hence, this study, with a much older population demonstrated a relationship between integrity, here a proxy for identity, and differing measures of cognitive sophistication.

With the third study, we return to adolescence and look in some detail at the relationship between epistemic and identity development. In this research with college students, we explored connections between epistemic development and identity formation. This relationship is initiated and highlighted when young persons are exposed to "a potent mixture of contradictory viewpoints and possibilities that together poison their well of natural certainty" (Chandler, 1987, p. 138). The process of recognizing the universality of subjectivity has been described as "pulling a small thread and unraveling the whole epistemic fabric of adolescence" (p. 149). In terms of identity formation, the problem becomes how the adolescent can come to make the necessary occupational and ideological decisions in the face of the newly-arrived-at sense of uncertainty. Epistemic growth begins with the realization that knowledge acquisition is a constructive process. If successfully completed, it should leave the individual free to act with some confidence in a newly created world of wholesale uncertainty (Boyes & Chandler, 1992).

Epistemic understanding refers to a person's assumptions about the nature of knowledge, where it is discovered, how it is produced, and how it may be maintained (Boyes, 1987). The construct of epistemic development and the resulting strategies dealing with doubt have been developed through a nomological network of research that can be traced through Perry (1970); Kitchener and King (1981); Kuhn, Pennington, and Leadbeater (1983); Kramer (1983); Boyes and Chandler (1992); and Chandler, Hallett, and Sokol (2002).

Perry (1970) pioneered the research on epistemic development by defining two criteria for growth: an acceptance of uncertainty and a commitment to resolve uncertainty. Based on these two criteria, Perry defined four strategies for dealing with epistemic doubt: simple dualism, complex dualism, relativism, and commitment in relativism. Kitchener and King (1981) expanded on Perry's research by dissecting the strategies and reorganizing them into three categories of thinking: prereflective, quasireflective, and reflective. These three categories were further described by subcategories that defined distinctions within the broader categories. Boyes and Chandler (1992) built on this research and formulated five strategies for epistemic development: naive realism, defended realism, dogmatism-skepticism axis, and post-skeptical rationalism. It is the dogmatism-skepticism axis that distinguishes their theory because it describes the realism-relativism-rationalism transformation differently from the other approaches. Although dogmatism and skepticism appear superficially different, they form an axis because they share the same underlying view of knowledge as inherently uncertain. In skepticism, this problem is dealt with by making decisions based on impulse or conformity to peers; in dogmatism, uncertainty is dealt with by following someone who claims to provide certainty.

Kramer (1983) extended the construct of epistemic development by suggesting that the construct consists of four epistemic strategies: *formistic-mechanistic* thought, a belief in a stable, unchanging perspective of knowledge determined and predictable by one-way linear causes (FM); *awareness of the relativistic* nature of knowledge, a belief that life is constantly in a state of flux and that truth is determined by context and pragmatism (AR); *acceptance of contradiction*, an acknowledgment of the inevitability of opposite perspectives, but without a synthesis of perspectives (AC); and *organicism*— an integration of contradiction into the dialectical whole (ORG). Organicism is an awareness of movement through forms wherein transition is seen as necessary to synthesize perspectives (Kramer, 1983, pp. 17–22). An individual traverses these epistemic strategies through a continuous process of growth that involves acceptance of multiple perspectives and yields increased confidence in resolving uncertainties about the world.

When we look at identity development we see a similar, but not identical, pattern as we see in epistemic development. An individual progresses through the identity statuses by means of exploring alternatives and making commitments. The person integrates childhood identifications with new perspectives based on their current experience as well as their anticipation of an adult future. Optimally, development proceeds toward a state of identity achievement wherein individuals construct their own identity. However, this initial identity formation process does not come with a lifetime guarantee. It continues throughout the life cycle as a continuous process dependent on successive disequilibrations, subsequent exploratory periods, and new or recommitments. Therefore, the essence of identity development consists of a continuity of process and change of content within a person during a life long journey of exploration and commitment. Bearing in mind the continuous and interwoven processes of epistemic and identity development, some expectations for different identity statuses' epistemic levels may be outlined.

FORMISTIC-MECHANISTIC STRATEGIES
AND THE FORECLOSED IDENTITY

At the beginning of the adolescent epistemological developmental process, the use of the formistic-mechanistic strategy of knowledge acquisition is expected to relate to the adoption of a foreclosed identity status. Persons using the FM strategy have a closed set of beliefs guided by unchanging principles; they find it difficult to recognize the legitimacy of differing opinions regarding important life issues. They trust in the dogma of authority and accept that right and wrong, correct and incorrect, sufficiently encompass their dichotomous world (Perry, 1970). Likewise, foreclosures have inflexible commitments to occupational roles, ideological beliefs, and interpersonal values without having explored alternatives or actively constructed their identities. They tend to be authoritarian and to adopt their parents' prescribed identity unexamined (Marcia et al., 1993). The formistic-mechanistic strategy was assumed to characterize foreclosures and serves to limit exploration in favor of unquestioning commitment.

THE ACCEPTANCE OF CONTRADICTION STRATEGY AND THE MORATORIUM IDENTITY

The acceptance of contradiction (AC) strategy was expected to characterize the moratorium identity status. Those employing the AC strategy recognize the contradictory implications of some of their possible choices but seem unable to resolve them, for example, idealism versus realism. Statements such as "the way things should be as opposed to the way things are" may be made (Kramer, 1983, p. 200). Those adopting this epistemic approach can account for multiple perspectives, but they remain only on the verge of commitment because of their difficulty in synthesizing conflicting viewpoints. In identity terms, moratoriums are described as conflicted, anxious, struggling, creatively directionless, and, sometimes, interpersonally exhausting (Marcia, 1986). The acceptance of contradiction strategy, characterized by the recognition of contrasting systems and the implications of opposites, may constrain the identity formation process to a moratorium status, which is marked by active and sometimes painful exploration, on the verge of consolidating commitments.

THE ORGANICISM STRATEGY AND THE ACHIEVED IDENTITY

The most advanced epistemic strategy involves the integration of contradiction into a dialectical whole and it is expected to be characteristic of identity achievements. A person using the organicism strategy (ORG) is conscious of movement through forms or stages and accepts the process of transition as normal. Such persons are able to synthesize conflicting perspectives and preserve all elements without loss to either their theses or antitheses (Kramer, 1983). Similarly, identity achievement persons have seriously explored the areas of occupation, ideology, and interpersonal values and have made consolidating commitments. Individuals in the achievement identity status show a high measure of self-confidence and openness to others' opinions (Marcia, 1986). It is important to note that "the identity process neither begins nor ends with adolescence ... the resolution of the identity issue at adolescence guarantees only that one will be faced with subsequent crises" (Marcia, 1980, p. 160). It is the openness and flexibility of this status that assures reconstruction of the identity contents throughout life. Therefore, an organicism epistemic strategy that accepts transitions through forms as normal and resolves conflict through synthesis appears to predispose the identity formation process to an identity achievement status that is reflective of both continuity and change as a result of exploration and commitment.

EPISTEMIC STRATEGY AND IDENTITY DIFFUSION

No specific epistemic strategy was expected to be associated with identity diffusions. In a sense, they have no particular strategy. The issues of "epistemological loneliness" (Chandler, 1987) either seem not to concern them sufficiently in order to adopt a strategy, or, perhaps, concern them too much. In any case, none of the foregoing strategies seems to fit them well. As Waterman (personal communication, November, 2000) put it, there must be a strategy preceding formistic-mechanistic, likely one that is more characteristic of pre-adolescents. In general, however, diffusions were expected to employ lower level strategies than were higher identity statuses.

The identity measure we used was the identity status interview for late adolescents (Marcia et al., 1993) administered to a final sample of 61 (48 females, 18 males) university undergraduate students (average age 21.0 years). Two measures of epistemic strategies were given: an "abstract" dilemma, "The Fifth Livian War" (Kuhn, Pennington, & Leadbeater, 1983); and a socio-emotional measure, an unwanted pregnancy problem (Söchting, 1991). Because identity occurs within an interpersonal, affective field, we thought that the relationships between a socio-emotional measure of epistemic strategy and identity might be greater than those between a more abstract measure and identity. Both the socio-emotional and abstract measures were scored according to Kramer's (1983) epistemic strategies and Kuhn et al.'s guidelines (1983). The probes that followed the two stories gave each subject a chance to state explicitly both how they "constructed" the problems and undertook to "resolve" the competing knowledge claims. Kramer defined a set of criteria with which to determine subjects' uses of particular epistemic strategies. Kuhn et al.'s guidelines refer to probes and criteria used specifically in scoring the Fifth Livian War dilemma (Kuhn et al., 1983). Participants' statements were evaluated according to the presence or absence of differentiation, acknowledgment of discrepancies, reconciliation, subjective perspectives, and multiple interpretations of the dilemmas. Participants were assigned both global and dimensional (on a 1-9-point scale) positions on each of the epistemic strategies, which, in developmental order, were: *formistic-mechanistic* (FM), *awareness of relativism* (AR), *acceptance of contradiction* (AC), and *organicism* (ORG). The global score was based on the highest dimensional score. If there were two dominant strategy scores, the raters' overall impression was used to break the tie.

To determine interscorer reliability, 20 randomly chosen abstract and socio-emotional dilemmas were independently rated by two trained raters. On the abstract measure the overall *tau*b = .774. Dimensional scores were averaged over the four strategies and had Pearson's r = .79. On the socio-emotional measure the overall global scores *tau*b = .792 and the Pearson's r for the dimensional scores was .74.

Seventeen identity status interviews were independently rated by two trained raters. Overall global scores *tau*b = .847. Dimensional scores were averaged over the four statuses and had a Pearson's r =. 79.

Our results concerning the place of the identity statuses in different epistemic strategies are found in Tables 5.1a and 5.1b. Participants in the higher identity statuses were found more frequently in the higher epistemic levels, both on the abstract and social measures. In order to calculate a Kendall's Tau on the relationship between strategies and identity statuses, each status was assigned a 1-4 rating from lowest to highest. A significant positive relationship was found between overall identity development and level of epistemic strategy as measured by the abstract problem (*tau*b = .287, N = 66, p = .007 [2-tailed]) and by the socio-emotional problem (*tau*b = .267, N = 66, p = .013 [2-tailed]). In general, the more advanced the late adolescent participants were in identity, the more advanced they were in epistemic level. This result corresponds to similar previous findings by Boyes and Chandler (1992). However, we obtained some anamolous findings for diffusions. Although they were most prevalent in the relativism and contradiction strategies, this may reflect less their epistemic advancement than a superficial similarity between their noncommitted, noninvolved "style" and the skeptical emphases within the AR and AC strategies (see Berzonsky, 1989).

TABLE 5.1a
Identity Status by Abstract Epistemic Level

	Abstract Measure of Epistemic Development				
					Total
	Formistic	*Relativism*	*Contradiction*	*Organicism*	
Identity					
Diffusion	1	4	2	1	8
Foreclosure	6	17	3	1	27
Moratorium	2	10	10	2	24
Achievement	1	1	2	3	7
Totals	10	32	17	7	66

TABLE 5.1b

Identity Status by Socio-emotional Epistemic Level

	Socio-emotional Measure of Epistemic Development				
					Total
	Formistic	Relativism	Contradiction	Organicism	
Identity					
Diffusion	1	2	4	1	8
Foreclosure	8	13	5	1	27
Moratorium	1	9	9	5	24
Achievement		2	1	4	7
Totals	10	26	19	11	66

Because both identity status and epistemic strategy was scored on a continuous as well as a categorical basis, it was possible to correlate these two measures. These correlations are found in Table 5.2. As expected, there was a significant positive relationship between foreclosure and formistic-mechanistic epistemic strategy on the socio-emotional measure. Unexpectedly, there was also a significant positive relationship between foreclosure scores and the awareness of relativism strategy on the abstract measure. In general, significant negative relationships were found between foreclosure and the two highest reasoning styles on both the abstract and social measures.

TABLE 5.2

Correlation Matrix Identity Status by Epistemic Level

	Epistemic Strategies:[a]							
	(ABS) 5th Livian War and (SOC) Pregnancy Measures							
	Formistic		Relativistic		Contradiction		Organicism	
	ABS	SOC	ABS	SOC	ABS	SOC	ABS	SOC
Identity Status								
Diffusion	.15	−.052	.074	.084	.081	.122	−.051	−.194
Foreclosure	.14	.295[b]	.393[b]	.16	−.391[b]	−.107	−.337[b]	−.382[b]
Moratorium	−.125	−.182	−.2	−.015	.312[b]	.127	.063	.132
Achievement	−.125	−.079	−.324[b]	−.280	.334[b]	−.023	.313[b]	.478[b]

[a]The correlations for the abstract and socio-emotional measures were formistic-mechanistic $r = .35$, Awareness of Relativism $r = .25$, Acceptance of Contradiction $r = .38$, Organicism $r = .28$. These effect sizes show that there was not sufficient overlap between the two measures to combine them. Furthermore, there is something to be gained by leaving them independent of one another when relating them to identity.

[b]Correlation is significant at the 0.0167 level (two-tailed) (alpha prime = 0.0167 and alpha = 0.05).

Moratorium scores were related significantly positively to the acceptance of contradiction strategy on the abstract, but not on the socio-emotional measure. Identity achievement scores were positively correlated with higher reasoning styles on the abstract measure, but only with organicism on the socio-emotional measure. No significant relationships were found between diffusion scores and epistemic strategy.

An interesting finding emerged for moratoriums, some of whom might be expected to soon move into achievement, others to have just left foreclosure. They were evenly split between the use of the lower epistemic strategy of passive awareness of relativism and the higher more active strategy of acceptance of contradiction (see Table 4.1). Because we had dimensional scores for all identity statuses for all subjects, we were able to look at differences between the two moratorium epistemic groups in their other identity status scores (i.e., their scores on achievement, foreclosure, and diffusion). We found that the moratoriums employing the higher acceptance of contradiction strategy had higher identity achievement scores than did the lower (awareness of relativism) strategy moratoriums, whereas the lower (awareness of relativism) strategy moratoriums had higher foreclosure scores. Thus, it appeared that epistemic strategy was discriminating between higher and lower developmental levels *within* the moratorium identity status. To our knowledge, this is the first time that such a fine-grained developmental distinction has been made within a particular identity status.

The fact that no differences were obtained in this study for the identity diffusion dimension suggests that what we are dealing with when we investigate the relationship between epistemic strategies and identity development is a phenomenon that occurs at higher levels of identity formation; that is, when identity exists (as in foreclosure), or is being disequilibrated and reformulated (moratorium), or has been constructed following a period of exploration (identity achievement). We speak sometimes of "postformal" thought; perhaps, diffusions are at "pre-mechanistic/formistic" levels.

Another possibility is that had we used Chandler's dogmatism-skepticism scoring scheme, we might have found some interesting results for diffusions. Perhaps, diffusions and foreclosures share a realization that they lack certainty in making decisions, but they deal with this problem very differently: Foreclosures put their faith in an authority; diffusions throw up their hands and make decisions by flipping a coin or doing what their friends are doing.

Psychotherapists and counselors who are concerned with change and growth may be interested in more applied implications of our findings of relationships between cognitive sophistication, epistemic strategies, and identity development. Persons in the higher identity statuses, moratorium and achievement, are not necessarily "happier" than foreclosures; moratoriums, in their disequilibrated state of identity crisis, certainly are not. But whatever suffering they are undergoing is more meaningful in identity development terms than is diffusions' inner emptiness. The change and growth involved in adolescent moratorium and achievement, and in moratorium-achievement cycles beyond adolescence, seems to be more developmentally significant, more reflective of the potentials for human growth, than the more contented, but rigidly defended stasis of foreclosure.

The key to both identity and epistemic development seems to be exploration: cognitive, experiential, and behavioral. But for successful exploration to occur, it is necessary to have those familial and social conditions that make exploration safe and meaningful. Safe exploration may even mean, in Erikson's words, allowing an adolescent to "touch bottom." In which case, we adults are the ones who must remain on the edge of the pool to pull the young person up if we see that they are too slow in surfacing. Of course, that requires that we, as generative figures have sufficient time and attention free from our own conflicts and unmet needs to be vigilant and effective lifeguards. We do not think that either young children or adolescents need "encouragement" to explore, that comes naturally. But they do need a fairly secure context within which to do it. On the other hand, too much security is also not conducive to identity development. For example, "accelerated programs" that focus solely on training persons to enter one occupational area as quickly as possible, programs that do not offer thought-provoking educational opportunities, are unlikely to provide encouragement and support for exploration, an important element in both epistemic and identity growth. Finally, for exploration and commitment to be ultimately meaningful, there must be available and rewarding social niches to accommodate a variety of identity contents.

REFERENCES

Bartholomew, K., & Horowitz, J. M. (1991). Attachment styles among young adults: A test of a four category model. *Journal of Personality and Social Psychology, 61,* 226–244.

Berzonsky, M. D. (1989). Identity style: Conceptualization and measurement. *Journal of Adolescent Research, 4,* 267–281.

Boyes, M., & Chandler, M. J. (1992). Cognitive development, espitemic doubt, and identity formation in adolescence. *Journal of Youth and Adolescence, 21*(3), 277–304.

Budner, S. (1962). Intolerance of ambiguity as a personality variable. *Journal of Personality, 30,* 29–50.

Chandler, M. J. (1987). The Othello Effect: Essay on the emergence and eclipse of skeptical doubt. *Human Development, 30,* 137–159.

Chandler, M. J., Hallett, D., & Sokol, B. (2002). Competing claims about competing knowledge claims. In B. K. Hofer & P. R. Pintrich (Eds.), *Personal epistemology: The psychology of beliefs about knowledge and knowing* (pp.145–168). Mahwah, NJ: Lawrence Erlbaum Associates.

Erikson, E. H. (1959). *Identity and the life cycle*. New York: International University Press.

Gibbs, J. C., Bassinger, J. D., & Fuller, D. (1992). *Moral maturity: Measuring the development of sociomoral reflections*. Hillsdale, NJ: Lawrence Erlbaum Associates.

Hearn, S. (1993). *Integrity, despair, and in between: Toward construct validation of Erikson's eighth stage*. Unpublished doctoral dissertation, Simon Fraser University, Burnaby, BC, Canada.

Hearn, S., Saulnier, G., Strayer, J., Glenham, M., Koopman, R., & Marcia, J. E. (under revision). *Between integrity and despair: Toward construct validation of Erikson's eighth stage*. Department of Psychology, Simon Fraser University, Burnaby, BC, Canada.

King, P. M., & Kitchener, K. S. (1994). *Developing reflective judgment*. San Francisco: Jossey-Bass Publishers.

Kitchner, K. S., & King, P. M. (1981). Reflective judgment: Concepts of justification and their relationship to age and education. *Journal of Applied Developmental Psychology, 2*, 89–116.

Kramer, D. A. (1983). *Structural and developmental features of relativistic and dialectic thought across the adult life-span*. Unpublished doctoral dissertation, Philadelphia, PA, Temple University.

Kuhn, D., Pennington, N., & Leadbeater, B. (1983). Adult thinking in developmental perspective: The sample case of juror reasoning. In P. Baltes & O. Brim (Eds.), *Life-span development and behavior* (Vol. 5, 157–195). New York: Academic Press.

MacKinnon, J. L., & Marcia, J. E. (2002). Concurring patterns of women's identity status, styles, and understanding of children's development. *International Journal of Behavioral Development, 26*, 70–80.

Main, M., Kaplan, N., & Cassidy, J. (1985). Security in infancy, childhood, and adulthood: A move to the level of representation. In I. Bretherton & W. Waters (Eds.), Growing points in attachment theory and research. *Monographs of the Society for Research in Child Development, 50*(1–2, Serial No. 209), 66–104.

Marcia, J. E. (1966). Development and validation of ego-identity status. *Journal of Personality and Social Psychology, 3*, 551–558.

Marcia, J. E. (1980). Identity in adolescence. In J. Abelson (Ed.), *Handbook of adolescent psychology* (pp. 159–187). New York: Wiley.

Marcia, J. E. (1986). Clinical implications of the identity status approach within psychosocial developmental theory. *Cadernos de Consulta Psicologica, 2*, 23–34.

Marcia, J. E. (1994). Ego identity and object relations. In J. M. Masling & R. F. Bornstein (Eds.), *Empirical perspectives on object relations theory* (pp. 59–103). Washington, DC: American Psychological Association.

Marcia, J. E. (1999). Representational thought in ego identity, psychotherapy, and psychosocial developmental theory. In I. Sigel (Ed.), *Theoretical perspectives in the development of representational thought* (pp. 391–414). Mahwah, NJ: Lawrence Erlbaum Associates.

Marcia, J. E., Waterman, A. S., Matteson, D. R., Archer, S. L., & Orlofsky, J. L. (1993). *Ego identity: A handbook for psychosocial research*. New York: Springer-Verlag.

Perry, W. G. (1970). *Forms of intellectual and ethical development in the college years*. New York: Holt, Rinehart and Winston.

Rapaport, D. (1959). The structure of psychoanalytic theory: A systematizing attempt. *Psychological Issues* (Monograph No. 6). New York: International Universities Press.

Sameroff, A. J., & Feil, L. A. (1984). Parental concepts of development. In I. Sigel (Ed.), *Parental belief systems: The psychological consequences for children* (pp. 83–105). Hillsdale, NJ: Lawrence Erlbaum Associates.

Saulnier, G. (1998). *Maturation of thought: Advanced construct validation of Erikson's either stage*. Unpublished doctoral dissertation, Simon Fraser University, Burnaby, BC, Canada.

Söchting, I. (1991). *Are moral reasoning, sex role orientation and prosocial behavior linked?* Unpublished thesis, Simon Fraser University.

Whitbourne, S. K. (1986). *The me I know: A study of adult identity*. New York: Springer-Verlag.

Chapter 6

Self-Regulation and Children's Theories of Mind

Louis J. Moses
University of Oregon

Stephanie M. Carlson
University of Washington

Classical taxonomies of the self carve out three related but nonetheless distinct facets of developing personhood: self-conception, self-esteem, and self-regulation (Harter, 1983). When we think about relations between the self and theory of mind (ToM), what likely comes to mind most readily is how changes in children's self-conceptions might affect their emerging theories of mind, or vice versa. My awareness of my own mental states ought to have ramifications for how I conceive of other minds (Harris, 2000), and my theories about the minds of others ought to change the way I conceive of my own (Gopnik, 1993). Less obvious, perhaps, is that children's developing ability to *regulate* the self might have implications for their theories of mind. Our aim in this chapter is to present the case that developments in self- regulation are indeed intimately bound together with advances in children's appreciation of mental life. Along the way we describe findings from an ongoing series of studies designed to illuminate potential relations between these two core aspects of human ontogeny.

DEVELOPMENT LINKS BETWEEN THEORIES OF MIND
AND SELF-REGULATION

If one were to ask parents and teachers to list the relative weaknesses of preschool children, toward the top of that list two items would likely emerge. First, it is plain to anyone that preschoolers are lacking in self-control: They have a very hard time resisting temptation, delaying gratification, and keeping their emotions and behavior in any sort of reasonable check. Second, it is equally plain that preschoolers are poor perspective-takers: They have great difficulty figuring out what people feel and think, often egocentrically assuming that others share their own seemingly accurate view of the world.

Self-regulation and theory of mind appear, then, to share something of the same developmental timetable. This commonality has been consistently verified in more formal research. The preschool years are a period of major growth in self regulatory skills. Following the pioneering work of Luria (1966), marked developmental changes in preschoolers' ability to regulate the self have been reliably documented (e.g., Gerstadt, Hong, & Diamond, 1994; Kochanksa, Coy, & Murray, 2001; Kochanska, Murray, Jacques, Koenig, & Vandegeest, 1996; Reed, Pien, & Rothbart, 1984; Zelazo, Frye, & Rapus, 1996). As they mature, preschoolers become increasingly adept at tempering or delaying their responses when the situation demands it, at suppressing them altogether when necessary, and at directing their attention away from salient distracters in contexts requiring selective attention.

At the same time a wave of remarkable change is sweeping through children's theory of mind. For example, 3-year-olds consistently flounder on measures assessing their understanding that beliefs can be false (Wimmer & Perner, 1983), that appearances may not reflect reality (Flavell, Flavell, & Green, 1983), and that different individuals may perceive a scene in different ways (Flavell, 1978). These younger preschoolers frequently state that beliefs and appearances always match reality, and that only a single perspective on any state of affairs is possible. Yet, by the time they are 5, children have an appreciation of these matters that, in some important respects (though by no means all), is not unlike that of adults.

Of course, the mere fact that two skills emerge in parallel is no guarantee that they are linked in any fundamental way. However, further circumstantial support for an association between self- regulation and theory of mind comes from two other sources. First, skills in these areas appear to be underpinned by common neural processes. The prefrontal cortex has long been viewed as the seat of executive, regulatory processes (Luria, 1973; Rothbart & Posner, 1985)—deficits in such processes, for example, are classically associated with damage to the frontal lobes. Recent imaging work suggests that the frontal lobes may be implicated in thinking about mental states as well (e.g., Frith & Frith, 1999; Sabbagh & Taylor, 2000; Siegal & Varley, 2002; Stuss, Gallup, & Alexander, 2001). Second, it is well known that individuals with autism have deficits in ToM (e.g., Baron-Cohen, 1995). Less well known, perhaps, is that these individuals also have quite profound executive deficits (e.g., McEvoy, Rogers, & Pennington, 1993; Russell, 1997), again raising the possibility that self-regulation and ToM share a common neural substrate, and perhaps a common conceptual core.

HOW MIGHT SELF-REGULATION AFFECT THEORY OF MIND DEVELOPMENT?

The ability to control or regulate the self might influence theory-of-mind development in one of two ways (Moses, 2001; Russell, 1996). A first possibility is that self-regulation simply affects the *expression* of theories of mind. That is, young children might already have developed rudimentary concepts of mind but be unable to make effective use of these concepts because they cannot flexibly direct their attention to appropriate aspects of the situation. Rather, in the absence of sufficiently developed self-control, their attention might simply be captured by whatever is most salient in the context. Certainly, it is clear from the structure of many ToM tasks that *some* level of self-control is necessary for success. In such tasks children are confronted with a choice between two competing, and potentially interfering, states of affairs. In Wimmer and Perner's (1983) classic false belief task, for example, Maxi develops a false belief about the location of his chocolate by virtue of the fact that he is absent when it is moved to a different location. Children must then predict Maxi's action on the basis not of the real situation but of his mistaken representation of that situation. Unfortunately, however, the actual state of affairs may be so salient in young children's minds, their knowledge of where the chocolate is so vivid, that they cannot resist referring to it, whether or not they have any understanding of false beliefs. And the same potentially disruptive conflict is present in almost all variants of the false belief task, as well as in many other ToM tasks. In deception tasks (e.g., Carlson, Moses, & Hix, 1998; Russell, Mauthner, Sharpe, & Tidswell, 1991), for example, children must mislead another individual by indicating not the actual location of a desirable object but a different, empty location. Similarly, in appearance–reality tasks (e.g., Flavell et al., 1983), either the appearance or the reality of a stimulus is typically dominant, and hence may be difficult to suppress.

A second, more radical possibility is that a certain level of self-regulation is critical for the very *emergence* of mental state concepts. Specifically, unless children have some ability to disengage attention from salient stimuli, it is difficult to imagine that they could even entertain the possible existence of a realm of abstract mental representation. Indeed, an organism without the ability to distance itself from whatever is dominant in the current context could hardly be said to have a notion of perspective at all (cf. Piaget, 1926; Sigel, 1993). In this view, then, the capacity to reflect on the mental states of self and other cannot begin to burgeon until control of the self is sufficiently in hand.

In what follows we aim to advance four claims about self-regulation and ToM. First, the fact that these abilities share a common developmental timetable is no accident: Self-regulation and ToM are indeed tightly linked in the preschool period. The second claim is that two aspects of self-regulation are fundamental to this relation: Inhibitory control, the capacity to suppress thought processes or actions that are not relevant to the goal or task at hand (Rothbart & Posner, 1985); and working memory, a system for temporarily holding in mind and processing information (Baddeley, 1986). The third claim is that inhibitory control interacts with conceptual content: The need for inhibitory control depends heavily on the conceptual context. And the final claim is that advances in self-regulation are critical for the emergence of theory of mind, not just its expression. Each of these claims has been tested in a series of correlational studies, all resting on the premise that if self-regulation and ToM are linked, then children who are more advanced in one domain should be more advanced in the other.

ARE SELF REGULATION AND ToM GENUINELY LINKED?

In a first, large-scale correlational study of these issues we gave a sample of 107 3- and 4-year-olds multi-task batteries measuring ToM and inhibitory control across two sessions (Carlson & Moses, 2001). The ToM battery comprised eight tasks measuring deceptive pointing, false belief understanding (both location false belief tasks and contents false belief tasks were included), and the appearance–reality distinction. The inhibitory battery included 10 tasks classified into two distinct subtypes. Conflict inhibition tasks required children to inhibit an inappropriate prepotent response while activating a conflicting novel response. For example, in the Bear/Dragon task (Kochanska et al., 1996; Reed et al., 1984) children needed to perform whatever actions a bear puppet requested (e.g., "touch your nose") but not to perform those requested by a dragon puppet ("touch your tummy"). Here, the prepotent response is to comply with all requests and the conflicting response is to comply with only a subset of them. Delay inhibition tasks required children simply to inhibit responding for a period of time. For example, in the Gift Delay task (Kochanska et al., 1996) children needed to face away from the experimenter for a period of 60 seconds while she noisily wrapped a gift for them. The conceptual basis for the conflict/delay distinction was subsequently confirmed empirically in a factor analysis.

The findings from this study strongly supported the first of our claims: The inhibitory battery was highly correlated with the ToM battery $r = .66$, $p < .001$). Other recent studies have reported similarly high correlations (e.g., Frye, Zelazo, & Palfai, 1995; Hughes, 1998a, 1998b; Hughes, Dunn, & White, 1998; Perner & Lang, 2000). Moreover, the correlations were uniformly high for the four ToM task types (deception, contents false belief, location false belief, and appearance–reality). These correlations ranged from .47 to .57, $ps < .001$. We also found that these correlations with ToM were consistently higher for conflict inhibition than for delay inhibition, a point to which we return later.

Nevertheless, it remained possible that these correlations, strong as they are, were a by-product of some more general developmental factor. However, the relation between the inhibitory control and ToM batteries remained significant even when we controlled for age, sex, and verbal (ability) $r = .41$, $p < .001$), and the same was true with respect to the individual ToM task types (rs ranged from .20 to .31, $ps < .05$). Hence, the association cannot be due to the possibility that developmental advances in both domains *coincidentally* occur in the same age range, or the fact that successful performance in both areas requires some verbal ability. Rather, it appears that these tasks share a much more central theoretical core.

Importantly, we found that the relation persisted when still other factors were statistically controlled. These factors included measures of symbolic play and family size (number of siblings) which are known to relate to either or both theory of mind and inhibitory control (Elias & Berk, 1999; Ruffman, Perner, Naito, Parkin, & Clements, 1998; Taylor & Carlson, 1997). They also included mental state control tasks designed to be similar in formal structure to the ToM tasks except that children were questioned not about mental states but rather about the previous location of an object or the previous contents of a container. Finally, in subsequent work (Carlson, Moses, & Breton, 2002), we have found that the relation remains significant even when a very broad measure of intelligence, including both verbal and performance aspects, is controlled. The link between self-regulation and ToM appears to be highly specific.

Perhaps the most prominent explanation for developmental changes in children's appreciation of mental life in the preschool period is that they are replacing inadequate theories with more adaptive ones. Specifically, younger children are believed to suffer from a conceptual deficit of one kind or another: For example, they are often said to altogether lack concepts of belief, mental representation, or even representation in general (e.g., Gopnik & Wellman, 1994; Moses & Flavell, 1990; Perner, 1991). Older preschoolers, it is argued, have developed a more adequate theory incorporating the missing concepts. Given the strength of the relation we obtained between inhibitory control and ToM, however, the question arose as to whether there was a need to invoke conceptual changes at all. Perhaps, regulatory factors might actually account for all the variance shared by ToM tasks in the preschool period. This was not the case, however. The relations between the four theory-of-mind task types and the aggregated ToM battery (item-total corrected) persisted, not only when age, sex, and verbal ability were held constant, but when inhibitory control was partialled as well (partial rs ranged from .22 to .35, ps < .05). Factors other than inhibition—possibly pure conceptual changes—are clearly implicated in ToM development.

WHAT ASPECTS OF SELF REGULATION ARE IMPLICATED IN ToM?

While our initial findings bolstered the case for a specific relation between self-regulation and ToM that was not a spurious byproduct of extraneous factors, it left open what aspects of self regulation might be most critical. We had focused on inhibitory control but self-regulation subsumes a variety of other executive processes thought to be relevant to the monitoring and control of thought and action. We have begun to address this issue by assessing whether inhibitory control continues to relate to ToM when other regulatory abilities are controlled.

One such ability is planning, a core component of the executive/regulatory system (Frye, 1999). Planning ability, at least in the sense of future-oriented thinking, would also seem to be implicated in theory-of-mind reasoning. To be successful on many ToM tasks children must not only inhibit prepotent responses, but they must also look ahead to what the naïve character is likely to think or do based on his or her intentions. Consistent with this analysis, correlations have indeed been found between ToM and planning (Hughes, 1998b; Bischof-Köhler, cited in Perner & Lang, 1999). To assess the specificity of the relation between self-regulation and ToM, it is therefore important to consider children's planning ability in addition to their inhibitory control.

In our initial study (Carlson & Moses, 2001), we had included a motor sequencing task (adapted from Welsh, Pennington, & Groisser, 1991). In this task children were shown a musical keyboard with four differently colored keys. They were instructed to press each key in a row with their index finger, repeating the sequence as many times as they could over a period of 10 seconds. The task assesses motor speed and motor planning, but has relatively light inhibitory demands. Performance on the motor sequencing task was related to theory of mind in raw correlations. However, the relation disappeared once age and verbal ability were controlled. Moreover, the relation between inhibition and ToM remained when motor sequencing was held constant, providing preliminary evidence that the link between self-regulation and ToM might be specifically mediated by inhibitory control.

In a subsequent study (Carlson, Moses, & Claxton, 2004) we examined the potential role of planning in theory of mind more broadly. A sample of 3- and 4-year-olds completed standard ToM measures (appearance–reality and false belief), a delay inhibition task (gift delay), two conflict inhibition measures (bear/dragon and whisper tasks), and two planning tasks.[1] In the Tower of Hanoi task (Simon, 1975; Welsh, 1991), children were required to transfer disks (monkeys) onto pegs (trees) so that the disks were arranged in exactly the same manner as an experimenter's disks, while adhering to a set of rules (e.g., a larger disk cannot be placed on top of a smaller disk). The level of difficulty increased with each successful trial. In a second planning task—Truck Loading (Fagot & Gauvain, 1997)—children acted as mail carriers whose job was to deliver party invitations to every house on the block (miniature houses on a poster board). The catch was that they could only drive the mail truck around the block once and in only one direction. Therefore, if they were planful, they would load the invitations onto the truck in the reverse order to which they needed to be delivered. The number of houses on the block increased with each successful trial.

Both the conflict inhibition battery and the planning battery were significantly related to ToM, $rs = .50$ and $.39$, $ps < .001$ and $.01$, respectively. Confirming the different pattern for conflict and delay tasks we had found earlier (Carlson & Moses, 2001), delay inhibition was not significantly related to ToM. Of greatest theoretical interest, however, was the finding that, in partial correlations controlling for age and verbal ability, only conflict inhibition remained significantly related to ToM, $r = .34$, $p < .03$. The relation between planning and ToM fell below significance in an analysis of this kind. Moreover, the relation between conflict inhibition and ToM persisted over and above planning ability as well as age and verbal ability, $r = .32$, $p < .04$. Although further research incorporating still other aspects of self-regulation remains to be done, these findings clearly move some distance toward isolating inhibition as the central factor linking self- regulation to ToM.

A SIMPLE INHIBITORY ACCOUNT

How might we explain the relations between self-regulation and ToM? A straightforward account might be framed as follows: Young preschoolers do have a theory of mind, but they have great difficulty expressing it because they cannot inhibit their knowledge of reality in standard ToM tasks. But a simple inhibitory account faces at least three major difficulties. First, as we have seen, not all inhibitory tasks relate strongly to ToM, suggesting that inhibition, per se, might not be the critical factor. Second, some ToM tasks appear to have prepotent response options but are relatively easy for preschoolers: Simple inhibition cannot explain the *sequence* of ToM development. And third, some ToM tasks do not appear to have prepotent response options but are nevertheless relatively difficult for preschoolers: Simple inhibition cannot explain the *generality* of ToM development. We address each of these challenges to the inhibitory account in turn.

INHIBITION, WORKING MEMORY, AND ToM

Recall that we had included both conflict and delay tasks in our earlier studies. The conflict tasks were consistently stronger predictors of ToM than were the delay tasks (see also Hala, Hug, & Henderson, 2003). Conflict and delay tasks differ along a number of dimensions. However, the dimension of greatest relevance, we think, is working memory (see Carlson & Moses, 2001; Carlson, Moses, & Breton, 2002). Most delay tasks simply require children to inhibit responding (e.g., to wait until the experimenter gives the signal); in contrast, conflict tasks require children to inhibit an inappropriate response while activating a conflicting response. The fact that the conflict tasks require conflicting alternatives to be held in mind suggests that the working memory demands are greater than for delay tasks. And, in this respect, the conflict tasks are like ToM tasks—ToM tasks require children to hold in mind two situations (real and represented) and to inhibit one of them. If this analysis is correct, we would expect correlations with working memory to be substantially higher for conflict inhibition than for delay inhibition.

We tested this hypothesis in a recent study (Carlson et al., 2002) in which we gave preschoolers working memory measures in addition to inhibitory measures (the conflict and delay tasks mentioned earlier) and ToM measures (false belief and appearance–reality). The working memory measures consisted of a backward digit span task (Davis & Pratt, 1996) in which children were asked to repeat a list of single-digit numbers in reverse order; a similar backward word span task; and a dual counting and labeling task (Gordon & Olson, 1998) in which children were asked to enumerate *and* state the name for each of three objects (e.g., "One is a shoe, two is a spoon, three is a car.").

As in our earlier studies, we found that conflict inhibition was more strongly related to false belief performance than was delay inhibition (see Table 6.1). Moreover, consistent with our analysis of the inhibitory tasks, working memory was significantly related to conflict inhibition but not to delay inhibition, and this was true both for raw correlations (rs = .54 and .14, respectively) and partial correlations controlling for age and IQ (rs = .35 and .07, respectively). But this raised the possibility that what was central to the self-regulation–ToM relation was not inhibition but rather working memory. Indeed, a number of studies have obtained moderate correlations between working memory and ToM (Davis & Pratt, 1996; Gordon & Olson, 1998; Keenan, 1998; Keenan, Olson, & Marini, 1998; Hughes, 1998a). Perhaps, then, conflict inhibition tasks relate to ToM *only* in virtue of the working memory requirements common to both kinds of measures.

To test this possibility we examined the relations between conflict inhibition and ToM, and between working memory and ToM. If inhibition is implicated over and above working memory, then the correlations for the inhibition tasks should be higher than those for the working memory tasks. Consistent with the inhibitory hypothesis, we found that although the raw correlations between false belief and both conflict inhibition and working memory were significant, only that between false belief and conflict inhibition remained so when age and intelligence were controlled (see Table 5.1). Moreover, when working memory was controlled in addition to age and intelligence, the relation between conflict inhibition and false belief remained significant.[2]

Our interpretation of these findings is as follows. Acquiring and expressing mental state concepts requires both working memory and inhibitory skill. Effective social cognition is not possible unless one is able to hold in mind relevant perspectives (working memory) and to suppress irrelevant ones (inhibition). Hence, tasks that pull heavily for *both* inhibition and working memory (conflict inhibition tasks) relate strongly to ToM. In contrast, those that make demands only on inhibition (e.g., delay tasks) or only on working memory (e.g., span tasks) relate much less strongly to ToM.

Our proposal is consistent with others suggesting that prefrontal functions involve an interaction between inhibitory processes and working memory (e.g., Diamond, 1991; Roberts & Pennington, 1996). According to Roberts and Pennington's interactive framework, for example, strong but

TABLE 6.1

Raw and Partial Correlations (Controlling for Age and IQ) Between False Belief and Measures of Conflict Inhibition, Delay Inhibition, and Working Memory

Measure	False belief	
	Raw correlation	*Partial correlation*
Conflict Inhibition	.52***	.30*
Delay Inhibition	.17	.09
Working Memory	.39*	.03

Note. All tests two-tailed. $N = 47$, except for correlations including delay inhibition, where $N = 46$; *$p < .05$; ***$p < .001$.

misleading prepotencies (hence heavy inhibitory demands) require correspondingly strong working memory activations to avoid falling prey to the prepotency. Thus, breakdowns in working memory should increase the likelihood of succumbing to incorrect prepotent responses. Our findings of a significant relation between conflict inhibition and working memory, and a specific relation between ToM and measures tapping both inhibition and working memory, are consistent with this theoretical account. They are also compatible with Diamond's (1991; Diamond & Taylor, 1996; Gerstadt et al., 1994) proposal according to which tasks that place demands on both working memory and inhibition are a better index of prefrontal cortex development than those that place demands on working memory alone. In that respect, Gerstadt et al. (1994) found that preschoolers could remember the rules to say "day" when presented with one abstract design and to say "night" when presented with another. However, they had considerable difficulty when required to say "day" in response to a moon card and "night" in response to a sun card. While both tasks impose working memory demands, only the latter imposes substantial inhibitory demands.

INHIBITION INTERACTS WITH CONCEPTUAL CONTENT

A second challenge to the simple inhibitory account lies in the fact that some ToM tasks appear to have prepotency and yet are relatively easy for preschoolers. A striking fact about theory of mind development is that an appreciation of different mental states emerges in a clear sequence. Pretense emerges early, toward the end of infancy (Leslie, 1987); desire understanding is present in 2-year-olds (Wellman & Woolley, 1990), and possibly earlier (Repacholi & Gopnik, 1997); but an appreciation of beliefs is not well developed until children are 3 or 4 (Wellman, Cross, & Watson, 2001). This sequence is apparent even in well-controlled experimental studies in which the content and structure of the tasks is closely matched for each mental state. For example, Lillard and Flavell (1992) told children stories in which a protagonist either thought, wanted, or pretended X. Children then learned that Y was in fact the case. They were then simply asked what the protagonist thought, wanted, or pretended. Similarly, Gopnik and Slaughter (1991) investigated children's understanding of changes in their own mental states. At Time 1 children either thought, wanted, or pretended X. The situation then changed such that they discovered that X was not the case, their desire for X was satiated, or they switched from pretending X to pretending Y. As a result, at Time 2, children ended up thinking, wanting, or pretending Y. The critical test question concerned children's earlier mental state—what they had thought, wanted, or pretended at Time 1 (just a few seconds before).

The common finding in studies like these is that belief tasks are relatively hard for preschoolers, pretense tasks are relatively easy, and desire tasks are somewhere in between. The pressing theoretical question is then to account for the order of emergence in children's understanding of these mental states. But, on the face of it, successful performance on all of these tasks would seem to require the inhibition of prepotent responses, no matter what specific mental state is involved. Recognizing another's false belief, unfulfilled desire, or pretense requires suppressing what I know about the conflicting true state of affairs. Similarly, recognizing my earlier beliefs, desires, or pretense requires backgrounding my current mental state and recovering an earlier, now outdated state of mind. However, if prepotency must be overcome when any of these mental states needs to be inferred, then we might expect that inhibitory control would be required for understanding all of them. If so, that would limit the explanatory force of the inhibitory account because it would be powerless to explain the sequence of ToM development. That is, although inhibition might impose a global constraint on ToM development, it would be irrelevant to any of the theoretically interesting developmental variation in the emergence of different ToM concepts.

But would we really expect inhibition to be implicated equally in children's appreciation of all of these mental states? On the simple inhibitory account outlined earlier the answer must be yes: All cases require the inhibition of prepotent knowledge about reality. However, an *interactive* inhibitory account makes a different prediction. On this account, inhibitory demands interact with conceptual content. What's prepotent in one conceptual context is not in another. Specifically, when beliefs are at issue, reality is likely to be highly salient because the very point of belief is to faithfully represent how things actually stand in the world (Carlson et al., 1998; Moses, 1993). The temptation to collapse beliefs onto reality is therefore likely to be strong. Hence, the inhibitory demands in belief tasks should be heavy. In contrast, in the case of pretense, reality is likely to be much less seductive because the very point of pretense is to create a counterfactual situation. As a result, there is likely to be much less pressure to collapse the pretend state onto the true state of affairs. Hence, the inhibitory demands in pretense tasks should be relatively light. Finally, desires appear to fall somewhere in between beliefs and pretense with respect to the prepotency of reality. Although we might well like our desires to match reality, we do not achieve this by changing our desires but rather by trying to change the world: The pressure to align is not on our desires but rather on reality (Searle, 1983). Consequently, those desires should be at least as salient as the true state of affairs. Hence, the inhibitory demands in desire tasks should be substantially lighter than those in belief tasks, though perhaps not as light as those in pretense tasks.

On the interactive hypothesis, then, inhibitory control should relate strongly to belief, moderately to desire, and weakly to pretense. Moses, Carlson, Stieglitz, and Claxton (2003) recently tested this hypothesis by giving children matched mental state tasks adapted from Lillard and Flavell (1992), and Gopnik and Slaughter (1991), as well as a subset of inhibitory tasks from our earlier work. The findings confirmed the interactive account (see Table 6.2). At the level of raw correlations, inhibition was strongly related to belief understanding, and moderately related to desire understanding, but not significantly related to pretense understanding. Further, when age, sex, and verbal ability were controlled, inhibition remained significantly related *only* to performance on the belief tasks (the correlation with pretense was now virtually zero). These findings represent strong evidence against a simple inhibitory account and, conversely, powerful support for an account in which inhibitory control interacts with conceptual content.

In a related line of work (Sabbagh, Moses, & Shiverick, 2003), one of us has looked at how inhibitory control relates to children's understanding of false belief (a mental representation) versus their understanding of so called "false" photographs (a non-mental representation). In a false photograph task, a photo is taken of an object at Location *X*. The object then moves to Location *Y*. The critical question concerns the location of the object *in the photograph*. Like the false belief task, this is a difficult task for preschoolers (Zaitchik, 1990), and it was initially argued that this common difficulty may arise because children are in the process of developing a general concept of representation, not just a concept of mental representation (Perner, 1991). However, performance on false belief tasks is only weakly correlated with that on false photo tasks (Davis & Pratt, 1996), suggesting that the source of difficulty on each task type might be quite different. An interactive inhibitory account can help to make sense of this pattern. Unlike beliefs, photos are typically not intended to mirror current reality; rather they mirror the state of affairs at the time at which they were taken. Whereas

TABLE 6.2

Raw and Partial Correlations (Controlling for Age, Sex, and Verbal Ability) Between Inhibitory Control and Measures of Belief, Desire, and Pretense Understanding

	Inhibitory control	
Measure	*Raw correlation*	*Partial correlation*
Belief	.53***	.42*
Desire	.33*	.16
Pretense	.25	−.04

Note. All tests two-tailed. *N* = 45 for raw correlations; *N* = 40 for partial correlations; *p* < .05; ***p* < .001.

we would like our beliefs to continually update, we would be dismayed if our prized photo albums possessed this property. And so, as in the case of the various mental states discussed earlier, the prepotency of current reality is different for beliefs and photographs: Current reality should be prepotent for beliefs but not for photographs.

Consistent with this hypothesis, we have found that preschoolers' inhibitory control relates to their performance on false belief tasks but not to that on false photograph tasks, again suggesting that inhibitory control interacts with conceptual content. In this research we also examined the relation between inhibitory control and performance on a false sign task. In this task (adapted from Parkin & Perner, 1996) a sign was intended to indicate the location of the protagonist. At some point, however, the protagonist moved to a new location, rendering the sign misleading. Children were then questioned as to where the sign indicated the protagonist was. We hypothesized that the inhibitory demands of the false sign task would be similar to those of the false belief task because, unlike photographs, there is normative pressure on both beliefs and signs to accurately reflect the current state of affairs (and hence that state should be prepotent in both cases). Our findings bear out this hypothesis: Although inhibition is unrelated to performance on the false photograph task, it relates just as strongly to performance on the false sign task as to performance on the false belief task (Sabbagh et al., 2003).

As an aside, these data have some relevance to our understanding of cognitive deficits in autism. As mentioned earlier, individuals with autism have deficits in both ToM and executive abilities. However, although these individuals routinely fail false belief tasks, they have little difficulty with false photograph tasks (Leslie & Thaiss, 1992). These data have been thought to rule out the hypothesis that executive deficits are central to ToM deficits in autism. That is, it has been argued that autistic individuals' difficulties on false belief tasks could not arise from executive problems because the need to inhibit knowledge of reality is equally present in photo tasks on which they have little difficulty (Leslie & Thaiss, 1992). However, given our findings that inhibitory control relates to performance on false belief but not false photograph tasks, it is entirely unsurprising that individuals with autism would find false photos much easier to process than false beliefs: The false photo task imposes minimal inhibitory demands in comparison to the false belief task, and is therefore not a fair index of autistic individuals' executive abilities. A much stronger test of the role of executive factors in ToM deficits in autism would involve determining whether individuals with autism have just as much difficulty with the false sign test—which our findings indicate does have a substantial executive component—as with the false belief task. If they did, an executive account of ToM deficits in autism would remain in the running; if not, support for a domain specific account of those deficits would be enhanced.

SELF-REGULATION AFFECTS THE EMERGENCE
OF ToM AS WELL AS ITS EXPRESSION

A final problem for a simple inhibitory account arises from the fact that some ToM tasks do not have obvious prepotency but are nevertheless very difficult for preschoolers. For example, in O'Neill and Gopnik's (1991) sources-of-knowledge task, an object is hidden in a tunnel and then children discover its identity either by looking in the tunnel, by feeling the object through the tunnel, or by being told what the object is (see also Gopnik & Graf, 1988). They are then asked how they came to know the object's identity. This task is hard for preschoolers, but when they err, their errors are largely unsystematic. In contrast to false belief tasks, in which children err consistently by responding in terms of the true state of affairs, in the sources-of-knowledge task they are not biased toward a particular, incorrect response. For example, they are not predisposed to state that they saw the object irrespective of how they discovered its identity. Similarly, in Moore, Pure, and Furrow's (1990) mental state uncertainty task children hear one puppet state, for example, that he *thinks* a target object is in the red box while another states that he *knows* the object is in the blue box. Children are then simply asked where the object is. This task is again difficult for preschoolers (and correlated with false belief performance) but children's errors are once more largely random: Across trials they do not mistakenly favor the incorrect "think" option.

It seems then that these tasks have no built-in prepotency and so should not impose a heavy inhibitory burden. However, if inhibitory control relates only to a limited class of the ToM skills that develop in the preschool period then its explanatory scope would be much reduced. It would be unable to account for the quite *general* nature of the ToM changes that occur in the preschool years.

But would we really expect inhibitory control to relate only to those ToM tasks that have prepotent response options? The answer depends on how we view the relation between self-regulation and theory of mind. At the outset we suggested two possibilities in this regard. First, as the simple inhibitory account asserts, self-regulation might affect the expression of ToM capacities that are already present in some form. In this view, children's failures on many ToM tasks may stem from problems translating conceptual knowledge into successful performance. If self-regulation has its impact largely with respect to ToM expression, then we would not expect a relation between inhibitory control and ToM tasks that do not exhibit prepotency. If there is no prepotency *in the task* then there should be no inhibitory demands, and hence no relation.

However, we also noted a second possibility wherein self-regulation might affect the very emergence of ToM capacities. A certain level of executive, regulatory ability may need to have developed before children could even construct complex concepts of mental life. It is certainly difficult to imagine how children could acquire such concepts without some capacity to reflect on thought and action, some ability to distance themselves from the immediate situation, some ability to inhibit their own salient knowledge. On this account, then, there might well be a relation between self-regulation and ToM tasks that do not exhibit prepotency. Even though measures like the sources and certainty tasks are not subject to prepotency effects, success on these tasks nonetheless requires that children possess concepts of knowledge and belief and, on the emergence view, inhibitory control is necessary for the construction of such concepts. Hence, a relation between inhibition and these non-prepotent ToM tasks would be expected.

We tested these competing hypotheses by giving preschool children both ToM tasks with prepotent response options (e.g., false belief, appearance–reality tasks) and ToM tasks without such options (sources and certainty tasks), and then examining how these different task types relate to inhibitory control (Moses et al., 2003). Our findings are consistent with the view that self-regulation has an impact at the point of ToM emergence rather than simply the point of ToM expression. Inhibitory control related just as strongly to the ToM tasks that did not show prepotency ($r = .48$) as to those that did ($r = .52$) (see Perner, Lang, & Kloo, 2002, for similar findings). Of course, it is always possible that, despite their similarity, the correlations with inhibition arose for different reasons. Perhaps, for example, the prepotent ToM tasks correlated with inhibition because of common inhibitory demands, whereas the nonprepotent tasks correlated with the inhibitory tasks because of either (a) their shared general cognitive demands or (b) their shared working memory demands. Both of these alternatives can be ruled out, however. With respect to the first possibility, the pattern of correlations remained the same when age, sex, and verbal ability were statistically controlled. With respect to the second, the pattern remained the same when children's performance on a working memory task—Gordon & Olson's (1998) counting and labeling task—was similarly held constant.

The fact that the correlations with inhibition were no higher for the prepotent ToM tasks than for the nonprepotent tasks might be viewed as not only supporting an emergence account, but as entirely ruling out an expression account (see Perner & Lang, 1999). While the pattern of correlations is certainly consistent with the possibility that executive "task" factors play little role in performance on ToM tasks, other evidence indicates that they may. Specifically, when the inhibitory demands of ToM tasks are directly manipulated, the effects on children's performance are sizeable (see, e.g., Carlson et al., 1998; Hala & Russell, 2001; Leslie & Polizzi, 1998; see also, Moses, 2001). For this reason, it seems likely that self-regulation may affect both the emergence and the expression of children's theories of mind.

CONCLUSIONS

To summarize, our findings support the four claims made earlier. First, self-regulation and ToM are indeed tightly linked in the preschool period. The finding is exceptionally strong, highly replicable, and robust in the face of a variety of relevant controls. Any theory that hopes to explain theory-of-mind development in the preschool years will need to somehow account for findings of this sort.

Second, working memory and inhibitory control appear to be jointly implicated in the relation between self-regulation and ToM. Both the ability to hold conflicting perspectives in mind and the ability to inhibit one's own salient perspective are crucial in mental state attribution.

Third, inhibitory control interacts with conceptual content: What's prepotent in one conceptual context may not be in another. This fact may in part explain why children understand some mental states (pretense, desire) before others (belief), and why understanding certain non-mental representations (e.g., photos) is unrelated to understanding mental representations (beliefs).

Finally, the effects of self-regulation are felt at the point of ToM emergence as well as the point of ToM expression. Self-regulation is a crucial enabling factor for ToM development rather than a mere "performance" factor.

In conclusion, the self appears to impact children's appreciation of mental life through a nonobvious route: via self-regulation. Our proposal is that self-regulation is necessary but not by any means sufficient for advances in children's theories of mind. A fully functioning executive/regulatory system could never, by itself, deliver concepts of mental life. Nonetheless, our findings indicate that immaturities in that system may well represent a powerful constraint on the theories of mind young children can acquire and flexibly deploy.

ENDNOTES

[1]Children were also given a third planning task—Kitten Delivery (adapted from Fabricius, 1988). Performance on this task was uncorrelated with the other planning tasks and so it was not included in the planning battery. The pattern of results remains virtually the same, however, if it is included.

[2]The pattern of findings was different for appearance–reality. Both conflict inhibition and working memory were significantly related to appearance–reality. However, neither of these relations survived once age and intelligence were held constant.

REFERENCES

Baddeley, A. D. (1986). *Working memory.* Oxford, MA: Clarendon Press.

Baron-Cohen, S. (1995). *Mindblindness: An essay on autism and theory of mind.* Cambridge, MA: MIT Press.

Carlson, S. M., & Moses, L. J. (2001). Individual differences in inhibitory control and children's theory of mind. *Child Development, 72,* 1032–1053.

Carlson, S. M., Moses, L. J., & Breton, C. (2002). How specific is the relation between executive function and theory of mind? Contributions of inhibitory control and working memory. *Infant and Child Development, 11,* 73–92.

Carlson, S. M., Moses, L. J., & Claxton, L. J. (2004). Individual differences in executive functioning and theory of mind: An investigation of inhibitory control and planning ability. *Journal of Experimental Child Psychology, 87,* 299–319.

Carlson, S. M., Moses, L. J., & Hix, H. R. (1998). The role of inhibitory control in young children's difficulties with deception and false belief. *Child Development, 69,* 672–691.

Davis, H. L., & Pratt, C. (1996). The development of children's theory of mind: The working memory explanation. *Australian Journal of Psychology, 47,* 25–31.

Diamond, A. (1991). Developmental time course in human infants and infant monkeys, and the neural bases of inhibitory control in reaching. *Annals of the New York Academy of Sciences: Part 7. Inhibition and executive control, 608,* 637–704.

Diamond, A., & Taylor, C. (1996). Development of an aspect of executive control: Development of the abilities to remember what I said and "Do as I say, not as I do." *Developmental Psychobiology, 29,* 315–334.

Elias, C., & Berk, L. E. (1999, April). *Self regulation in young children: Is there a role for sociodramatic play?* Poster presented at the biennial meeting of the Society for Research in Child Development, Albuquerque, NM.

Fabricius, W. V. (1988). The development of forward search planning in preschoolers. *Child Development, 59,* 1473–1488.

Fagot, B. I., & Gauvain, M. (1997). Mother–child problem solving: Continuity through the early childhood years. *Developmental Psychology, 33*(3), 480–488.

Flavell, J. H. (1978). The development of knowledge about visual perception. In C. B. Keasey (Ed.), *Nebraska symposium on motivation (Vol. 25).* Lincoln: University of Nebraska Press.

Flavell, J. H., Flavell, E. R., & Green, F. L. (1983). Development of the appearance–reality distinction. *Cognitive Psychology, 15,* 95–120.

Frith, C. D., & Frith, U. (1999). Interacting minds—A biological basis. *Science, 286,* 1692–1695.

Frye, D. (1999). Development of intention: The relation of executive function to theory of mind. In P. D. Zelazo, J. W. Astington, & D. R. Olson (Eds.), *Developing theories of intention* (pp. 119–132). Mahwah, NJ: Lawrence Erlbaum Associates.

Frye, D., Zelazo, P. D., & Palfai, T. (1995). Theory of mind and rule-based reasoning. *Cognitive Development, 10,* 483–527.

Gerstadt, C. L., Hong, Y. J., & Diamond, A. (1994). The relationship between cognition and action: Performance of children 3.5–7 years old on a Stroop-like day–night test. *Cognition, 53,* 129–153.

Gopnik, A. (1993). How we know our minds: The illusion of first-person knowledge of intentionality. *Behavioral & Brain Sciences, 16,* 1–14.

Gopnik, A., & Graf, P. (1988). Knowing how you know: Young children's ability to identify and remember the sources of their beliefs. *Child Development, 59,* 1366–1371.

Gopnik, A., & Slaughter, V. (1991). Young children's understanding of changes in their mental states. *Child Development, 62,* 98–110.

Gopnik, A., & Wellman, H. M. (1994). The theory theory. In L. Hirschfeld & S. Gelman (Eds.), *Mapping the mind: Domain specificity in cognition and culture* (pp. 257–293). New York: Cambridge University Press.

Gordon, A. C. L., & Olson, D. R. (1998). The relation between acquisition of a theory of mind and the capacity to hold in mind. *Journal of Experimental Child Psychology, 68,* 70–83.

Hala, S., Hug, S., & Henderson, A. (2003). Executive functioning and false belief understanding in preschool children: Two tasks are harder than one. *Journal of Cognition and Development, 4,* 275–298.

Hala, S., & Russell, J. (2001). Executive control within strategic deception: A window on early cognitive development? *Journal of Experimental Child Psychology, 80,* 112–141.

Harris, P. L. (2000). *The work of the imagination.* Oxford, UK: Blackwell.

Harter, S. (1983). Developmental perspectives on the self system. In E. M. Hetherington (Ed.), *Handbook of child psychology: Vol. 4. Socialization, personality, and social development* (pp. 275–386). New York: Wiley.

Hughes, C. (1998a). Executive function in preschoolers: Links with theory of mind and verbal ability. *British Journal of Developmental Psychology, 16,* 233–253.

Hughes, C. (1998b). Finding your marbles: Does preschoolers' strategic behavior predict later understanding of mind? *Developmental Psychology, 34,* 1326–1339.

Hughes, C., Dunn, J., & White, A. (1998). Trick or treat? Uneven understanding of mind and emotion and executive dysfunction in "hard-to-manage" preschoolers. *Journal of Child Psychology and Psychiatry, 39,* 981–994.

Keenan, T. (1998). Memory span as a predictor of false belief understanding. *New Zealand Journal of Psychology, 27,* 36–43.

Keenan, T., Olson, D. R., & Marini, Z. (1998). Working memory and children's developing understanding of mind. *Australian Journal of Psychology, 50,* 76–82.

Kochanska, G., Coy, K. C., & Murray, K. T. (2001). The development of self-regulation in the first four years of life. *Child Development, 72,* 1091–1111.

Kochanska, G., Murray, K., Jacques, T. Y., Koenig, A. L., & Vandegeest, K. A. (1996). Inhibitory control in young children and its role in emerging internalization. *Child Development, 67,* 490–507.

Leslie, A. M. (1987). Pretense and representation: The origins of "theory of mind." *Psychological Review, 94,* 412–426.

Leslie, A. M., & Polizzi, P. (1998). Inhibitory processing in the false belief task: Two conjectures. *Developmental Science, 1,* 247–253.

Leslie, A. M., & Thaiss, L. (1992). Domain specificity in conceptual development: Neuropsychological evidence from autism. *Cognition, 43,* 225–251.

Lillard, A. S., & Flavell, J. H. (1992). Young children's understanding of different mental verbs. *Developmental Psychology, 28,* 626–634.

Luria, A. R. (1966). *Higher cortical functions in man.* New York: Basic Books.

Luria, A. R. (1973). *The working brain: An introduction to neuropsychology.* New York: Basic Books.

McEvoy, R., Rogers, S. J., & Pennington, B. F. (1993). Executive function and social communication deficits in young, autistic children. *Journal of Child Psychology and Psychiatry, 34,* 563–578.

Moore, C., Pure, K., & Furrow, D. (1990). Children's understanding of the modal expression of certainty and uncertainty and its relation to the development of a representational theory of mind. *Child Development, 61,* 722–730.

Moses, L. J. (1993). Young children's understanding of belief constraints on intention. *Cognitive Development, 8,* 1–25.

Moses, L. J. (2001). Executive accounts of theory of mind development. *Child Development, 72,* 688–690.

Moses, L. J., Carlson, S. M., Stieglitz, S., & Claxton, L. J. (2003). *Executive function, prepotency, and children's theories of mind.* Manuscript in preparation, University of Oregon.

Moses, L. J., & Flavell, J. H. (1990). Inferring false beliefs from actions and reactions. *Child Development, 61,* 929–945.

O'Neill, D. K., & Gopnik, A. (1991). Young children's ability to identify the sources of their beliefs. *Developmental Psychology, 27,* 390–397.

Parkin, L. J., & Perner, J. (1996). *Wrong directions in children's theory of mind: What it means to understand belief as representation.* Unpublished manuscript, University of Sussex.

Perner, J. (1991). *Understanding the representational mind.* Cambridge, MA: MIT Press.

Perner, J., & Lang, B. (1999). Development of theory of mind and executive control. *Trends in Cognitive Sciences, 3,* 337–344.

Perner, J., & Lang, B. (2000). Theory of mind and executive function: Is there a developmental relationship? In S. Baron-Cohen, H. Tager-Flusberg, & D. Cohen (Eds.), *Understanding other minds: Perspectives from autism and developmental cognitive neuroscience* (pp. 150–181). Oxford, UK: Oxford University Press.

Perner, J., Lang, B., & Kloo, D. (2002). Theory of mind and self control: More than a common problem of inhibition. *Child Development, 73,* 752–767.

Piaget, J. (1926). *The language and thought of the child.* New York: Harcourt, Brace.

Reed, M., Pien, D. L., & Rothbart, M. K. (1984). Inhibitory self-control in preschool children. *Merrill Palmer Quarterly, 30,* 131–147.

Repacholi, B. M., & Gopnik, A. (1997). Early reasoning about desires: Evidence from 14- and 18-month-olds. *Developmental Psychology, 33,* 12–21.

Roberts, R. J., Jr., & Pennington, B. F. (1996). An interactive framework for examining prefrontal cognitive processes. *Developmental Neuropsychology, 12,* 105–126.

Rothbart, M. K., & Posner, M. I. (1985). Temperament and the development of self-regulation. In L. Hartlage & C. F. Telzrow (Eds.), *The neuropsychology of individual differences: A developmental perspective* (pp. 93–123). New York: Plenum.

Ruffman, T., Perner, J., Naito, M., Parkin, L., & Clements, W. A. (1998). Older (but not younger) siblings facilitate false belief understanding. *Developmental Psychology, 34,* 161–174.

Russell, J. (1996). *Agency: Its role in mental development.* Mahwah, NJ: Lawrence Erlbaum Associates.

Russell, J. (Ed.). (1997). *Autism as an executive disorder.* New York: Oxford University Press.

Russell, J., Mauthner, N., Sharpe, S., & Tidswell, T. (1991). The "windows task" as a measure of strategic deception in preschoolers and autistic subjects. *British Journal of Developmental Psychology, 9,* 331–349.

Sabbagh, M. A., Moses, L. J., & Shiverick, S. M. (2003). *Executive functioning and preschoolers' understanding of false beliefs, false photographs and false signs.* Manuscript under review.

Sabbagh, M. A., & Taylor, M. (2000). Neural correlates of theory-of-mind reasoning: An event-related potential study. *Psychological Science, 11,* 46–50.

Searle, J. (1983). *Intentionality.* Cambridge, UK: Cambridge University Press.

Siegal, M., & Varley, R. (2002). Neural systems involved in "theory of mind." *Nature Neuroscience Reviews, 3,* 463–471.

Sigel, I. E. (1993). The centrality of a distancing model for the development of representational competence. In R. R. Cocking & K. A. Renninger (Eds.), *The development and meaning of psychological distance* (pp. 141–157). Hillsdale, NJ: Lawrence Erlbaum Associates.

Simon, H. A. (1975). The functional equivalence of problem solving skills. *Cognitive Psychology, 7,* 268–288.

Stuss, D. T., Gallup, G. G., Jr., & Alexander, M. P. (2001). The frontal lobes are necessary for "theory of mind." *Brain, 124,* 279–286.

Taylor, M., & Carlson, S. M. (1997). The relation between individual differences in fantasy and theory of mind. *Child Development, 68,* 436–455.

Wellman, H. M., Cross, D., & Watson, J. (2001). Meta-analysis of theory of mind development: The truth about false belief. *Child Development, 72,* 655–684.

Wellman, H. M., & Woolley, J. D. (1990). From simple desires to ordinary beliefs: The early development of everyday psychology. *Cognition, 35,* 245–275.

Welsh, M. C. (1991). Rule-guided behavior and self-monitoring on the Tower of Hanoi disk-transfer task. *Cognitive Development, 6,* 59–76.

Welsh, M. C., Pennington, B. F., & Groisser, D. B. (1991). A normative-developmental study of executive function: A window on prefrontal function in children. *Developmental Neuropsychology, 7,* 131–149.

Wimmer, H., & Perner, J. (1983). Beliefs about beliefs: Representation and constraining function of wrong beliefs in young children's understanding of deception. *Cognition, 13,* 103–128.

Zaitchik, D. (1990). When representations conflict with reality: The preschooler's problem with false beliefs and "false" photographs. *Cognition, 35,* 41–68.

Zelazo, P. D., Frye, D., & Rapus, T. (1996). An age-related dissociation between knowing rules and using them. *Cognitive Development, 11,* 37–63.

Part III

SELF, MIND, AND CULTURE

Chapter 7

Self and Power in the World of Romance: Extending Sociogenic Theories*

Dorothy Holland
University of North Carolina, Chapel Hill

Anthropology's engagement with concepts of self and subjectivity has changed radically. Over the last 30 years, in response to a watershed period that we call the critical disruption, the discipline recast its core concept of culture and refigured the significance of discourses and practices of the self. Anthropologists now place greater emphasis on the conditions that cultural imaginaries and powerful institutions set for self-formation and grant greater recognition to the ways that gender, class, race, and other social divisions refract day-to-day experiences and the selves that take shape in them. In turn, they insist that all these social forces—discursive imaginaries, durable institutions and formative divisions—are refracted and transfigured by daily experience and the selves that transact and register it.[1]

My chapter begins with a brief overview of earlier conceptions of self in anthropological thinking and then turns to examine more recent theory by means of an ethnographic study of self and power in the cultural world of romance. The analysis is meant to reflect a conceptualization of self—a cul-

---

*Parts of this chapter were reproduced using modified segments of Holland, Lachicotte, Skinner, & Cain (1998). Reprinted by permission of the publisher from *The sexual auction block*, in D. C. Holland, W. S. Lachicotte, D. Skinner, & C. Cain, pp. 144–177, Cambridge, MA: Harvard University Press. Copyright © 1998 by the President and Fellows of Harvard College.

tural-historical, social practice theory of self and identity—that my colleagues and I have produced from the works of Vygotsky, Bakhtin, and Bourdieu (Holland, Lachicotte, Skinner, & Cain, 1998; Holland & Lave, 2001; Lachicotte, 2002; Skinner, Pach, & Holland, 1998). The goal is to extend sociogenic theories of the self in light of the past 3 decades of critical debate: to bring issues of power, domination, and liberation explicitly to bear on social self-fashioning.

CULTURAL DISCOURSES AND PRACTICES OF THE SELF

Everywhere—in Nepal, for example, or in American Samoa—there are ways of talking about what anthropologists take to be a person's self (or selves). That is, there are conventional means for conceptualizing and representing a complex set of entities and processes thought to be intrinsic to, although not necessarily within the skin of, a person that shape his or her action. These intrinsic capacities are implicated in reflexivity, in the stances that a person sometimes takes to objectify, monitor, and evaluate his or her own behavior.[2] Nepalis and Samoans have ways of talking about selves, but their discourses differ from those prevalent in the United States. They also engage in activities thought to affect the self, "practices of the self," that are not common in the United States. Decades of anthropological research confirm the existence of a great variety of such discourses, practices, concepts, means, and modalities of the self [3] (Geertz, 1973; Harris, 1989; Levine, 1982, pp. 291–304; Marsella, DeVos, & Hsu, 1985; Shweder & Bourne, 1984; White, 1992).

One of the major questions to be raised about this cultural cornucopia is its significance. How, if at all, do these culturally specific discourses and practices inform the selves that are their object? In the history of anthropological theories of the self, theorists have taken up different positions on the ontological status of these self discourses and practices. Their stances have shifted profoundly over time, as have their intellectual projects, with issues of power and domination emerging relatively recently.

Before the 1970s, anthropological work on culture and the self (and other cross-cultural inquiries) developed primarily through a dialogue, sometimes implicit, sometimes explicit, between universalist and culturalist perspectives. At the crux of the dialogue is the status attributed to specific discourses and practices of the self. For those who embrace the theoretical priority of the "natural self," culture is subordinate to universal properties of human psychology. The human self is, first and foremost, a complex of natural, species-given, structures and processes. Perceptible to scientific probing, the natural self exists beneath the sometimes dazzling, but always thin overlay of cultural expression, of the ways of enacting and talking about the self—much as the species-given human body exists beneath culturally variable kinds of clothing and bodily adornment. As viewed by universalists, culturally variant discourses and practices are mildly interesting, but mostly inconvenient and scientifically quaint, coverings of the universal self.

The countervailing culturalist position attributes much more significance to culturally specific concepts of the self. For the culturalists, these concepts, discourses and practices of the self are indicators of the contours of a pervasive cultural logic that shapes the self in profound ways. From this stance, cultural discourses and their relationship to the self are like that of a bottle to the liquid it contains. Self-discourses and practices must be scrutinized for they are clues to the contours of the bottle—the culture—that shapes the malleable self.

Twenty-five or 30 years ago, powerful crosscurrents began to disrupt the universalist-culturalist debate. Anthropology entered into a period of incorporating feminist and other critical social theories, a move that demanded reexamination of the discipline's relations with its subjects. The field came under sustained criticism from within. The critiques reflected on the collaboration of anthropologists with colonial powers (e.g., Asad, 1973), for example, and on the tendency of anthropological fieldwork to focus myopically on males and male activities (e.g., Reiter, 1975; Weiner, 1976).

Often drawing explicitly on Foucault, this body of work highlighted the entanglement of power with knowledge and implicated scientific knowledge in its critique. Cultural forms—including descriptions or representations of other cultures, especially those espoused by powerful elites or otherwise associated with authority and legitimacy—were no longer regarded as benign or neutral. Rather they were conveyances of power that entered into the shaping of the very objects they described. Feminists, for example, began to see the cultural discourses of older ethnographies as representing the perspective of the more powerful members of the society. They began to question cultural forms as impositions, pushing women and men to behaviors and subjectivities that are compatible with the same structures and institutions that favor members of some social categories over others (e.g., Abu-Lughod, 1991).

These critical stances had a number of ramifications in anthropology. For one, representations of cultures as holistic, coherent, integrated, timeless wholes became suspect. It could no longer be taken for granted that everyone subscribed equally, regardless of social position, to the cultural tenets elucidated in the ethnography. Skeptics asked whether those who lacked power took a different stance toward "the" culture than did those in power and argued that cultural meanings were perspectival. Accounts of culture that ignored the importance of social position became suspect of unwittingly, if not surreptitiously, silencing those who lacked privilege and power. Anthropology is now much more reticent to treat the cultural discourses and practices of a group or people as though they were indicative of one underlying cultural logic or essence equally compelling to all those raised in its folds. Instead, contest and struggle over power and the cultural meaning that supports and constitutes it have been brought to the foreground.

SUBJECTIVITY AND SELF
IN THE WAKE OF THE CRITICAL DISRUPTION

In addition to refiguring culture as an object of study, the critical disruption in anthropology and other human sciences intervened powerfully in dialogues about the self *per se*. The critical disruption has, to put it mildly, interfered with questions posed both from the universalist and especially from the culturalist positions. Social constructivist theory, some versions of which are referred to as discourse or post-structuralist theory, emphasizes the historical production of subjects and subjectivities. Selves are conceived to be socially constructed through the mediation of powerful discourses and their artifacts—census forms, curriculum vitae, etiquette protocols, DSM-III diagnostic categories of mental disorders, educational diagnostics that label some children "at risk," and the like. Such genres require people to present themselves according to categories obligatory to the form. Resistance to such affordances is possible, but those subject to the form are limited to two choices: to comply or resist.

With the advent of social constructionism, stances toward cultural forms and their relationship to self shifted. Discourses and practices of the self were no longer treated as inconsequential coverings of the universal self. But neither were they considered reflections of core cultural themes that shape existence much as a container shapes the liquid poured into it. Instead, self discourses and practices are now seen as "tools of the self," which, when forcefully applied, cause the self to assume the shape of first this, then that social artifact.

Of even greater consequence, the critical disruption fatally undermined important taken-for-granted, Enlightenment notions of the prototypic self as coherent, rational, and originary. Foucauldian arguments hold instead that persons are profoundly subject to the social and political conditions in which they exist. State power, although once instrumental in the production of modern or Enlightenment understandings of subjectivity, is not in our current historical era conducive to producing a coherent, rational self, especially for those people most vulnerable to its ministrations. Regimes of power set profound conditions for the possibilities of self. This recognition calls for an alternative model of self, one that admits power relations, allows multiple, fragmentary, and scarcely developed selves, and puts the historical production of lives and subjectivity in the forefront of intellectual projects to be researched (Henriques et al., 1984, 1998).

The critical disruption stimulated two major lines of inquiry in subsequent anthropological studies related to self and identity, lines that differed primarily in the sorts of tools of the self that attracted research attention. The first focused on representations of cultural and social groups and the politics of those representations; the second, on culturally distinct tools of the self and their shaping of personal experience. Regarding the former, the topic of cultural and social identities has become a high priority in the discipline. Inquiry addresses the hegemonic discourses and practices that construct ethnic, race, and gender categories and the consequences of those representations for the people and groups they purport to describe.

Of more immediate relevance to this section, the second line of study represents a revitalization of anthropologists' interest in self and subjectivity (Holland, 1997; Whittaker, 1992). The older, pre-1970s, functionalist paradigms of culture encouraged a view of the relation of culture to self as seamless, especially for pre-industrial societies. Culture theorists saw in ritual performances templates for managing personal experience and subjectivity. Most members of a culture would learn these templates through participation in these obligatory performances and practices, and, in the end, embrace and enact the cultural principles that (thus) ruled their lives (e.g., Eggan, 1974). As Marcus and Fischer (1986) pointed out, the demise of these older paradigms of culture, while making the self a risky topic, also make it an intriguing one. The divergent positions that developed subsequently in the 1970s, were as likely to find in cultural practices and discourses a source of personal problems and difficulties that people tried to relieve (e.g., Crapanzano, 1980). People were no longer conceived simply as personifications of core cultural themes and the questions anthropologists asked about experience and subjectivity changed. A series of innovative ethnographic studies of self and personhood ensued. Although these ethnographic studies were not themselves always in theoretical accord, they did agree that self discourses and practices were significant in the very constitution of those selves.[4]

Michelle Rosaldo's (1980) *Knowledge and Passion: Ilongot Notions of Self and Social Life* provides a good example. The book presents Rosaldo's efforts to understand Ilongot men's motivation for headhunting, or, to put it differently, her effort to understand Ilongot masculine selves and the ways in which taking a human head was for them a key experience in becoming a man. Rosaldo refused to short-circuit her process of understanding by reducing the activities of headhunting to a utilitarian logic. Such logic, one that counts the worth of action according to its utility in obtaining socially defined goods, would have explained head hunting as an effort to achieve status. Rosaldo also refused to reduce the Ilongot perspective to a Freudian logic, or to any scheme that demanded that she ignore the particular Ilongot discourses and practices that had to do with headhunting. Similarly, she was determined not to follow the more accustomed anthropological route, devoting herself solely to a semiotic analysis of the symbols used in rituals and myths. She wanted instead to know the things important to the Ilongot themselves: why, for instance, did men tell her, in a matter-of-fact manner, that *liget*, an emotion word, sometimes translated into English as anger, is the reason for beheadings (p. 24)? She could not, in pursuit of such questions, bypass Ilongot talk about headhunting because those were the discourses and practices that people used both to communicate their experiences to others and to understand themselves (e.g., p. 36).

These ethnographic studies of selves, identities, and personhood attend more explicitly to culture than does the social constructivist or poststructuralist approach, but they clearly depart from the older culturalist arguments about self. Selves are not seen simply as emerging from pervasive cultural logics, but rather as forming over time in relation to a range of *specific cultural activities* such as headhunting in the Ilongot study or, in the case of the example presented in this chapter, practices of romance and attractiveness. Holland et al. (1998) refer to these activities as creating cultural or "figured" worlds. Specific selves or identities form in relation to the discourses and practices that construct the cultural worlds they engage. In the remainder of the chapter I refer to these selves as *sociogenic*, a term which signals a reliance on George Herbert Mead, Lev Vygotsky, M. M. Bakhtin, Pierre Bourdieu, and other theorists who consider selves to be socially formed—that is, formed in social practices and expressed in the terms of specific cultural genre.

SOCIOGENIC VERSUS SOCIAL CONSTRUCTIVIST CONCEPTIONS OF THE SELF

Sociogenic and social constructivist theories of the self are alike in considering culturally variant, socially inflected discourses and practices of the self central to self-formation. Yet, they differ in several respects of import to contemporary debates. Whether these differences are ultimately reconcilable or not, each approach raises legitimate challenges for the other. I argue that sociogenic theories are productively augmented by combining their recognition of the potential in these historical and sociocultural tools of self-fashioning for human agency with a social constructivist concern with power and domination. First, however, I invite the reader to imagine the cultural world of romance as it was constructed on two college campuses, one, a historically black university; the other, historically white, in the American South circa 1980.

THE CULTURAL WORLD OF ROMANCE AND ATTRACTIVENESS

The largest of our studies of campus culture, a multi-year project involving an extended ethnographic component and a survey, followed a group of women in their careers through the universities. At the onset of the project, the women were in their first year of college life. The course of the study showed (as we researchers could have remembered) that student activities and culture, especially for women, revolved around gender relations interpreted according to the popular ideology of romance (Holland & Skinner, 1987; Holland & Eisenhart, 1990).

For many Americans, romance and attractiveness may seem to be an obvious way to interpret gender relations involving sex. Yet narratives and practices of romantic interactions are decidedly cultural, not natural, with a history dating back, at least, to the performances, songs and poems of courtly love staged by aristocrats of what is now the south of France in the 11th and 12th centuries (Holland et al., 1998, pp. 239–247).[5] Cultural constructions have to be learned and their related practices mastered. The women in our study were both learning more about romance and attractiveness and taking part in the communities of practice that made the world of romance a central feature of daily student life on campus. They were developing their own senses of themselves as romantic and sexual actors. In the process, they and their fellow students knew, used, learned, and created a huge vocabulary of gender-marked terms—jerk, jock, prick, hunk, Susie sorority, bitch, and fox—all of which were names for persona in the cultural world of romance (Holland & Skinner, 1987). When students used these terms, they presumed that their talk would be understood in relation to a simplified world of heterosexual cross-gender relationships. The central narrative of the figured world specifies a typical progress of events:

An attractive man ("guy") and an attractive woman ("girl") are drawn to one another.

The man learns and appreciates the woman's qualities and uniqueness as a person.

Sensitive to her desires he shows his affection by treating her well. E.g., he buys things for her, takes her places she likes, and shows that he appreciates her and appreciates her uniqueness as a person.

She in turn shows her affection and interest and allows the relationship to become more intimate.

This narrative also presupposes the motives or purposes of such relationships:

The relationship provides intimacy for both the man and the woman.

The relationship validates the attractiveness of both the man and the woman.

And, it allows and accounts for some exceptions:

In some cases, the attractiveness or prestige of the man is less than that of the
woman. He compensates for his lower prestige by treating her especially well.

If the woman's attractiveness is the lower of the two, she compensates by
permitting a greater degree of intimacy and by being satisfied with less good
treatment from the man.

The names for types of men and women, which had initially attracted our attention, turned out to be tools for socially positioning those people who, for the most part, caused problems in the taken-for-granted progress of male/female relations posited by the cultural narrative. Men used "bitch," for example, to insult and rein in women who overvalued their attractiveness relative to the men's, women who expected a lot of good treatment and offered little affection and intimacy in return. "Nerds" were men who were neither attractive nor sufficiently "tuned in" to know what a woman might like. Moreover, they were too insensitive to make up for their lesser attractiveness by treating a woman well.

More than a few times, again belying the popular conception that romance is natural, the women in our study happened into uncomfortable, unpleasant situations. These experiences, whether their own or those of friends, affected their developing sense of themselves as romantic actors and attractive women. A flavor of this aspect of the world of romance is conveyed in this excerpt from Karen, one of the women in our study. She was describing things that had happened since the last interview.

Karen: A friend of mine [Annette] invited us ... to a party in the
        dorm. And, she told us that there'd be ... a couple of people
        there that she really liked a lot: guys, that is ... and ... when
        we got there ... the main one she wanted to see ... I mean ...
        he didn't even hardly acknowledge her presence. He
        practically didn't even speak to her .... And it just sort of
        messed up the whole party—mainly for her, and because of
        that, it messed it up for all of us. I expected ... some real nice
        guys. I thought they'd be really glad to see her. But they
        [weren't] ... the one she wanted to see acted real stuck-up, as if
        she wasn't even there .... He ignored her .... She'd be
        standing practically beside him, and he wouldn't say anything.

Later the interviewer asked why the man, Sam, had acted the way he did.

Karen: I don't know ... maybe she just had it in her head that he
        liked her ... and he was just trying to talk to this other girl

or something. But he did act, he acted sort of too good for
her, you know?

Annette was upset in the ensuing days. Karen, in describing her plight,
explained that Annette was trying to reason out Sam's actions:

Interviewer: What were some of the ways she reasoned it out?
Karen: Um, well, she thought at first maybe because he was with
        that girl, he didn't want to talk to anybody else. And, but
        then, he was talking to other girls that were walking by, and
        um, then she was thinking, maybe he was mad at her, but
        she didn't know why, you know, she was just thinking of
        different stuff like that.
Interviewer: Did you think of any things like that too?
Karen: Uh, not really, I, I, it's gonna sound terrible. I thought, well
        he just didn't want to, didn't want to see her at all, 'cause he
        just didn't, I don't know, what I thought was that, he was like
        I said before, he was some big jock on campus, you know,
        and he just wanted the real, just certain girls around him,
        you know.
Interviewer: What … what kinds?
Karen: Really pretty.

Karen's embarrassment in telling this story was palpable. Her discomfort
draws our attention to the significance of attractiveness. Karen was clearly
embarrassed to say explicitly that her friend was not pretty enough for Sam's
tastes and so he treated her badly. It was as though Annette had something to
be ashamed of, and Karen's hesitancy marked that shame. And, although
Annette was obviously ruminating over Sam's behavior, Karen did not try to
save her time and worry by explaining what was (to Karen) very clear. As the
cultural narrative implies and this incident underscores, attractiveness is a
pivotal aspect of the cultural world of romance. It is the basis for women's
claims to good treatment by men. Otherwise, why should Annette's not being
pretty enough for a big jock on campus be a cause of embarrassment?

One of the striking features of this account is the intensity of Karen's, and
presumably Annette's, emotional involvement with Sam's behavior. Reactions
to these and other such incidents make it clear that much was at stake when it
came to romance. Identification with and investment of self in the cultural
world of romance was a very serious matter for many of the women. This intensity and degree of involvement returns us to a question that separates sociogenic and social constructivist theories of the self: How is the investment of self
in cultural constructions of romance (evident in our ethnographic study of
women's engagement with romance) to be understood?

SOCIOGENIC SELVES

At odds about the fundamentals of personal makeup, the two theories—
sociogenic and social constructivist—do not account for the investment of
selves in social worlds in the same way. In responding to the critical disruption—to the questions left by Foucault's successful demolition of the Western,
integral and originary subject—post structuralist scholars such as Hall
(1996), Butler (1990), and Henriques, Hollway, Urwin, Venn, and
Walkerdine (1998) draw on psychoanalytic theory to create an account of self
as both subject to molding by powerful discourses and yet partly independent
of social forces. In contrast, my colleagues and I have chosen a theoretical
path based in Mead's sociality and Vygotsky's mediated developmentalism.
Instead of understanding people's entanglement in romance and attractiveness as a result of psychodynamic forces, we see crucial aspects of their
selves—their identities—as culturally and socially formed through practice
in cultural worlds.

Vygotsky's understandings of human development and of the role of
semiotic mediation in it ultimately account for how humans can be both
bound in relations of power and yet retain the possibility of agency. For
Vygotsky, the key to truly human existence was the ability to escape enslave-
ment to the happenstance of environment. The means of escape were two-
fold. Just as humans modify the environment physically—thanks to their
production of, and facility with, tools—they also modify the environment's
stimulus value for their own mental states through the production and use
of signs. Humans intervene and mediate their activity technically *and* semiotically. The heuristic development afforded by semiotic mediation becomes over time a means, albeit a *modest* means, of gaining voluntary
control over one's behavior.

One of our major concerns has been to extend Vygotskian ideas of self-
management and self-organization through the concept of identity. Although Vygotsky himself stressed the construction of "higher psychological
functions" such as thinking in situations of recall, the idea of mediating devices is applicable, beyond the domains of memory, problem solving and
inferencing, to processes of self organization and management (1978, pp.
56–57; Wertsch, 1985, pp. 61–66). Luria (cited in Cole, 1985, p. 149), for
example, discusses the semiotic mediation of will, and Vygotsky (1997)
himself sketched the development of a "logic of emotion." Through signs
and words children learn to talk about, compare, classify, and thus manage
their own emotions. These ideas inform recent studies of, and popular notions about, artifices for modulating emotion. We suggest that his ideas be
extended toward a concept of identity as a "higher order" semiotic mediator, organizing one's thoughts, feelings, intentions and ultimately activity
around a sense of who one is or wants to be or not be in the social world.

Identities are organizations of the self brought about in practice by the use of discourses and practices as tools for self management; that is, identities are semiotically mediated organizations of thoughts, intentions, and feelings in particular fields of activity. They are a key, higher-order means through which people care about what is going on around them and by which they try to direct their own behavior. Through objectifications of the sort of person one wants to be one can try, at first consciously, later in more routine fashion, to realize the sense of self in daily life.

These identities figuratively and relationally link the intimate or personal world with the collective space of cultural forms and social relations. The social psychologist Kenneth Gergen (1994) captured the flavor of this double-sidedness of the self when he wrote: "Narratives of the self are not personal impulses made social, but social processes realized on the site of the personal" (p. 210). We are interested in identities, the imaginings of self in worlds of action, as social products. Indeed, we begin from the premise that identities are lived in and through activity and so must be conceptualized as they develop in social practice. But we are also interested in identities as psychohistorical formations that develop—sometimes thickening, possibly atrophying through experience—over a person's lifetime, populating intimate terrain and motivating social life.

Our notion of identity, with its Vygotskian extension via "tools of identity," has a second source. It is an adaptation, for the purposes of anthropology and cultural studies, of sociogenic concepts of personhood developed within the American school of social psychology that claims G. H. Mead (1910, 1912, 1913, 1925, 1934) as its founder. Mead began with humans' instinctual abilities to coordinate actions, and traced the subsequent career of this coordination to the foundation of humans' distinctive engagement with social life. A person acquires the ability to take the standpoint of the other as she learns to objectify herself according to culturally interpreted qualities of performance in and commitment to social identities (e.g., drawing from the cultural activities of romance: a sexy woman, someone who is engaged, unattractive, a woman men like, a feminist).[6] Such objectifications, especially those to which she is strongly emotionally attached and committed, become the foundations, in our social practice theory of self and subjectivity, of her pro-active identities.

I can now present the difference between social constructivist and sociogenic theories more clearly. Identities are important in both theories, as is accounting for engagement with social and cultural worlds. In Hall's (1996) words:

> The notion that an effective suturing of the subject to a subject-position requires, not only that the subject is `hailed`, but that the subject invests in the position, means that suturing has to be thought of as an *articulation*, rather

than a one-sided process, and that in turn places *identification*, if not identities, firmly on the theoretical agenda. (p. 6)

We entertain a different possibility for "suturing" the person to social position. In our cultural historical, or to use the more popular term, sociocultural perspective, persons form over time in practice through and around the cultural forms by which they are identified, and identify themselves. Our metaphor is not "suture," which makes the person and the position seem to arrive preformed at the moment of suturing, but "co-development"—the linked development of persons, cultural forms and social positions within historical worlds. Instead of relying on psychodynamic sources as the only ones standing between the person and determination by powerful social forces, sociogenic conceptions look to people's cultural productivity. In social movements and activism, especially, people articulate new cultural imaginaries whose identities may become tools, means of diverting the personal and social force of oppressive forms. But, even in everyday life, people collectively and individually produce objectifications of self that they in turn use in their efforts to reshape their own behavior.[7]

FORMING A SELF IN THE WORLD OF ROMANCE

Let us return now to the specific question of women's investment in the world of romance. A cognitivist paradigm, which guided our initial studies of student culture, yielded information about an important cultural resource—images of different types of men and women—used for describing others and imagining oneself, and an account of the horizon of meaning against which the women understood many of their encounters with men. The women were learning about a cultural world of romance, populated by a set of agents (in the case of the world of romance: attractive women, boyfriends, lovers, fiancés) who engaged in a limited range of meaningful acts or changes of state (flirting with, falling in love with, dumping, having sex with) as moved by a specific set of forces (attractiveness, love, lust). Though productive, the cognitivist paradigm proved inadequate for grasping the emotional investment of self that women were making as they became more deeply engaged in the cultural constructions of romance and sex on campus. They were not only learning to practice romance and to figure it in the manner of their peers, but were also coming increasingly to "grow into" it. They were coming to embody the cultural world of romance and to care intensely about what happened in that world and to take responsibility for how their own romantic interactions turned out.

Most importantly, they were developing an identity—a sense of themselves as participants, or, in some cases, studied nonparticipants, in romance. Growing into and embodying the world meant coming to interpret and feel oneself and others as romantic actors. For most, it also eventually meant acting as an agent in romance even to the point of generating new terms for romantic actors, constructing meaningful stories and incorporating and modifying images from the media into local communities of practice.

Sociogenic theories build on Vygotsky's recognition that cultural artifacts can serve as tools of self management and even as levers of self-reconstruction and thus agency, yet they introduce a means of human agency that is appropriately reserved. Semiotic mediation and the associated development of identity clearly take time and depend on the availability of cultural resources and a social context in which those resources are performed. By emphasizing the developmental aspects—including the possibility of "fossilization" (the routinization and abbreviation of the social production of activity in habits of mind and body) and its contrary, the moments of self-recognition and awareness that respond to disruptions of the social context, Vygotsky provides a nuanced notion of durable forms of self-organization. Thus, in harmony with the critical disruption, we have an account of self that is profoundly rooted in cultural activities and socially differentiated discourses.

A CRITIQUE OF SOCIOGENIC THEORIES

Despite the compatibility of sociogenic theories with the lessons of the critical disruption, they are vulnerable to challenges from social constructivists. In one of the first works of critical psychology inspired by Foucault, Henriques et al. (1984/1998) critique Mead and Vygotsky for ignoring social forces that transcend social interaction. They include a story to illustrate these forces.

Some years ago in several Puerto Rican towns, young children suddenly began to mature sexually. Young girls—some as young as four—began to develop breasts. Local cultural notions of maturation were thrown into disarray and age-specific practices toward these children became confused. As it turned out, the children's diets contained supplements derived from the feed given to the chickens that were a mainstay of local subsistence. The supplements, growth hormones added by the U.S. corporate supplier in order to increase "turnaround" and thus profit, had worked not only in the chickens, but also in the children.

The point of the story was simple: the children's bodies/minds and the taken-for-granted notions of maturation informing adults' interactions with them depended on more than the local context of social interaction. They also depended on material interventions and social conditions set by powerful agents—in this case, global corporations. To ignore these relations of power is to miss forces that clearly shape local life and to mistake local cultural interpretations and social interactions as more determinant than they are. Henriques et al. recognized Mead's and Vygotsky's sociogenic theories of mind as superior to most psychological accounts, but faulted them ultimately for neglecting the powerful institutions that intervened in minds/bodies and social interactions.

Selves, Henriques et al. argued, are embedded in relations and regimes of power, as are the social interactions that inform them. Hence, any adequate sociogenic theory of the self must make a place for social and political forces—institutional powers—that set the conditions for social interaction and for self. Because they failed to theorize regimes of power, Meadian and Vygotskian theories of self and social interaction remained ad hoc, unable to account for externalities, and so prone to fall back on the kind of ahistorical, asocial subjectivity that Foucault had effectively dismissed.

Henriques et al. concluded that these shortcomings made sociogenic theories less than useful in accounting for the historical nature of lives and subjectivities—despite their openness to social and cultural life. Instead Henriques et al. espoused a theory of self founded in psychoanalytic theory and in the recognition of the pervasiveness of powerful discourses and practices that "push" the self into various social constructions. The foreword of their 1998 edition voices a similar critique of more recent psychological studies of self-authoring. Although acknowledging a kind of symbolic "bootstrapping"—the kind of indirect agency achieved through semiotic mediation, Henriques et al. nonetheless impugn the work for inattention to the constraints powerful institutions set on this bootstrapping.

We, too, find sociogenic approaches disappointing for their inattention to power and privilege in social life. Unlike Henriques et al., we choose to augment, rather than abandon, the sociogenic theories inspired by Mead and Vygotsky. After all, Henriques et al. themselves adopt a transfigured or extended version of psychoanalytic theory and they provide no argument that sociogenic theories preclude such an extension. In Bourdieu's theory of practice (1977, 1990) and in Bakhtin's appreciation of the orchestration or strategic incorporation of powerful others in self-fashioning (1981, 1990, c.f. Voloshinov, 1986),[8] we find compatible remedies for the oversights of power that mar sociogenic theories. Bourdieu and Bakhtin combine the Marxian problematic that nourished Vygotsky with the phenomenological concerns shared by Mead and by symbolic-interactionism.[9] On these bases Bourdieu introduces concepts, such as "modes of domination" and "symbolic violence", that make "symbolic power" and its institutional supports an integral element of everyday social and personal life. Thus, he argues that sensitivities to symbolic power develop as integral aspects of the self.

In our modified sociocultural approach, what we call a social practice theory of self and identity, we follow the development of historically contingent selves within local fields of activity, a process circumscribed and infiltrated by relations of power. Our ethnographic studies of the development of self and personhood in the cultural world of romance provide an example of the utility of Bourdieu's concepts in capturing the workings of power in self-fashioning.

ROMANTIC SELVES IN RELATIONS OF POWER

In practice, relations of power and position intersect with the figuring of activities according to a cultural imaginary. Bourdieu has shown part of this process in his various studies of cultural activities from Algeria to France. These activities involve the possibility of face-to-face and institutional domination, incidents of violence of a symbolic sort at least, and the loss or gain of "symbolic capital" (Bourdieu, 1977, 1990; Ortner, 1995). Symbolic violence is Bourdieu's term for the denigration, even invalidation, of a person's bases for claiming social value. Such denigration reflects negatively on the person's social standing and ability to command respect. The greater a person's symbolic capital, the greater the esteem and legitimacy *automatically* credited to what he or she says or how he or she dresses or looks or what he or she does. People with low social credit must work against expectations to achieve the same deference, respect and positive regard.

All of these cultural activities including romance on the campuses we researched or academic pursuits in the French schools studied by Bourdieu, the kinds of symbolic capital they afford (attractiveness, brilliance), and the relations of power they underwrite, are culturally and historically specific. The symbolic capital particular to each is not an essential characteristic of the person, but rather the shifting outcome, the product or accounting of activity: how the person is treated and allows him or herself to be treated. At first we thought of attractiveness as it was conceived and expressed by those in our study—and in the ubiquitous advertisements about hair, skin, clothes, diets—as an intrinsic characteristic of a person, a set of qualities—looks and demeanor—that some had naturally, others cultivated, and many lacked. Upon closer examination, however, attractiveness turned out to be more a product of his or her relations and activities. It was drawn from, and counted on, the attractiveness of those to whom he or she appealed and how he or she fared in romantic/sexual encounters.

Through each of his encounters with women, a man's attractiveness was affirmed, increased or diminished, according to the outcome. The same was true for women. What kind of men did she go out with? Were they attractive or not? Did they treat her well, or as though she were nothing special? Although "attractiveness" is a noun, it would be better to speak more often about its verb-like qualities, if we used a verb that meant, "to make attractive." I "make you attractive," you "make me attractive," she "makes him attractive" and so on. As argued by various feminists (e.g., Connell,

1987; Willis, 1991; Yanagisako & Collier, 1987) for gender, this phrasing de-essentializes the quality by revealing its social-relational dynamics—the continually negotiated constructions and reconstructions that create attractiveness and attractive people. Sam's treatment of Annette made her less attractive and therefore less deserving of good treatment from other men.

From Bourdieu's theory, Annette's encounter with Sam is the type of episode in which people become familiar with the language of social claims, sensitive to signs of recognition, aware of who has the authority to impose the symbolic capital of notoriety and respectability or its opposite, and able to calculate how much of a chance one is taking in making such a claim. In the course of these experiences people develop a sense of the value of their symbolic capital, where they stand, and when they should censor their own actions, silence themselves, hide their desires and lower their expectations (Bourdieu, 1977).[10] What made matters worse in the Annette case—and no doubt intensified Karen's embarrassment about the incident—was Annette's public proclamations about her interest in Sam. She had publicly and boldly proclaimed her attraction to Sam, and, by approaching him, had in effect laid claim to a comparable attractiveness of her own, only to have it demolished by his disinterest. When it came to the game of romance, at least as viewed from Karen's eyes, Sam's behavior communicated that Annette was not in his league, and, because Annette had made her claims public, it was hard to ignore their refutation.

VULNERABILITY TO SYMBOLIC VIOLENCE

Men, too, were vulnerable to having their attractiveness insulted by women, to having their social worth belittled, to bearing the brunt of symbolic violence. Women could accept their gifts, their attention, and their good treatment, and still not reciprocate with any show of affection. They could refuse to allow the relationship to become more emotionally or physically intimate. Women could insult them verbally as well, referring to them as "pricks," "nerds," "creeps," and other unappealing names. Nonetheless, our studies showed that women's treatment by men had a greater impact upon evaluations of women's social worth than the relationship reversed. That is, the gender ideology discussed here turned out to have more importance for women than it had for men. On the face of it, the narrativized romantic/sexual relationship that constitutes the core meanings of the world of romance and sex—the pairing of attractive people who give and get equally from each other, and the expected outcome of intimacy and prestige for both—seems to favor neither the woman nor the man. But, in the student world of the late 1970s and early 1980s, equality was not the rule. Women's attractiveness and prestige were far more dependent on their relationships to men than vice versa. Men had diverse sources of symbolic capital. Men on the basketball team and men of (potential) wealth, for example, had sources of attractiveness and prestige that were largely independent of the ways that women treated them. There was no such alternative source for women. Participation on sports teams—no matter how many championships the teams won—simply added little to women athletes' attractiveness to male students; the same was true for women's participation in student government or in performance groups. Thus, with regard to the symbolic capital of attractiveness, women had more at stake in how men treated them than men had in how women responded to them.

Men were also at an advantage in another way. They were more often in *positions* of control over material and symbolic resources from which they could dominate women by (inappropriately, from the woman's perspective) treating them as (potential) romantic/sexual partners of lesser attractiveness than themselves.

In the course of the open-ended, periodic interviews that we conducted, the women told us about many incidents involving actual or potential romantic/sexual partners, especially the upsetting ones in which men had made them or a friend of theirs feel bad. Annette's story was one of these. They also talked about other incidents in which they or a friend had been, by their own assessment, inappropriately treated as a romantic/sexual partner by a professor or boss. Unlike Annette, who willingly sought Sam as a romantic partner, the women in the classroom and workplace stories neither sought out, nor desired romantic involvement with their bosses and teachers.[11] In the incidents of symbolic violence I consider next, men "called out" the figured world of romance and sex in the workplace, thus transfiguring the field of interaction.

In explicating this sort of symbolic violence, I take advantage of a video depiction of such an event. Instead of considering an incident that was recounted to me, I have chosen to analyze a videotaped *simulation* of such an incident. The video captures the importance of gestures and spatial positioning better than any of the accounts provided by the women in the study. It is useful in particular for understanding the ways in which the gendered identities of the world of romance are evoked clandestinely in the workplace—for understanding how, in other words, gender relations in the workplace become complicated by the ambiguous intermingling of two figured worlds.

The video clip was part of a televised special program on sexual harassment in the workplace. The simulated incident was arranged for the program by a social psychologist, John Pryor, in order to illustrate his research on men who sexually harass women in the workplace and on the conditions under which men are likely to harass (Pryor, LaVite, & Stoller, 1993). What I want to discuss is not what the narrator points out about the behavior of the men in the incident. Rather it is how the women in our studies, who had come to inhabit the world of romance and attractiveness, might have interpreted this behavior. In order to avoid awkward, conditional phrasings I treat the participants as though they had developed the ways of figuring gender relations that we described in our studies.

> **Narrator's Voice**: *During a psychology class, Dr. Pryor recreated one of his more revealing studies.*

[Two men, the Experimenter, John, and Mr. Williams, the "Computer Trainer," walk up to a desk with a computer; they shake hands.]

> **John, the Experimenter** *[to Mr. Williams, the "Computer Trainer"]: What we're going to do here, I'm trying to evaluate a program I've developed for the Department of Office Management. OK?*

[The "Computer Trainer" sits down at the desk and the Experimenter sits on the edge of the desk.]

> **Narrator's Voice**: *In this scenario, a graduate student who is actually participating in the experiment leads the research subject to believe that he will be training undergraduate women to use a computer.*

> **Experimenter** *[to Mr. Williams]: What you're going to do is instruct the girl that's going to be coming in here on how to correct these mistakes. OK?*

> *Now I don't know if you noticed the girl out in the hall, but the girls that are being sent down here by the Department of Office Management are real foxy.*

> **Narrator's Voice**: *In reality the real purpose of the experiment was to see if the research subject would harass given the opportunity.*

[The Experimenter goes out and calls "Cindy." "Cindy" comes in. The "Computer Trainer" stands up.]

> **Experimenter**: *Cindy! It is Cindy isn't it? I'm John. How are you? [They shake hands.]*

> **"Cindy"**: *I'm fine, thank you.*

> **Experimenter**: *Don't I know you from somewhere? You look like an old girlfriend of mine. [He still has her hand. "Cindy" laughs.] I want you to come on over here. Cindy, this is Mr. Williams.*

["Cindy" and Mr. Williams shake hands.]

> **Mr. Williams**: *Hi, Cindy.*

Experimenter: Mr. Williams will basically be your boss here for the next fifteen minutes. So all's you have to do is listen to what Mr. Williams has to say and follow his instructions. OK? OK?

["Cindy" sits down at the desk to be trained.]

Narrator's Voice: By the design, the graduate student, who is really part of the research design, purposively harasses the woman—setting an example for the "Computer Trainer" to do the same.

[The Experimenter, John, is standing behind "Cindy." He puts his hands on her bare shoulders—she has on a "boat-top" sweater. He leaves his hands on her bare shoulders as he says the following:]

Experimenter [to "Cindy"]: Make yourself comfortable, then just follow Mr. Williams' instructions and you'll be doing OK. OK? [She nods her head, yes.]

Experimenter [to Mr. Williams]: And you remember that you're going to fill out an evaluation sheet?

Mr. Williams [to the Experimenter]: Yeah. OK.

Experimenter: OK.

Mr. Williams: OK, thanks a lot.

[The Experimenter leaves Mr. Williams and "Cindy" alone.]

Narrator's Voice: Left alone, and left to believe that sexual harassment is permitted and even condoned, the "Computer Trainer" takes full advantage of the situation.

"Computer Trainer": You want me to give you the sentence now?

[He is standing behind the chair. He looks at his paper, then puts his right hand on the chair behind "Cindy's" right shoulder.]

"Cindy": OK .... What'd I ...

Mr. Williams: It's number 3. Just hit number 3 up here.

[Still behind her, somewhat right of center, he reaches around her left side with his left hand, and hits the key. When he removes his hand from the keyboard, he grasps her shoulder.]

"Cindy": Do I have to hit return?

Narrator's Voice: Although this is a recreation, similar behavior was observed during 90% of the experiments.

Mr. Williams: That's good.

"Cindy": OK. and ?

Mr. Williams: Just use those. Those are fine.

Narrator's Voice: *Shannon Hoffman, who participated in the real studies [and has just played Cindy in the simulation], remembers feeling vulnerable because of the permissive situation created by the men in charge.*

[Mr. Williams kneels by Cindy's right side and leaves his left arm around her. A few seconds later he pats/rubs her back.]

Mr. Williams: And that's all you really need to do. Just hit the letter and you'll be fine.

For those who have grown into the figured world of romance that we described from our studies, the incident is a complicated one of symbolic violence.

The initial conversation between the two men set the stage for the incident. It drew on the discourse of romance to construct the woman as an object of desire. Of equal importance, the experimenter, in the process of figuring the woman, gendered both himself and the other man. The experimenter said to the recruited computer trainer, "Now, I don't know if you noticed the girl out in the hall, but the girls that are being sent down here by the Department of Office Management are real foxy."

In the world of romance as figured on the two study campuses, circa 1980, one's partner, or those to whom one was attracted, reflected back on one's own attractiveness. In the taken-for-granted case outlined in the cultural narrative, those who were equally attractive were attracted to one another.[12] "Hunks" were not attracted to "nags" or "dogs" or "cows," but to "foxy girls" or "dolls," and likewise, "foxy girls" were not attracted to "jerks," "nerds," "wimps," or "turkeys." Still the attribution—exactly who was a "hunk" and who was a "creep"—varied by participant and was not fixed in stone. There were no absolute measures of attractiveness; there was no authority that could definitively assess who was and who was not attractive. Instead, attractiveness was a symbolic capital attested to, aggrandized, or devalued by the attractiveness of those one approached and the treatment one received from them.

By labeling the women as "foxy," the experimenter evoked the world of romance and a comparison of the women "being sent down by the Department of Office Management" according to their attractiveness. He construed her as a prestigious object of desire, and, thus, when he later approached her in an intimate way, he cast himself as an attractive, desirable man. Here was a "foxy" woman with whom he could be familiar.

With his "foxy" aside, the experimenter drew the computer trainer into the figured world of romance and sexuality as well. He gendered the computer trainer by implying that he (the trainer) would participate—with the experimenter and from the same, desirable position—in the world of male/female relations. He implied not only that they (experimenter and computer trainer) were heterosexual, but also that they shared standards of taste in women and were roughly on par in attractiveness. Had the other man been gay, the experimenter's remark itself might have constituted an incident of symbolic violence, a painful reinforcement of the hegemony of heterosexuality in which homosexuals are relegated to marginality and invisibility, if not actual opprobrium. For the woman, there were two sorts of insult, two aspects to the symbolic violence.

A GENDERING INSULT

In the two men's interactions with the woman, we observe gestures through which they invoked the world of romance and sex. The experimenter said to the woman, "Don't I know you from somewhere? You look like an old girlfriend of mine." He put his hands on her in an intimate manner, an intimacy that was unexplained by any prior history. "It is Cindy, isn't it?" he asked. His gestures and phrases, and the later physical intimacy of the computer trainer, all invoked a clandestine discourse, a discourse that opened a space within the workplace that was ambiguously, if at all, governed by the work at hand, or the figured relations of occupational specialization and merit. The workspace was instead infused with gender relations, interpreted according to the model of romance, and peopled by types who were relevant to that world.

Yet the work went on; the experimenter continued training. The sexual world was always close to the surface, threatening to overwhelm the ostensible activity, but the discourse remained submerged, clandestine. Hence, here and in the incidents described to us, it was difficult for the women to contest or refuse such a gendering. Especially in cases where gestures and innuendo were the language of choice, the evocation of the world of sex and romance could be counter-charged to the woman. Should she too blatantly or explicitly avoid the unwanted intimacies and communicate her refusal too forcefully, she could be accused of reading meaning into gestures inappropriately, of seeing something that no one else sees, or of fantasizing that she is attractive enough to be the object of a man's desire. She could be accused of purposefully evoking the world of romance herself. Her clothes, her makeup, her posture, and her movements could be scrutinized as cues, and put forward as evidence of her desire. Why did "Cindy" have on a sweater that left the tops of her shoulders bare?

When it was frequently invoked despite a woman's wishes, in this incident and the others described to us, the discourse of romance constituted a refusal to treat her as worker or student, on a par with other students or workers. It was a refusal to accord the woman any value independent of her attractiveness. This is a widespread strategy of male resistance to the incorporation of women into traditionally male worksites (Weston, 1990). The situation simulated in the video clip is more complex. The work went on; the computer trainer continued the training, yet he did so in such a way that the world of romance and sexuality infiltrated the activity at hand, giving all acts a double significance. The incidents women described to us were similar. Sometimes they were even more blatant, and sometimes more ambiguous.

Some of the women were learning through experience that their vulnerability to what we have called the "sexual auction block," apropos the student world of gender relations, extended into the workplace and the classroom. They were vulnerable to a form of symbolic violence in which they could be "reconstituted," without their invitation or permission and before their fellows, from student or worker to object of desire and token of attractiveness.

AN INSULTING GENDERING

There was more to the violence in this incident: the gendering not only denied the woman's value as a worker; the gendering itself (its substance or content) was one that undermined her symbolic capital in the world of romance.

Read from the cultural world of romance, a woman's attractiveness supposedly determined how men would treat her. Attractive woman received attention, gifts, and intimacy and gained access to whatever social and material amenities the men wished to share. Unattractive women either received ill treatment from attractive men or else settled for relations with unattractive, less prestigious men.

There were ways to make up for mismatches in attractiveness. A relatively unattractive man could still succeed with a relatively attractive woman if he treated her especially well. He could be exceptionally sensitive to her, especially creative and clever in pleasing her. In just this way, expectations for good treatment became a language of claims to relative attractiveness. A woman who seemed to expect a lot of special treatment, with little demonstration of affection on her part, was interpreted as claiming to be more attractive than her partner. If the man felt a woman was demanding too much, that she was overrating her own attractiveness relative to his, he could retaliate by calling her a "bitch." By the same token, if the man expected intimacy and demonstrations of affection and admiration, and yet treated the woman as though she were simply an object—ignoring her or otherwise treating her badly—he was interpreted as claiming that she was less attractive than him.[13]

These points are relevant to the incident depicted in the video clip. Both men continued to be intimate with the woman, though she had given no indication that she desired intimacy with them. Except for the experimenter's fleeting acknowledgment that she looked like the type of woman he was willing to have as girlfriend—an accolade that is more or less valuable depending on one's assessment of his attractiveness—neither man did anything for her that counted as good treatment in the world of romance. They gave no indication of sensitivity to her wishes. They gave no sign that they saw her as a special person. Nor did they do anything for her in the way of special favors. By the standards of the figured world of romance, they were claiming to be prestigious, desirable males whose attractiveness was so much greater than the woman's that she could expect no special treatment from them at all. In short, they played out the entitlements of men possessing large amounts of symbolic capital, men of great attractiveness and high prestige. And, in the process, they devalued the woman's symbolic resources; they implied by their actions that, in comparison to them, she had the lesser capital.

Women in our study often talked about such incidents in the course of their (potential) romantic/sexual involvements. They described many situations in which they felt demeaned by men's treatment. The incidents, in other words, had the themes just elucidated: their (potential) boyfriends and lovers enacted positions of greater entitlement and thus cast the women as relatively unattractive. The women complained of being treated as though they were only one of a crowd of women, many of whom would "do" just as well. They also objected to men's expectations that they would jump into intimate relations with little prelude. They disliked being made to feel as though they were simply props that men used to demonstrate status to their buddies. The incidents that occurred in the classroom or the workplace were similarly insulting, but even harder to manage. At parties and social events, in dating relationships, a woman could counter, effectively or not, a man's view of his superior attractiveness. She could publicly label him a "prick" or a "jerk" or a "nerd." Or she could simply leave, without much fear of damaging retaliation on his part.

The women in our study were not so ready to insult the symbolic capital of men in positions of authority. Obviously, potential retaliation from a boss or an instructor could be much more damaging. Compared to men of their peer groups, bosses and instructors had more means at hand to impose "their vision of the divisions of the social world and their position within it." (Bourdieu, 1985, p. 732). It was difficult, indeed dangerous, to retaliate effectively because the boss or employer had an independent source of attractiveness/prestige as a result of his position. It was also difficult because of the double-talk nature of the clandestine discourse.

THE PIN UP CALENDAR

Another incident, drawn from an account told to me, shows some of the same elements of the case portrayed in the video. It points even more clearly to the ways in which positional aspects of identity and the sensitivities developed in the process of growing into the world of romance and sex can render women vulnerable to acts of symbolic violence.

The incident comes from a paper that a woman wrote in one of my classes. The paper concerned the history of pin-up calendars, but it also included a brief tale of the author's experience with such a calendar.

> In 1985, I was a manager at a new car automobile dealership in .... One day I entered the parts department for a consultation with the manager [of that department]. As the door closed behind me I turned and without warning came face to face with a very large "pinup" calendar sponsored by a tool company and displaying a bikini-clad, buxom woman whose exaggerated body positioning and seductive gaze infused the image with clear, culturally-coded sexuality ...."

Although this incident seems quite different from the one simulated in the video, Eva's continuing description suggests a similarity. She wrote: "I felt my face flush with anger and shame as the ground holding me on an equal level with my fellow manager shifted beneath my feet." Eva's situation can be analyzed along the same lines as in the video's incident. Interpreted from the same popular ideology of romance and its dynamic of attractiveness, the perceptible evocation of a figured world made Eva's situation as potent and insulting as the woman's in the video. The "pin-up" on the calendar recalled the world of romance and attractiveness. The space that was ostensibly a workplace was infused with gender relations, interpreted according to the model of romance and sexuality. In that space, Eva's superior position as manager of the car dealership, relative to her colleague, the parts manager, was rendered less potent. Instead, their positions in the world of romance and sexuality, that is, of a woman in relation to a man, were brought to the fore. To the extent that she had to occupy that position, the basis for her claim to superior status as a worker was vitiated. She experienced a form of symbolic violence.

The similarity with the video incident goes even farther. Not only was Eva exposed to a gendering insult, but, just as in the case of the video clip, the gendering was also an insulting one. The means of symbolic violence were different; the outcomes were similar. In the video simulation, "Cindy" suffered an insulting gendering when the men treated her as having little attractiveness relative to them. In order to understand how Eva underwent an insulting gendering, we must realize that gender labeling redounds

upon the classifier *and* the addressee, the person "listening" to the classification. Eva wrote, in the brief discussion of her experience, "the image defined a standard of beauty and a role by which to judge women, leaving me
... physically substandard." The calendar's picture of the woman in the bikini evoked a ranking of women according to attractiveness—a ranking in
which Eva felt devalued. As with gender typing by words—the use of "foxy"
in the video—so too the image on the calendar, reflected on the person
observing (the visual addressee of) it.

Eva's analysis could be extended by the recognition that the parts manager was making a claim about his own tastes and attractiveness. He implied
that he was attracted by handsome women, and so was a handsome man.
The calendar evoked a three-way ranking of Eva, the woman in the bikini,
and the man—a ranking in which the man was elevated as Eva was put
down. The parts manager had created a gendering space that offered him,
the man, claim to the symbolic capital of attractiveness. Women entering
the space were "invited" to feel disempowered.

Eva's response to the pinup calendar shows that the positional aspects of
her identity as a woman in the figured world of romance have become disposition. By growing into the world of romance, she had developed a sensitivity to threats to her social worth, to her symbolic capital of attractiveness.
Her disposition—to see herself through the figured world and to be vulnerable to insults of her attractiveness—affected her, and was easily triggered,
even in a situation that was supposedly divorced from romance.[14] Bourdieu
(2000, pp. 169–170) illuminates the social significance of reactions such as
Eva's when he writes:

> The practical recognition through which the dominated, often unwittingly,
> contribute to their own domination by tacitly accepting, in advance, the lim-
> its imposed on them, often takes the form of *bodily emotion* (shame, timidity,
> anxiety) .... It is betrayed in visible manifestations such as blushing, inarticu-
> lacy, clumsiness, trembling, all ways of submitting, however, reluctantly, to
> the dominant judgment, sometimes in internal conflict and 'self-division',
> the subterranean complicity that a body slipping away from the directives of
> consciousness and will maintains with the violence of the censures inherent
> in the social structures.

POWERFUL INSTITUTIONS AND CULTURAL IMAGINARIES: SETTING CONDITIONS FOR ROMANTIC SELVES

It is clearly easy to create spaces of practice, figured by the world of romance
and attractiveness, in which males are especially privileged and women are
especially at risk of symbolic violence. Easement to privilege in a particular
community of practice—the peer groups that we studied in the late 1970s

and early 1980s, for example—is more or less likely to be realized, depending on conditions set by powerful institutions and collective imaginaries. In the United States, men have on average enjoyed more varied sources of symbolic capitalization than have women, and they are still more likely to occupy positions that control the distribution of material and symbolic resources. When this historical advantage is reproduced in local situations—as it was in the collegiate cultural activities we studied, then women remain more dependent on men's treatment of them for their social worth than the reverse.

Pryor's findings, reported in the video clip, could also be interpreted along the same lines. The experimental conditions set up a situation in which simply being a (heterosexual) male gave all the (heterosexual) men who participated symbolic capital and its attendant entitlements, relative to the women. In the interpretation given by the video's narration, the experimental conditions established a "permissive situation." The men anticipated no sanction for initiating intimacy with the woman. We can augment or better specify Pryor's analysis by drawing on the popular imaginary of romance and attractiveness. The experimental conditions established a space of "male privileging" that had two characteristics. First, male/female relations were interpreted according to the figured world of romance and attractiveness. Recall how the experimenter called out this world through his comments and actions. Second, the conditions created a space that afforded men greater symbolic capital, greater attractiveness and prestige, than women. The comments and actions of the experimenter, from his position of authority, not only evoked the world of romance, they also positioned him and his male trainer as attractive/prestigious, relative to the woman. Recipients of this authoritatively given capital, the men had reason to expect the woman to treat them as though they were attractive males.[15]

Since the time of the studies described in this chapter, there have been organized efforts by activists to stop unwanted sexual advances. These efforts and the politics surrounding them have brought legal and quasilegal means, and the associated forces of the state, to bear in new ways on local gender relations. Largely "owned" by women, the resulting discourses of sexual harassment provide a remedy of sorts beyond the individual woman's attempts to counter or dissuade a man from involving her in unwanted relations.[16] They have at least created new "tools of positioning and identity"—beyond "prick," "jerk," and like insults—for interpreting and naming the parties to acts of symbolic violence undertaken in clandestine or submerged romantic fields.

This discourse of sexual harassment affords a woman a new cultural resource to turn the playing field of romance more to her advantage, redefining the incident from one of her inappropriate and degrading gendering into one of *his* negative gendering, of outlawing and ostracizing the man.

Had Eva's encounter with the bikini-clad woman on the calendar happened now, and not in 1985, she would, perhaps, have been moved to counterattack. Instead of feeling devalued because she failed to meet standards of physical appearance, Eva might have figured the situation as one in which she was the would-be victim of sexual harassment. She might have tried to turn the parts manager's office into a place that discomforted him, because the space *he* had created did not meet standards of acceptability. She could have called out the cultural world of predatory sex offenders by hanging an anti-harassment poster over his pin-up calendar. Whether his response to her poster would have been as intense as hers to his calendar, and whether *his* response would have been one of self monitoring and censorship depend, of course, on the extent to which he had grown into the world of meaning that makes sexual harasser s intelligible and their acts despicable.

Notwithstanding the potential of sexual harassment policies as resources against symbolic violence, it must also be noted that the popular ideology of romance is thoroughly entangled with other powerful institutions that affect (and effect) gendering and the cultural world of romance. Sexual harassment discourses may offer a means of fighting insulting genderings, but they shed little light on, and give little relief from, a veritable preoccupation that many of us have with our own attractiveness and with projects of self-beautification.

Capitalism has accelerated the fetishization of the symbolic capital created in the popular ideology of romance—attractiveness—by circulating representations of female beauty which few women can match, yet which are taken up and applied to self and others (Haug, 1986; Willis, 1991). The advertisements of the cosmetics and apparels industries alone—not to mention the ways in which attractiveness, romance, and sexuality are harnessed to sell other products—clearly intensify and shape, and are in turn intensified and shaped by, the pivotal role accorded attractiveness in the figured world of romance. Although not a focus of our study, the peer activities and discussions devoted to beautification would have been hard to miss. The women spent large segments of time improving and evaluating their own looks, weight, hair, skin, clothes, and so forth.[17]

Powerful institutions and cultural imaginaries thus constitute the conditions for local social interaction, inflecting social relations with power. Through mediation, these institutions and imaginaries become sensitivities of the self, constituting an identity as a romantic/sexual, gendered person.

CONCLUSIONS

In this chapter I have argued that theories of the self, including the sociogenic theories championed by the sociocultural school, must be capable of accounting for the formation of self in social interactions suffused by power.

So much we have learned from the critical disruption. There must be an account of the means by which the social orders underwritten by powerful institutions and cultural imaginaries come to be refracted in selves formed under their aegis. While those who criticize sociogenic theories for their lacunae with respect to power have often imported psychodynamic theory for the task of explaining how people become intimately entangled and self invested in exploitative relations of power (Henriques et al., 1998), my colleagues and I have proposed instead a cultural-historical or sociocultural, social practice theory of self.

We treat discourses and practices of the self—in a manner consistent with both recent anthropological ethnographies of self and personhood and Vygotsky's emphasis on semiotic mediation—as the media around which socially and historically positioned persons develop their subjectivities over time in culturally constructed activities. We employ Bourdieu's notion of domination by "symbolic violence" as a constant reminder that the selves forming in these worlds develop vulnerabilities to power of various forms. It may be the powers of the state or of corporations and other powerful institutions, enforced by the virtually compulsory discourses and practices they generate. It may be the less grand power of those cultural forms produced and imparted in the course of mundane, "low-level" struggles that maintain gender, race, class, and other social hierarchies. Selves are drawn in their compass and develop sensitivities (dispositions in Bourdieu's terms) to signs of symbolic power and to circumstances in which their own symbolic capital is likely to be devalued denigrated (or not) should they act. Meadian and Bakhtinian notions of sociability and Vygotskian ideas of development are compatible with, and productively extended by, these ideas.

Together sociogenic theories and Bourdieu's appreciation of symbolic power create a more adequate account of human activity as both a personal *and* a social creation. Of special benefit to this goal, sociogenic accounts of sociability and development recognize people's abilities to produce or appropriate cultural forms, which they can then use to modify their own behavior. This everyday capacity to intervene symbolically and thus to alter the conditions under which one acts helps to solve the riddle of how people who grow into worlds of power are yet sometimes able to transfigure them. The case of romance is a good case in point. We can show through a social practice theory of self and identity, the complex "sensitivities," the susceptibility to domination, which people develop through cultural forms deployed as tools of identity and positioning, such as a "pin-up calendar" or tokens of attractiveness. Yet that is only half the story. We can also recognize and explain the simultaneous possibilities of liberation granted by the production and circulation of new discourses and practices like those of sexual harassment. By such means women forge a new figured world or platform for identifiable social action and thus new grounds for agency beyond the cultural world of romance and attractiveness: a new ground for self-fashioning.

ENDNOTES

[1]Acknowledgments: My special thanks to Cynthia Lightfoot, Michael Chandler, and Chris Lalonde for inviting me to present this paper at a plenary session at the 30th Annual Meeting of the Jean Piaget Society for the Study of Knowledge and Development. My session was the first so I benefited from participants' comments for all 3 days of the conference. Colleagues, especially the co-authors of the publications of mine that I cite, collaborated in developing the theoretical ideas in this chapter. William Lachicotte provided valuable feedback on the chapter, as well; so did Cynthia Lightfoot. The ethnographic research project depended on the great skills of the research associates that worked with me, especially Margaret Eisenhart. Finally, I deeply appreciate the women in the study. Their gift of time and their openness made the study possible.

[2]Roughly built from characteristics shared by the many meanings of "self" in the anthropological literature, this definition alludes to Ito's (1987, pp. 46–47) fuller one: First, *self* has (1) a reflexive quality, the ability to distinguish, evaluate and objectify self and other; and (2) a dynamic quality, the apperceptive ability to understand, interpret, manipulate, and incorporate sensory judgments. Self is both executor and object of judgments, discriminations, creativity and order. Besides Ito (1987), see also White (1992), Harris (1989), and Fogelson (1982). A more detailed exposition of this section of the chapter is given in Holland (1997).

[3]In a similar vein, historians, for example, Stallybrass (1992), document changing concepts of self and action in earlier historical eras.

[4]"Tool" is not the best of words (Holland, 1997) for these discourses and practices. Tool implies that the control of a user. Instead, we need a concept that conveys the "indeterminacy" and polysemous nature of tools (see Smolka, de Góes, & Pino, 1997).

[5]Ethnographic studies in many countries—Taiwan, the Dominican Republic, Vietnam, Indonesia, and Uganda, among others—indicate that cultural imaginaries of romance have been promulgated more recently through the global circulation of cultural forms—print, movies, television, and music—and directed powerfully in advertisements toward material wants and, sometimes, toward goals of the state. These capitalist and/or state projects have encouraged romantic love, originally a culturally and historically specific set of cultural constructions, worldwide, cultivating emotional and material experiences of a particular kind of bonding—at least in fantasy (see, e.g., Adrian, 2003).

[6]In a major development of the Meadian tradition on which we draw, McCall (1987), Stryker (1987), and others have expanded their vision of the social and cultural bases for possible identities. Besides social roles, crosscutting "master-statuses" of race, ethnicity, class, gender and sexuality are now recognized

as possible bases, as are salient cultural conceptions of personality (e.g., an aggressive person).

[7]Whether the psychodynamic account of the person, to which Hall alludes, and the sociohistorical account that we develop here are compatible remains an open question. In the relationship that he draws between psychodynamic forces and investment in social institutions, Bourdieu (2000, pp. 164–167) emphasizes humans' fundamental desire for recognition, a desire that could conceivably be linked to Mead's notions of sociability. Because of the changing political and cultural climate in Soviet Russia, Bakhtin (Voloshinov, 1927/1987) and Vygotsky had complex and complicated relations with psychodynamic theory, and kept their distance from it (van der Veer & Valsiner, 1991). They give us little help with this question.

[8]Unfortunately, there is insufficient space to do more than allude to Bakhtin's contributions here. See Holland et al. (1998), Holland and Lave (2001), and Lachicotte (2002).

[9]Bakhtin and Vygotsky also shared common roots. They were both strongly influenced by the vibrant intellectual life of early post-revolutionary Soviet Union. They were informed by a common stock of concepts, such as "inner speech," and attuned to the concerns identified in the linguistics, literary criticism, and art circles of the day. For more, see Wertsch, 1985, 1991, and Holland et al., 1998.

[10]These senses and dispositions developed through practice are positional or relational aspects of identities (Holland et al., 1998, pp. 125–143). Especially because they are usually mediated by displays of emotion and other forms of unintentional, indirect communication and not explicitly stated or objectified, they are difficult to modify. Vygotsky's notions of semiotic mediation provide a means by which such reactions can be manipulated if not controlled.

[11]Many of the tellers had a vivid, seemingly emblematic, memory of at least one such experience, a memory still evocative of a number of mixed and unresolved feelings—anger, embarrassment, guilt, and helplessness. Their stories, similar to the accounts of the women in the study, were "readings" of incidents according to the figured world of romance and attractiveness.

[12]By "taken-for-granted case," I mean the situation that constituted the standard of meaning. Unless faced with explicit indication to the contrary, participants to a discussion assumed that particular cases fit the taken-for-granted case.

[13]In this figuring of sexual relations, it might be noted, rape constituted an ultimate form of ill treatment (Holland & Eisenhart, 1990; Holland et al., 1998).

[14]Susceptibility to domination is a necessary partner for the practice of symbolic power. Bourdieu (2000, p. 69) writes, "being the result of the inscription of a relations of domination into the body, dispositions are the true principle of the acts of practical knowledge and recognition of the magical frontier between the dominant and the dominated, which the magic of symbolic power only serves to trigger off."

[15]The most unsettling aspect of Pryor's findings is how little effort it took to create a situation in which a high percentage—over a third in one group and

90% in the other—of the men involved felt entitled to treat the woman as though she possessed considerably less social worth than they. It sadly corroborates other cases, such as those all too frequent episodes in which male athletes, misusing the attractiveness and prestige attributed to them, act out their entitlement by mistreating women (Sanday, 1990). Although one might be tempted to think of them, or men in general, as sexual harassers at heart, that is, as intrinsically or essentially sexual harassers, my point is a different one. That so many of the men in the experiment were "successfully" gendered and easily led to act out the liberties of greater attractiveness, suggests dispositions formed in relation to the a historically specific, cultural construction of romance. Evidently, the ideology of romance was a potent part of these men's experience; thus the world of heterosexual romance and sexuality was easily "triggered" for them and receipt of indications of attractiveness sufficient to have them take on the superior position of an attractive man relating to a less attractive, less prestigious woman.

[16]Bakhtin's emphasis on the social image of languages, dialects and cultural forms is important here. The groups that become associated with a genre affect the deference paid to it and vice versa. The idea of sexual harassment is still on trial, so to speak. Its legitimacy and feasibility as a remedy is still being popularly assessed in discussions such as those surrounding the Anita Hill/Clarence Thomas hearings, in cultural productions such as *Oleanna*, a play by David Mamet (1992), and in everyday incidents that might invoke the discourse.

[17]Romantic practices are also confounded with other fields of power that profoundly affect the playing field of cross-gender relations. Clearly women and men in the United States are advantaged as participants in the world of romantic and sexual relations differentially according to race, class, age and sexual orientation. Popular and other media represent attractive femininities that are, for example: ageist, constructing younger forms as beautiful; racist, putting a societal premium on white features; and classist, promoting as distinctive those forms of beauty that depend on wealth. These race, class, and age privileges are not determined by the figured world of romance and attractiveness, but are mediated and potentiated by it.

REFERENCES

Abu-Lughod, L. (1991). Writing against culture. In R. G. Fox (Ed.), *Recapturing anthropology* (1st ed., pp. 137–162). Santa Fe, NM: School of American Research.

Adrian, B. (2003) *Framing the bride: Globalizing beauty and romance in Taiwan's bridal industry.* Berkeley: University of California.

Asad, T. (Ed.). (1973). *Anthropology and the colonial encounter.* London: Ithaca Press.

Bakhtin, M. M. (1981). *The dialogic imagination: Four essays by MM Bakhtin* (M. Holquist, Ed.; C. Emerson & M. Holquist, Trans.). Austin: University of Texas Press.

Bakhtin, M. (1990). *Art and answerability* (M. Holquist & V. Liapunov, Eds.; V. Liapunov, Trans.). Austin: University of Texas press.

Bourdieu, P. (1977). *Outline of a theory of practice* (R. Nice, Trans.). Cambridge, UK: Cambridge University Press.

Bourdieu, P. (1985). The social space and the genesis of groups. *Theory and Society, 14,* 723–744.

Bourdieu, P. (1990). *The logic of practice* (Eng, Ed.; R. Nice, Trans.). Stanford, CA: Stanford University Press. (Originally published 1980)

Bourdieu, P. (2000). *Pascalian meditations.* Stanford, CA: Stanford University Press.

Butler, J. (1990). *Gender trouble: Feminism and the subversion of identity.* New York: Routledge.

Cole, M. (1985). The zone of proximal development: Where culture and cognition create each other. In J. Wertsch (Ed.), *Culture, communication, and cognition: Vygotskian perspectives* (pp. 146–161). Cambridge, UK: Cambridge University Press.

Connell, R. W. (1987). *Gender and power: Society, the person and sexual politics.* Palo Alto, CA: Stanford University Press.

Crapanzano, V. (1980). *Tuhami: Portrait of a Moroccan.* Chicago: University of Chicago Press.

Eggan, D. (1974). Instruction and affect in Hopi cultural continuity. In *Education and cultural process: Toward an anthropology of education* (pp. 311–332). New York: Holt, Rinehart & Winston.

Fogelson, R. D. (1982). Person, self, and identity: Some anthropological retrospects, circumspects, and prospects. In B. Lee (Ed.), *Psychosocial theories of the self* (pp. 67–109). New York: Plenum Press.

Geertz, C. (1973). *The interpretation of cultures* (pp. 412–453). New York: Basic Books.

Gergen, K. (1984). An introduction to historical social psychology. In K.J. Gergen & M. M. Gergen (Eds.), *Historical social psychology* (pp. 3–36). Hillsdale, NJ: Lawrence Erlbaum Associates.

Hall, S. (1996). Introduction: Who needs identity? In S. Hall & P. du Gay (Eds.), *Questions of cultural identity* (pp. 1–17). London: Sage.

Harris, G. G. (1989). Concepts of individual, self, and person in description and analysis. *American Anthropologist, 91,* 599–612.

Haug, W. F. (1986). *Critique of commodity aesthetics: Appearance, sexuality and advertising in capitalist society* (R. Bock, Trans.). Minneapolis: University of Minnesota Press.

Henriques, J., Hollway, W., Urwin, C., Venn, C., & Walkerdine, V. (1998). From the individual to the social: A bridge too far. In *Changing the subject: Psychology, social regulation and subjectivity* (pp. 11–25). London: Methuen. (Originally published 1984)

Holland, D. (1997). Selves as cultured: As told by an anthropologist who lacks a soul. In R. Ashmore & L. Jussim (Eds.), *Self and identity: Fundamental issues.* Cambridge, UK: Oxford University Press.

Holland, D. C., & Eisenhart, M. A. (1990). *Educated in romance: Women, achievement, and college culture.* Chicago & London: The University of Chicago Press.

Holland, D., Lachicotte, W. J., Skinner, D., & Cain, C. (1998). *Identity and agency in cultural worlds.* Cambridge, MA: Harvard University Press.

Holland, D., & Lave, J. (Eds.). (2001). *History in person: enduring struggles, contentious practive, intimate identities.* Santa Fe, NM: School of American Research Press.

Holland, D., & Skinner, D. (1987). Prestige and intimacy: The cultural models behind Americans' talk about gender types. In D. Holland & N. Quinn (Eds.), *Cul-

tural models in language and thought (pp. 78–111). New York: Cambridge University Press.

Ito, K. L. (1987). Emotions, proper behavior (hana pono) and Hawaiian concepts of self, person, and individual. In A. B. Robillard & A. J. Marsella (Eds.), *Contemporary issues in mental health research in the Pacific Islands* (pp. 45–71).

Lachicotte, W. S., Jr. (2002). Intimate powers, public selves: Bakhtin's space of authoring. In J. M. Mageo (Ed.), *Power and the self* (pp. 48–67). Cambridge, UK: Cambridge University Press.

LeVine, R. A. (1982). *Culture, behavior, and personality: An introduction to the comparative study of psychosocial adaptation.* Chicago: Aldine.

Mamet, D. (1992). *Oleanna.* New York: Vintage Books.

Marcus, G., & Fischer, M. (1986). *Anthropology as cultural critique: An experimental moment in the human sciences.* Chicago: University of Chicago Press.

Marsella, A., DeVos, G., & Hsu, F. L. (Eds.). (1985). *Culture and self: Asian and Western perspectives.* New York: Tavistock Publications.

McCall, G. J. (1987). In K. Yardley & T. Honess (Eds.), *Self and identity: Psychosocial perspectives* (pp. 89–103). Chichester, UK: John Wiley & Sons.

Mead, G. H. (1910). What social objects must psychology presuppose? *Journal of Philosophy, 7,* 174–180.

Mead, G. H. (1912). The mechanism of social consciousness. *Journal of Philosophy, 9,* 401–406.

Mead, G. H. (1913). The social self. *Journal of Philosophy, Psychology and Scientific Methods, 10,* 374–380.

Mead, G. H. (1925). The genesis of the self and social control. *International Journal of Ethics, 35,* 251–277.

Mead, G. H. (1934). *Mind, self and society.* Chicago: University of Chicago Press.

Ortner, S. (1995). Resistance and the problem of ethnographic refusal. *Comparative Studies in Society and History, 37*(1), 173–193.

Pryor, J. B., LaVite, C. M., & Stoller, L. M. (1993). A social psychological analysis of sexual harassment: The person/situation interaction. *Journal of Vocational Behavior, 42,* 68–83.

Reiter, R. (Ed.). (1975). *Toward an anthropology of women.* New York & London: Monthly Review Press.

Rosaldo, M. (1980). *Knowledge and passion: Ilongot notions of self and social life.* Cambridge, UK: Cambridge University Press.

Sanday, P. R. (1990). *Fraternity gang rape: Sex, brotherhood and privilege on campus.* New York: New York University Press.

Shweder, R. A., & Bourne, E. J. (1984). Does the concept of person vary cross-culturally? In R. A. Shweder & R. A. Levine (Eds.), *Culture theory: Essays on mind, self, and emotion* (pp. 158–199). Cambridge, UK: Cambridge University Press.

Skinner, D., Pach, III, A., & Holland, D. (Eds.). (1998). *Selves in time and place: Identities, experience, and history in Nepal.* Lanham, MD: Rowman & Littlefield.

Smolka, A. L. B., de Goes, A. C. R., & Pino, A. (1997). (In)determinacy and semiotic constitution of subjectivity. In A. Fogel, M. C. Lyra, & J. Valsiner (Eds.), *Dynamics and indeterminism in developmental and social processes* (pp. 153–164). Hillsdale, NJ: Lawrence Erlbaum Associates.

Stallybrass, P. (1992). Shakespeare, the individual, and the text. In L. Grossberg, C. Nelson, & P. Treichler (Eds.), *Cultural studies* (pp. 593–612). New York: Routledge.

Stryker, S. (1987). Identity theory: Developments and extensions. In K. Yardley & T. Honess (Eds.), *Self and identity: Psychosocial perspectives* (pp. 89–103). Chichester: John Wiley & Sons.

van der Veer, R., & Valsiner, J. (1991). *Understanding Vygotsky: A quest for synthesis* (1st ed.). Oxford, UK: Blackwell.

Voloshinov, N. V. (1986). *Marxism and the philosophy of language.* Cambridge, MA: Harvard University Press. (Originally published 1929)

Vygotsky, L. S. (1987). *Mind in society: The development of higher psychological functions.* Cambridge, MA: Harvard University Press.

Vygotsky, L. S. (1997). Child psychology. In *The collected works of L. S. Vygotsky,* Vol. 4. (R. Rieber, Ed.; M. Hall, Trans.). New York: Plenum Press.

Weiner, A. B. (1976). *Women of value, men of renown: New perspectives in Trobriand exchange.* Austin: University of Texas Press.

Wertsch, J. V. (1985). *Vygotsky and the social formation of mind.* Cambridge, MA: Harvard University Press.

Wertsch, J. V. (1991). *Voices of the mind: A sociocultural approach to mediated action* (1st ed.). Cambridge, MA: Harvard University Press.

Weston, K. (1990). Production as means, production as metaphor: Women's struggle to enter the trades. In F. Ginsburg & A. Lowenhaupt (Eds.), *Uncertain terms: Negotiating gender in American culture* (1st ed., pp. 137–151). Boston, MA: Beacon Press.

White, G. M. (1992). Ethnopsychology. In T. Schwartz, G. M. White, & C. A. Lutz (Eds.), *New directions in psychological anthropology* (pp. 21–46). Cambridge, UK: University of Cambridge Press.

Whittaker, E. (1992). The birth of the anthropological self and its career. *Ethos, 20*(2), 191–219.

Willis, S. (1991). *A primer of everyday life.* London: Routledge.

Yanagisako, S. J., & Collier, J. F. (1987). Toward a unified analysis of gender and kinship. In S. J. Yanagisako & J. F. Collier (Eds.), *Gender and kinship* (pp. 14–50). Stanford, CA: Stanford University Press.

Chapter 8

Theories of Self and Theories as Selves: Identity in Rwanda

David Moshman
University of Nebraska—Lincoln

The most genocidal hundred days in human history was arguably the period from April to July of 1994 when the Hutu Power government of Rwanda orchestrated the killing of some 800,000 Rwandans in an orgy of violence marked by people killing their neighbors with machetes. Noting that the killers were Hutu and that most of the victims were Tutsi, Western accounts of the genocide called up an image of ancient tribal hatreds erupting in uncontrollable mass killings. This picture was consistent with popular stereotypes of Africa, and thus plausible to many who knew little about Rwanda. It also provided moral cover to the various Western governments and international institutions that had tolerated or even facilitated the genocide, and was thus comforting to those who knew too much.

The account of the genocide provided by the Western media, however, had little relation to the reality of what had actually happened in Rwanda. Contrary to the early reports, the 1994 genocide was not due to tribal, racial, or ethnic differences. Rather, what happened in Rwanda is a story of ideology and identity (Berry & Berry, 1999; Des Forges, 1999; Gourevitch, 1998; Janzen & Janzen, 2000; Mamdani, 2001; Melvern, 2000; Newbury, 2002; Prunier, 2001; Smith, 1998; Waller, 2002).

To highlight the role of ideology and identity in the Rwandan genocide is to suggest an important role for social, cognitive and developmental psychology in understanding what happened. At the same time, attempting to

183

explain genocides and other catastrophic violations of human rights may require us to reconsider important aspects of psychological theory. In particular, for developmental psychologists concerned with identity formation, Rwanda is a sobering reminder that the construction of identity is not always a good thing.

In this chapter, I propose the concept of theory-as-self as a bridge between the developmental psychology of self-conceptions and the social psychology of identity in cultural context. I begin with a brief history of Rwanda, highlighting issues of identity central to the 1994 genocide. I then turn to the development of self-conceptions, especially the later emergence of explicit theories of self. Such theories, I argue, are used not only to *understand* oneself but, at least in some cases, to *define* oneself as a person. Thus, at least in a psychosocial sense, the theory *becomes* the self. This, I argue, is what it means for a self-conception to become an identity.

I suggest in this chapter that identities are theories of ourselves through which we consciously create ourselves. My identity, I will argue, is my explicit theory of myself as a person. Not only is it about myself, but it defines my "self," and thus becomes my self. Although identities are personal and social constructions, then, they are nonetheless quite real. Indeed, as the example of Rwanda will show, they can be matters of life and death.

GENOCIDE IN RWANDA

A small country in east-central Africa, the land of a thousand hills, Rwanda began as a kingdom in what is now its south-central region. Stronger than most of their neighbors, the Rwandans expanded their empire during the course of a centuries-long dynasty of what they regarded as sacred kings, each of whom was known, in turn, as the *Mwami*. The Mwami was the personification of *Imana*, the dynamic principle of life and fertility, who would "assure the fertility of land, cattle, and people by means of intricate royal rituals" (Smith, 1998, p. 744). The Mwami expected something in return, relying on peasant labor to enrich his court. "Yet his reign," notes Smith (1998), "was not simply exploitive. In a patrimonial realm of this type, the king seeks legitimacy, not just domination. And for this, he must give as well as take" (p. 744). Kigeri Rwabugiri, for example, the last of the precolonial kings, routinely provided food for the needy from his granary, which was known as *rutsindamapfa*, the conqueror of famine.

Rwabugiri was thus popular with the lowly, and his reign, beginning in 1860, was widely deemed legitimate. Upon his death in 1895, however, there was a power struggle over the succession, and the royal drum, analogous to the crown of a European king, was claimed by Yuhi Musinga, whose lack of legitimacy as Mwami led to a series of revolts. Musinga retained power, but only with the help of Germany, whose explorers had first entered the country in 1894. Control of Rwanda gradually passed to Germany and then, with Germany's defeat in World War I, to Belgium. Musinga himself, although largely scorned by Rwandans, continued in the role of Mwami until 1931, when the Catholic Church, the religious arm of Belgian colonialism, "became tired of his insistence on the religious significance of Rwandan royalty" (Smith, 1998, p. 745). The "pagan monarch" was replaced with a young new king who led the population in a mass conversion to Catholicism that became known in missionary literature as the "Tornado" (Mamdani, 2001). The political and religious domination of Rwanda by the Belgian government and Catholic Church was now complete.

In establishing and consolidating their control over Rwanda, the Europeans exploited an existing social distinction between Hutu and Tutsi, assimilating it to a Christian worldview and elevating it to a guiding principle of Rwandan society. Thus a flexible distinction that had gradually shifted in meaning over the course of centuries suddenly became more rigid and more central to identity.

In the centuries prior to colonization, the Hutu/Tutsi distinction was a complex and evolving one, interlacing the diverse ancestries, physical appearances, economic niches, and social statuses of Rwandans. In general, a child of Hutu parents is deemed to be Hutu and a child of Tutsi parents is deemed Tutsi. Ancestry and physical appearance are sufficiently correlated to have generated widely shared cognitive prototypes concerning the physical appearance of Hutu and Tutsi: "for Hutus, stocky and round-faced, dark-skinned, flat-nosed, thick-lipped, and square-jawed; for Tutsis, lanky and long-faced, not so dark-skinned, narrow-nosed, thin-lipped, and narrow-chinned (Gourevitch, 1998, p. 50)."

Gourevitch hastens to add that "[n]ature presents countless exceptions" (p. 50). Not even Rwandans themselves can reliably differentiate Hutu from Tutsi on the basis of physical appearance. Hutu and Tutsi, moreover, have for centuries lived interspersed among each other, intermarried, spoken the same language, shared the same religious beliefs, and played multiple overlapping roles in Rwandan society. Anthropologists agree that they are not in any sense distinct tribes or ethnic groups. A tribe or ethnic group is "a small nation that may have its own religion, its own territory, its own culture and way of doing things, and its own language. The Hutu and Tutsi have none of these things" (Prunier, 2001, p. 109).

How, then, did the distinction between Hutu and Tutsi originate?

[T]he source of the distinction is undisputed. Hutus were cultivators and Tutsis were herdsman. This was the original inequality: cattle are a more valuable asset than produce, and although some Hutus owned cows while some Tutsis tilled the soil, the word Tutsi became synonymous with a political and economic elite. (Gourevitch, 1998, p. 48)

The colonizers assimilated this cultural reality to the racial worldview of late 19th century Europe:

> [W]hen the Europeans arrived in Rwanda at the end of the nineteenth century, they formed a picture of a stately race of warrior kings, surrounded by herds of long-horned cattle and a subordinate race of short, dark peasants, hoeing tubers and picking bananas. The white men assumed that this was the tradition of the place, and they thought it a natural arrangement.

> "Race science" was all the rage in Europe in those days, and for students of central Africa the key doctrine was the so-called Hamitic hypothesis, propounded in 1863 by John Hanning Speke .... Speke's basic anthropological theory, which he made up out of whole cloth, was that all culture and civilization in central Africa had been introduced by the taller, sharper-featured people, whom he considered to be a Caucasoid tribe of Ethiopian origin, descended from the biblical King David, and therefore a superior race to the native Negroids. (Gourevitch, 1998, pp. 50–51)

A complex mix of ideology and pragmatism resulted in a colonial system that enhanced Tutsi authority, within the overall context of colonial control, and led to a reification and racialization of the Hutu/Tutsi distinction that was substantially internalized by the Rwandans. "[W]hether they accept or reject it," observes Gourevitch, "few Rwandans would deny that the Hamitic myth is one of the essential ideas by which they understand who they are in this world" (1998, p. 53).

> The Belgians ... proclaimed the Tutsi to be racially superior to the Hutu; they ... said they were more beautiful and so much more intelligent. There was in fact a whole literature concerning the beauty and intelligence as well as the high administrative ability of the Tutsi. The Tutsi loved it, and the Hutu lived with the idea that they were ugly and stupid and that God had created them to labor under the leadership of the Tutsi. (Prunier, 2001, p. 112)

In the 1920s, Belgium dismantled the complex Rwandan administrative structure, a product of centuries of cultural evolution that allowed for a degree of local autonomy and permitted some Hutu some genuine authority and status. The traditional system was replaced by a more centralized hierarchical structure that left Hutu with little protection against increased exploitation by the Tutsi elite. Then in 1933-34, to further reinforce their ideological and administrative system, the Belgians conducted a national census and issued ethnic identity cards. Now 85% of Rwandans were officially designated Hutu, 14% were officially designated Tutsi, and 1% were officially designated Twa (the marginalized and oppressed descendants of the original pygmy inhabitants of Rwanda). The official assignation of identity was reinforced by systematic indoctrination in the colonial Catholic schools.

> Whatever Hutu and Tutsi identity may have stood for in the precolonial state no longer mattered; the Belgians had made "ethnicity" the defining feature of Rwandan existence. Most Hutus and Tutsis still maintained fairly cordial relations; intermarriages went ahead, and the fortunes of "*petits Tutsis*" in the hills remained quite indistinguishable from those of their Hutu neighbors. But, with every schoolchild reared in the doctrine of racial superiority and inferiority, the idea of a collective national identity was steadily laid to waste, and on either side of the Hutu-Tutsi divide there developed mutually exclusionary discourses based on the competing claims of entitlement and injury. (Gourevitch, 1998, pp. 57–58)

As Rwanda moved toward independence in the 1950s, exclusionary visions dominated debate regarding postcolonial political options. In a superficial sense, these competing visions fell at the opposite extremes of a political dimension extending from Tutsi control to Hutu control, with various accommodationist alternatives in between. Ideologically, however, the extremist alternatives were variations on the same colonial theme. Tutsi extremists advocated Tutsi control as the natural and legitimate consequence of what they took to be the established historical fact that the Tutsi were a Hamitic race from the north who, long before the arrival of Europeans, had justifiably taken control over the Hutu, an inferior Bantu race native to the Rwanda region. Hutu extremists rejected the premise of Tutsi superiority and the political conclusion of Tutsi supremacy but embraced the core premise of the Tutsi extremist argument—the Hamitic hypothesis that Hutu were the original Bantu inhabitants of Rwanda and Tutsi a distinct race of subsequent settlers. For Hutu extremists, the indigenous inhabitants of Rwanda, the Hutu, constituted the legitimate nation of Rwanda; as pre-European colonizers, the Tutsi were an alien race with no right to citizenship. Thus Hutu extremists

> heralded a native postrevolutionary republic in which the Tutsi would be tolerated only so long as they remained outside of the political sphere, whereas [Tutsi extremists] held on to the notion that the Tutsi were a civilizing influence with a right to rule precisely because they were different. In reality, these post-colonial twins, Bantu and Hamite, were ideological offspring of Rwanda's poisoned colonial past. (Mamdani, 2001, p. 131)

Meanwhile the Belgians, upset with the demands for independence from what they saw as an ungrateful Tutsi elite, decided to switch their allegiance over to the Hutu and leave Rwanda to its own devices. Abruptly reversing decades of policy, they installed Hutu in power and, in 1962, officially acknowledged Rwanda's independence.

The volatile period leading to independence saw, in 1959, the first political violence between Hutu and Tutsi. This escalated into a series of arsons, killings, and genocidal massacres by Hutu extremists that took the lives of thousands of Tutsi over the next 4 years. There followed several decades of relative calm. In the early years of postcolonial Hutu rule, Tutsi were politically disenfranchised as an alien race but the Tutsi elite still enjoyed the fruits of their continuing economic and educational advantages. After the bloodless coup of July 1973 by Major General Juvenal Habyarimana, the Tutsi were reconstrued as an indigenous ethnic group rather than an alien race, and were thus entitled to a role in the political sphere. The government marginalized Tutsi participation, however, on the basis of a conception of democracy as majority rule, which was taken to mean rule by the majority and thus Hutu rule. Tutsi were, moreover, increasingly restricted in the economic and educational domains as well. Significantly, although rejecting the colonial premise of Tutsi superiority, postcolonial Rwanda steadfastly maintained Belgium's ideological commitment to ethnic differentiation and continued the system of ethnic identity cards.

Even before the violence of 1959, large numbers of Rwandans, mostly Hutu, were living across the border in Uganda, Congo, Tanzania, and Burundi. Most had migrated for economic reasons or were descended from economic migrants from as far back as the late 19th century. Beginning in 1959, these expatriate Rwandans were joined by Tutsi refugees of the ethnopolitical violence in Rwanda. By 1990, the Rwandan diaspora had grown enormous and volatile, constituting more than 1.3 million people in Uganda alone. In October of that year, the Rwandan Patriotic Front (RPF), a Tutsi-dominated army of Rwandan exiles based in Uganda, launched an invasion of Rwanda.

Although the initial invasion was a dismal failure, continuing pressure from the RPF rekindled Hutu fears of Tutsi domination and rejuvenated the ideology that now became known as Hutu Power. President Habyarimana's efforts to find a place for Tutsi in Rwanda and his efforts to reach an accord with the RPF came under vigorous attack.

> Habyarimana spoke of the Tutsi as an ethnic group, not a race; as a *Rwandan*, and not an *alien*, minority. The claim that the Hutu constituted a democratic majority because they were the ethnic majority would have made no sense from the point of view of Hutu Power. Because for Hutu Power, the Hutu were not just the majority, *they were the nation*. This is why the birth of Hutu Power as an organized political tendency went alongside a comprehensive propaganda effort discrediting Habyarimana's effort at

reconciliation. Hutu Power had to undo Habyarimana's attempt to rehabilitate the Tutsi as an ethnic minority in Rwandan society. (Mamdani, 2001, p. 190, italics in original)

Through the radio station RTLM and the newspaper *Kangura*, an ongoing program of indoctrination in the ideology of Hutu Power was instituted.

> The propagandists built upon the lessons Rwandans had learned in school. It was hardly necessary even to repeat the basic assumption that Hutu and Tutsi were different peoples by nature, representatives of the larger and equally distinct "Bantu" and "Nilotic" ("Nilo-Hamitic," "Hamitic," or "Ethiopid") groups .... Those who married across group lines produced "hybrids" for children and people from one group who tried to pass for members of another were said to be like "beings with two heads." The radicals rejected the idea that Rwandans were a single people, charging that this concept was a Tutsi trick to divide and weaken the Hutu by destroying their sense of ethnic identity. As *Kangura* assured the Hutu, "You are an important ethnic group of the Bantu .... The nation is artificial but the ethnic group is natural." (Des Forges, 1999, pp.; 72–73)

Hutu with different views were now deemed guilty of treason. Hutu Power pop star Simon Bikindi excoriated those Hutu who failed to embrace Hutu Power, singing "I hate these Hutus, these de-Hutuized Hutus, who have disowned their identity, dear comrades ..." (quoted in Gourevitch, 1998, p. 100; McNeil, 2002, p. 59).

Massacres of Tutsi resumed, costing several thousand lives between 1990 and 1993. And in the course of this ideological shift, there was the turn toward genocide:

> The Hutu elite felt that they had made a mistake by sparing the women and children in 1963. Too many exiles had been allowed to flee, and now they were returning to take vengeance. Too many Tutsi had survived within Rwanda, and now they were taking too many resources and acting as a potential fifth column within the country. This time, the Hutu elite decided, they would deal especially with the women and children so that there would be no third round .... (Prunier, 2001, p. 115)

Beginning in January 1994, General Roméo Dallaire, commander of UN forces in Rwanda, repeatedly requested reinforcements and permission to act, arguing plausibly that a small force with an appropriate mandate could prevent the escalation of violence. He was explicitly denied authority to take action. Then, on April 6, President Habyarimana was assassinated when the plane in which he was returning to Kigali,

Rwanda's capital, was shot down, very likely by advocates of Hutu Power. Word went out across the country that the time had come. There was "work" to be done.

> Hutus young and old rose to the task. Neighbors hacked neighbors to death in their homes, and colleagues hacked colleagues to death in their workplaces. Doctors killed their patients, and schoolteachers killed their pupils. Within days, the Tutsi populations of many villages were all but eliminated, and in Kigali prisoners were released in work gangs to collect the corpses that lined the roadsides. Throughout Rwanda, mass rape and looting accompanied the slaughter. Drunken militia bands, fortified with assorted drugs from ransacked pharmacies, were bused from massacre to massacre. Radio announcers reminded listeners not to take pity on women and children. As an added incentive to the killers, Tutsis' belongings were parceled out in advance—the radio, the couch, the goat, the opportunity to rape a young girl. (Gourevitch, 1998, p. 115)

Many of the killings were exceptionally brutal. Victims were physically tortured, often by having parts of their bodies cut off, and some, rather than being finally killed, were simply left to die of their wounds. Some of the assaults were psychological:

> Assailants tortured Tutsi by demanding that they kill their own children and tormented Hutu married to Tutsi partners by insisting that they kill their spouses ....

> Assailants often stripped victims naked before killing them, both to acquire their clothes without stains or tears and to humiliate them. In many places, killers refused to permit the burial of victims and insisted that their bodies be left to rot where they had fallen. (Des Forges, 1999, p. 216)

Tens of thousands of women and girls were raped, often multiple times (Des Forges, 1999; Royte, 1997, reports 250,000). Many such attacks directly reflected the sexual side of the colonial ethnic ideology.

> Generally esteemed as beautiful, Tutsi women were ... said to scorn Hutu men whom they found unworthy of their attention. Many assailants insulted women for their supposed arrogance while they were raping them ....

> Assailants sometimes mutilated women in the course of a rape or before killing them. They cut off breasts, punctured the vagina with spears, arrows, or pointed sticks, or cut off or disfigured body parts that looked particularly "Tutsi," such as long fingers or thin noses. (Des Forges, 1999, p. 215)

For a hundred days the genocide raged on, killing an average of 8,000 people each day in a country of 8 million. Recognizing that the United Nations Genocide Convention requires action to prevent and punish genocide, the United States systematically eschewed the use of that term, deliberately obscured what was happening in Rwanda, and vigorously blocked any meaningful response by the UN Security Council. Meanwhile France, which had become Rwanda's primary European patron since independence, warned the RPF against any further military incursion. Defying the French government, the RPF continued south from the Uganda border and, when France decided against military confrontation, took control of Kigali and ended the genocide in July. By that time, however, the daily death toll, which was greatest in the first few weeks, had long been declining due to the rapidly diminishing number of Tutsi and political enemies left to be killed.

The RPF had from its earliest days proclaimed an ideology of national unity, teaching its recruits that they were "not Hutu, Tutsi nor Twa" (training notes quoted in Des Forges, 1999, p. 694). Decrying ethnic distinctions and conflicts, the RPF sang:

> It is the white man who has caused all that, children of Rwanda. He did it in order to find a secret way to pillage us. When they arrived, we were living side by side in harmony. They were unhappy that they could not find a way to divide us. They invented different origins for us, children of Rwanda: some were supposed to have come from Chad, others from Ethiopia. We were a fine tree, its parts all in accord, children of Rwanda. Some of us were banished abroad, to never come back. We were separated by this division, children of Rwanda, but we have overcome the whiteman's trap ... So, children of Rwanda, we are all called to unite our strength to build Rwanda .... (quoted in Des Forges, 1999, p. 693)

Regarding the majority of Hutu as political victims of the Hutu Power government, the victorious RPF maintained its nationalist ideology. In one of its first acts, the new government abolished the system of ethnic identity cards. After generations of colonial and post-colonial rule, no longer would the government of Rwanda officially identify its citizens as Hutu, Tutsi, or Twa.

National unity, however, was and remains a quixotic goal. Post-genocide Rwanda has been wracked by grief and outrage among survivors of the genocide, guilt and denial among perpetrators and bystanders, fears of reprisal among perpetrators and other Hutu, suspicions and tensions among neighbors, and widespread cynicism concerning the prospects for reconciliation. Its prisons are bursting with over 100,000 alleged perpetrators of genocide and its legal system lacks the resources to provide even minimal due process under these circumstances (Janzen & Janzen, 2000).

Rwandans have learned for generations to categorize themselves in ethnic terms. Even under the best of circumstances, it would be naive to think that such self-conceptions can simply be excised from the body politic. In addition to what continue to be construed as fundamental ethnic categories, the new government was faced with

> an elaborate grid of subcategories .... There were Hutus with good records, and suspect Hutus, Hutus in exile and displaced Hutus, Hutus who wanted to work with the RPF, and anti-Power Hutus who were also anti-RPF, and of course all the old frictions between Hutus of the north and those of the south remained. As for Tutsis, there were all the exiled backgrounds and languages, and survivors and returnees regarding each other with mutual suspicion; there were RPF Tutsis, non-RPF Tutsis, and anti-RPF Tutsis; there were urbanites and cattle keepers, whose concerns as survivors or returnees had almost nothing in common. (Gourevitch, 1998, p. 235)

In a political sense Rwanda remains an independent country, but in a psychosocial sense it is far from clear that it still exists, or can ever be recreated, as a nation.

> On April 30, 1997 ... Rwandan television showed footage of a man who confessed to having been among a party of *genocidaires* who had killed seventeen schoolgirls and a sixty-two-year-old Belgian nun at a boarding school in Gisenyi two nights earlier. It was the second such attack on a school in a month; the first time, sixteen students were killed and twenty injured in Kibuye.

> The prisoner on television explained that the massacre was part of a Hutu Power "liberation" campaign .... During [the] attack on the school in Gisenyi, as in the earlier attack on the school in Kibuye, the students, teenage girls who had been roused from their sleep, were ordered to separate themselves—Hutus from Tutsis. But the students had refused. At both schools, the girls said they were simply Rwandans, so they were beaten and shot indiscriminately. (Gourevitch, 1998, pp. 352–353)

THEORIES OF SELF

We will return to post-genocide Rwanda's continuing crisis of identity, including this account of the Rwandan schoolgirls. I will attempt at that point to shed some light on the 1994 genocide in Rwanda by drawing on cognitive and developmental considerations in identity formation. To set the stage for that analysis, I now present a conception of identity as an explicit theory of oneself as a person and a constructivist account of how people come to have such theories.

People have theories of many things, including theories of mechanical causality, theories of life, and theories of mind. Such theories range from the intuitive theories of young children to the formal theories of physicists, biologists, and psychologists, respectively. What all theories have in common that makes them theories is that they are structured and explanatory. A theory is a structure of knowledge organized in such a way that it goes beyond description to explain, whether convincingly or not, some set of phenomena.

Research indicates that even the knowledge of preschool children is sufficiently structured and explanatory to be usefully construed as consisting of theories (Flavell & Miller, 1998; Gopnik, Meltzoff, & Kuhl, 1999; Wellman & Gelman, 1998). Such theories are initially implicit in behavior rather than objects of consciousness, but over the course of childhood, adolescence, and early adulthood they become increasingly explicit, and the process of formulating and testing theories becomes increasingly conscious and deliberate. To be sure, there are also developmental changes in the content of our theories—in the substance of what we believe and in the organization of those beliefs. Much of conceptual development, however, consists of increasingly explicit knowledge about theories and theorizing in general and increasing consciousness and control with regard to our own theories and theorizing (Karmiloff-Smith & Inhelder, 1974/1975; Kuhn, 1999, 2000; Moshman, 1979, 1998, 1999, 2001).

To the extent that we are physical objects our theories of mechanical causality are, in part, theories of ourselves. Similarly, as living things, our theories of life are in part theories of ourselves. Even more clearly, perhaps, our theories of mind are theories of ourselves as psychological beings. Neither my theory of causality, my theory of life, nor my theory of mind, however, is a theory about me in particular. Even my theory of mind, as this term is generally understood, is a theory about the workings of minds in general, including but not limited to my own.

Nevertheless, I have considerable knowledge about myself in particular. This may include knowledge about my physical, biological, and psychological characteristics. Such knowledge about personal characteristics could be construed as derived from, associated with, or even part of my theories of causality, life, or mind. To the extent that my knowledge about various aspects of myself is integrated and enables me to understand my characteristics and behavior in a general way, however, we might usefully construe such knowledge as constituting a theory of self.

THEORIES AS SELVES

Theories of self, like theories of causality, life, and mind, are initially implicit in behavior rather than objects of consciousness. Over the course of development, however, theories of all sorts become increasingly explicit. Advanced theories of self, in particular, are explicit theories of who we are as persons. The persons who construct such theories are also the persons the theories are about. When we theorize about ourselves, then, we have some degree of control over the object of our theorizing.

This makes theories of self importantly different from most other theories. Theories in domains such as physics, chemistry, and biology are theories about physical, chemical, and biological realities that are not under the control of the theorist and thus are not influenced by the theory. I can determine what I believe about the speed of light, the boiling point of water, or the chemical structure of DNA, but my self-chosen beliefs do not alter the speed of light, the boiling point of water, or the structure of DNA.

My beliefs about myself, in contrast, may change me. In my effort to understand myself as a person, I may change myself in such a way as to make myself more understandable. As my theories and theorizing become increasingly explicit, I consciously try to organize myself in such a way that I can explain myself both to myself and to others. The result is that I become committed to behaving in a manner consistent with some coherent explanation of why I believe and do what I believe and do. Thus I maintain an explicit theory of who I am. We may call such theories *identities*.

An identity, then, is an explicit theory of oneself as a person (Moshman, 1999). My identity is an organized and explanatory account whereby I consciously construe myself as a rational agent—that is, as a being who acts on the basis of beliefs, values, and commitments of my own and who manifests some degree of unity across behavioral contexts and continuity over time. To see my self in this way, however, is to transform myself, to some degree, into precisely what I theorized myself to be.

There is both a general and a specific sense in which this is true. At a general level, if I deliberately and systematically construe myself as a rational agent I will try to act on the basis of a justifiable set of beliefs, values, and commitments and thus will attempt to rationally establish such beliefs, values, and commitments. To the extent that I am successful, I will in fact be more rational in my behavior, more consistent across behavioral contexts, and more continuous over time.

The specific content of my theory of self, moreover, may affect my specific characteristics and behaviors. To see myself as a political liberal, for example, may initially involve nothing more than a recognition that my beliefs on several current political issues are beliefs that are typically labeled liberal. Having labeled myself a liberal, however, I may go on to consider the relation of political liberalism to my moral beliefs, religious beliefs, career goals, social commitments, etc. I may commit myself to a liberal ideology that I believe explains and justifies my beliefs and behavior in a variety of domains. Liberalism, at this point, is not just a label for some collection of beliefs or a summary description of my behavior but a theory of what is central to who I am and a commitment to behave in ways consistent with that self-conception.

The formation of identity, in other words, is in large measure a process in which my theory about myself becomes my self, who I really am—if not in some ultimate metaphysical sense, at least in a deep psychological sense. I don't just find out who I already was but determine who I will be. Identity, then, is the self-conscious core of an advanced self. To the extent that I have an identity, my theory of self is not just a theory about some pre-existing self but, at a deep psychological level, *is* my self.

DISCOVERY, CREATION, AND CONSTRUCTION

An identity, then, is not only a theory of self but a commitment to be a particular kind of person. How do we come to have identities? Identity formation, I will argue, is a process of discovery, a process of creation, and, most fundamentally, a process of construction (Moshman, 1999). It is a process of discovery in that it involves learning about yourself but it is not simply a matter of locating a pre-existing self. It is a process of creation in that it involves determining who you will be, but it is not a free choice among limitless options. Rather, identity formation is most fundamentally the construction of a theory of self, and of a corresponding self, that are constrained but not determined by a variety of internal and external realities.

Suppose, for example, I see myself as a musician—or more specifically a pianist. I might initially encounter the term *pianist* as a label for people who play the piano, and thus as a label I can proudly adopt at my first piano lesson or upon attaining a level of competence that leads my teacher or parent to say "You're really getting to be a pianist." But unless I become devoted to the piano, being a pianist, or in some broader sense a musician, may never become part of my theoretical understanding of who I am as a person and thus may never be part of my identity.

Suppose being a pianist does become part of my identity. Perhaps after exploring other career options I become a musician, and specifically a pianist who play in local bars and/or in the great concert halls of the world. I come to see it as my central mission in life to bring rich musical experiences to diverse audiences. I might even come to believe that I was always meant to be a pianist and that, after several false starts, I have finally discovered who I really am.

My conception of my identity as something I discovered is not utterly misguided. I may indeed have long had musical and motor capacities, perhaps due to some combination of genetics and early experiences, that made it easier for me to achieve a high level of competence playing the piano than to achieve comparable levels of competence in most other domains. Coming to see myself as a pianist, then, may indeed have been a process of learning about myself. But it is not true that I have really been a pianist since birth or that I was destined to be a pianist regardless of circumstances. I am mistaken if I see the formation of my identity as the discovery of my real inner self or my one true role in life.

Alternatively, I may believe that I have freely created myself, that I could have been whoever I chose to be, and that anyone could choose, as I did, to be a pianist. This conception of identity as a creation, like the conception of identity as a discovery, does have merit. Everyone has options, and I could indeed have made different choices and commitments. But it is not true that one can be whoever one wants to be. Theorizing that one is a musician will not make it so. I cannot be a professional pianist if I do not have the right kinds of musical and motoric talents. Equally important, I cannot be a professional pianist in a society with no pianos, or in a society in which people like me are not allowed to play the piano.

A constructivist conception posits, in common with the identity-as-creation view, that identity is something we construct rather than a preformed self waiting to be discovered. Far from being free, however, this construction is highly constrained by inner and outer realities. I have some freedom to regard myself as a pianist even if I play no concerts, but whether I can construct a successful identity as a pianist will depend on my opportunities to play the piano, my success in developing pianistic abilities, and the reactions of others to my playing.

Suppose I do indeed see myself as a pianist and also, to return to an earlier example, as a liberal. As a matter of semantics it is easy enough to conclude that I am a liberal pianist, but with regard to identity this is but one of multiple options. I might see my liberalism as central to who I am and my piano-playing as something I do for fun, or even to earn a living, but as secondary to my fundamental commitment to liberal values. Alternatively, I might see myself fundamentally as a pianist and regard my liberal views as a basis for activities such as voting that I see as secondary to who I am. A third possibility is that I may construct an understanding of myself in which being a liberal and a pianist are inseparable parts of my fundamental sense of myself as a person who promotes peace, justice, and solidarity across cultures by spreading the joy of music, in which case I am indeed, in a deep psychological sense, a liberal pianist. Finally, both my liberal views and my piano playing may be secondary in my own mind to my fundamental theory of myself as, above all, a Muslim, or a physicist, or a Russian, or a mother. My identity may, moreover, consist of some theoretical coordination of these and/or other categorizations and commitments. Constructing an identity is not just a matter of categorizing myself along one or more dimensions but also a matter of coordinating these categorizations and/or choosing one or more of them as central to who I am.

My identity, then, is individual and self-constructed. It is not simply imposed by social or cultural circumstances through processes of coercion or indoctrination. Nevertheless, my choices are never free. Identities are always constructed in social and cultural contexts. Identities are constructed by interacting individuals in contexts where our choices join us within larger groups united by shared commitments. Identity formation is never just an imposition of culture on the individual but it is generally, at least in part, an effort to join with others and thus play a role in something larger and more enduring than oneself (Jenkins, 2001; McCauley, 2001).

Identity, I have argued, is best construed as an explicit theory of self that, to some degree, becomes the self. Even to the extent that my theory of self becomes my self, however, I cannot be whoever I wish simply by theorizing it. The construction of identity is a process of reflection, coordination, and social interaction in which I construct an explicit theory of who I am. My alternatives are always a function of inner and outer realities, limited by my personal characteristics and my social and cultural context. Almost always, however, there are multiple options, some better than others, and thus real choices and commitments to be made.

IDENTITY IN RWANDA

In the early 1990s, the Hutu Power newspaper *Kangura* exhorted the Hutu, "You are an important ethnic group of the Bantu .... The nation is artificial but the ethnic group is natural" (quoted in Des Forges, 1999, p. 73). Meanwhile, Hutu Power pop star Simon Bikindi musically denounced "these de-Hutuized Hutus who have disowned their identity" (Gourevitch, 1998, p. 100; McNeil, 2002, p. 59). Through such propaganda, Hutu Power ideologues relentlessly pressured Hutu to believe they were learning a fundamental truth about who they really were. They were not just Hutu rather than Tutsi but Hutu rather than Rwandan. Hutu and Tutsi might share Catholic religious beliefs and the language Kinyarwanda but such commonalities could never be a legitimate basis for solidarity. Identity formation, in the view of Hutu Power, was the discovery of one's essential Hutu identity. Thus "what had once been a fluid and tolerant situation came to deny individuals the right to choose their ethnopolitical identities, and when the genocide began in 1994, Hutus who were not allies of the ruling group were labeled traitors and slaughtered, too" (Chirot, 2001, p. 4).

Denial of one's essential ethnic identity was of course deemed illegitimate for Tutsi as well. Alison Des Forges tells of a child of three who in the course of the genocide "begged for his life after seeing his brothers and sisters slain. 'Please don't kill me,' he said. 'I'll never be Tutsi again.' He was killed" (1999, p. 212). Within the discovery paradigm, the promise is nonsense; only a child would think one could choose not to be Tutsi. You can lie about whether you are Tutsi, or even make a mistake about it, but if your ethnicity is a primordial reality then there is no choice to be made. Not only is Tutsi the correct label for you but it defines who you are as a person.

Almost always, however, there are indeed choices to be made. Faced with a distinction between Hutu and Tutsi, you can reject the dichotomy and identify yourself instead as Rwandan. Identity, it can be argued, is not a discovery but a creation. A three-year-old is too young to generate an explicit theory of self but adolescents and adults can determine their own identities through their own choices and commitments.

Even under the best of circumstances, however, such choices and commitments are far from free. Consider, for example, Hutu Power's insistence that the nation is "artificial" and the ethnic group "natural." This conceptualization reflects, as we have seen, the identity-as-discovery view that identity formation is a simple matter of finding out the truth about oneself. An advocate of the identity-as-creation view might respond by rejecting the distinction between "artificial" and "natural." All identities, it might be argued, are creations. No identity is more "natural" or more "artificial" than any other.

Such a response is too quick, however. Many African nations are indeed artificial in the sense that they are European creations, and many African ethnic groups are indeed natural in the sense that they are distinct cultural groups with centuries of independent history. In Rwanda, by contrast, the opposite is true: The nation is a natural social group with a centuries-long history, whereas the sharp bifurcation of Hutu from Tutsi is a 20th-century colonial imposition. Such facts of history do not require or determine particular identity choices, but they do render some choices more justifiable than others. A constructivist perspective enables us to see that identity formation is neither a straightforward discovery nor a free creation but rather a rational construction, a process of explicit theorizing constrained by historical, cultural, social, and personal realities.

In the years leading up to the 1994 genocide, for example, Rwandan expatriates in Uganda could think of themselves as Hutu or Tutsi, or could try, as many did, to forge new identities as Ugandans, but the social and political circumstances of Uganda made Hutu, Tutsi, and Ugandan identities difficult to construct and maintain. This was a critical consideration in the formation and ideology of the Rwandan Patriotic Front (RPF):

> In exile, we saw each other as Rwandans. Living outside Rwanda, you don't
> see each other as Hutu or Tutsi, because you see everyone else as strangers
> and you are brought together as Rwandans, and because for the Ugandans, a
> Rwandan is a Rwandan. (Tito Ruteremara, RPF political commissar, quoted
> in Gourevitch, 1998, p. 210)

Within Rwanda, in stark contrast, social and political constraints strongly and increasingly favored ethnic rather than national identities. In the context of the Rwandan genocide, moreover, it is immediately clear that the notion of identity as a free creation is far too glib. Cultural contexts set real constraints on choice.

Even under the most excruciating circumstances, however, there may be more than one option. Recall Philip Gourevitch's astonishing account, quoted earlier, of the schoolgirls in Gisenyi and Kibuye who, faced with a demand from an armed militia to sort themselves by ethnicity, chose instead to stand together as Rwandans. It would misconstrue the situation, and the students' response to it, to suggest that this is simply what they were or that it is simply a label they chose to apply to themselves. Identity cards having been abolished, any of the girls could have called themselves Hutu, and many could have saved their lives by doing so. By identifying themselves as Rwandan, they made themselves Rwandan.

You can't be a Rwandan by yourself, however. You can only be a Rwandan if there is such a thing as Rwanda, and Rwanda is only a social reality if there are multiple individuals who identify as Rwandans. Identities are both individual and collective. Our explicit theories of self simultaneously create our selves and create the collective realities that make those selves meaningful.

Does Rwanda still exist? Genocides are all too common, and yet every genocide is unique (Chalk & Jonassohn, 1990; Churchill, 1997; Fein, 1993; Jonassohn & Bjornson, 1998; Moshman, 2001). There is no precedent for what happened in Rwanda, and no way to know whether a country in which this has happened can survive as a nation. Construing yourself as Rwandan is an individual choice of identity but such a choice is meaningless unless others make the same choice. Thus choosing to be Rwandan is a collective act of solidarity. Rwanda as a social reality can only be founded on the decisions and commitments of people, individually and collectively, to see themselves as Rwandan, and to see this as central to who they are in the world.

As individuals, the schoolgirls in Gisenyi and Kibuye are unknown to us. We do not even know their names. What we do know is that, beyond their individual understandings and commitments, they committed themselves to a collective understanding that made them all part of something greater than themselves. In construing themselves as Rwandans, they momentarily recreated Rwanda, and died for it.

IDENTITIES THAT DON'T KILL

People find solidarity and meaning in belonging to groups. As we develop, we increasingly see ourselves as belonging not only to groups of people with whom we have face-to-face or other personal relationships (such as families, peer groups, school communities, church communities)

but to more abstract groups that are defined on the basis of shared characteristics and/or commitments associated with various categories of race,
ethnicity, language, religion, gender, profession, nationality, political
ideology, socioeconomic status, sexual orientation, and so forth. Most adolescent and adult self-conceptions coordinate multiple group affiliations
and personal values.

Some identities, however, are largely defined by membership in a particular category. In some such cases, moreover, the category itself is largely defined by shared hostility to an enemy group. Who we are, in such cases, is
defined by who we hate. In the extreme, these are what Maalouf calls "identities that kill" (2001, p. 30).

Although the existence of violent identities does not prove that identity
formation should be discourage, the prevalence of such identities and the
devastation they cause suggest reason for attention to what sort of identities
those around us are developing and caution about what sort of identities we
encourage. In this section I suggest we foster identities that are (a) self-constructed, (b) multifaceted, (c) moral, and (d) true.

Identity theory in the developmental tradition of Erikson (1968) has
generally advocated self-constructed identities. In particular, Marcia
(1966) distinguished "achieved" from "foreclosed" identities on the basis of
whether the identity is rationally chosen from multiple options rather than
a product of indoctrination. Research has supported the view that achieved
identities are more adaptive and/or mature (Marcia, Waterman, Matteson,
Archer, & Orlofsky, 1993). A case can be made, in fact, that only to the extent that an identity is self-constructed is it a genuine identity. My identity is
not just anyone's theory about me but my own theory about me, and my theory of self is more deeply my own if I have constructed it rather than had it
imposed upon me (Moshman, 1999).

Self-constructed identities are not necessarily less committed to groups
than are externally imposed identities. Rather than being imposed by the
group, however, self-constructed commitments are rationally constructed
by its members via processes of reflection, coordination, discussion, and interaction. Individual members, moreover, will generally have multiple
commitments that they coordinate in their own ways. Thus an important
benefit of self- constructed identities is that they are more likely to be multifaceted. "To the extent that ethnic, religious, or political groups are not
their only source of identity, people will be less likely to go along with
violent practices by them" (Staub, 2001, pp. 297–298).

From a societal point of view, moreover, multifaceted identities are associated with intricately interconnected social and ideological networks. Individuals with multifaceted identities will interconnect with each other in a
variety of ways rather than dividing into some small number of discrete, and
potentially hostile, groups. Two people may differ along a dimension im-

portant to one or both of them but nevertheless have something important to each in common. Multifaceted and intersecting identities provide the benefits of collective identity without sacrificing individual consciousness and control (Maalouf, 2001).

In Rwanda in the early 1990s, for example, systematic indoctrination in the Hutu Power ideology made it virtually unavoidable to see yourself as Hutu or Tutsi and extraordinarily difficult to see other categorizations and relations as equally legitimate bases for constructing a theory of self. If you were a Hutu doctor you were a Hutu who was a doctor, not a doctor who happened to be Hutu. When the Hutu were exhorted to do what had to be done with regard to the Tutsi, alternative bases for solidarity and action were difficult to imagine. Hutu doctors, teachers, and priests might have been less likely to kill their patients, students, and parishioners, respectively, if their professional identities had been stronger than their ethnic identities, and there might have been greater potential for national, linguistic, or religious solidarity across the Hutu/Tutsi divide if multiple dimensions of identity were deemed legitimate.

In promoting identity, then, we should attempt to foster self-constructed and multifaceted identities rather than externally imposed one-dimensional categorizations. There are also two additional characteristics of an ideal identity that, I argue, should be promoted: morality and truth.

To have a moral identity is to have an explicit theory of self whereby you see yourself as a moral agent—that is, as a person who acts of the basis of respect and/or concern for the rights and/or welfare of others (Bergman, 2002; Moshman, in press). Moral identity does not guarantee moral action—people who see themselves as profoundly moral often fail to perceive moral issues, to apply relevant moral principles, or to do what they should. Nevertheless, all other things being equal, people who see themselves as moral are presumably more likely to perceive moral issues, consider them seriously, and do what they deem correct. Your moral self-conceptions may be especially influential, moreover, if they are central to an explicit theory of who you are as a person.

If we want you to have a self-constructed and multifaceted identity, however, we cannot simply insert moral commitments or excise alternative values. Indeed, to the extent that a moral identity is externally imposed, one can question whether it is genuinely moral or a genuine identity. The challenge in promoting moral identity is to encourage the construction of multifaceted identities in which moral values and commitments play a central role.

Finally, one last characteristic of an ideal identity is its truth. This follows directly from the earlier definition of identity as a theory of self. A fundamental characteristic of theories is that they can be evaluated on the basis of truth. Such evaluations may not enable us to conclude that a complex theory is true, but we sometimes have sufficient evidence to conclude that one theory is better supported than another or even that a theory is demonstrably false. Like theories of any sort, some potential theories of myself provide better accounts than others of what I am really like and why I really do what I do. It is possible, moreover, that I might have an explicit theory of myself so discrepant with what I am really like and so ignorant of my actual motivations that I could be said to have a false identity (Moshman, in press).

Identities that kill are often false identities in that they are premised on false beliefs about self-relevant matters of biology, ancestry, and history. This is not to say that the truth will make us friends. In many cases, however, the truth makes it more difficult to justify extremist ideologies and to maintain one-dimensional identities.

Nevertheless, even in the interest of truth, we should resist the temptation to coerce commitment to particular ideologies and identities. Rather, we should promote an understanding of identity formation as a rational process and foster consciousness and control of one's choices and commitments. To the extent that we self-consciously construct our identities, we are more likely to create selves that are real and justifiable, not because these selves have always existed or because they are the only possible outcome of history but because we have rationally decided that this is who we will be.

The ideal atmosphere for identity formation, then, is one in which individuals are politically and socially free to construct diverse interpretations, coordinations, ideologies, and commitments. Within this setting, however, we must keep in mind, and must remind each other, that as rational agents we are not epistemologically or morally free to believe whatever we wish or to construct ideologies and identities that ignore or falsify history. We should aim to construct identities that are multifaceted and unique, but nonetheless rooted in morality and truth. With this in mind, let us return one last time to Rwanda.

HISTORY AND IDENTITY IN POSTGENOCIDE RWANDA

For generations to come, identities in Rwanda will be formed in the shadow of the 1994 genocide. Understandings of what happened and why will for many be central to identity formation. What Rwanda will be like will depend on how its past is understood.

Reconceptualization and denial follow genocide so routinely that they can reasonably be construed as its normative final phase (Churchill, 1997; Cohen, 2001; Moshman, 2001, in press). Rwanda has been no exception.

> After a century in which Rwandans had labored under the mystification and deceit of the Hamitic fable, whose ultimate perversity took the world-upside-down form of genocide, the RPF and its anti-Hutu Power allies de-

scribed their struggle against annihilation as a revolt of realists. "Honesty" was among their favorite words, and their basic proposition was that greater truth should be the basis of greater power. Under the circumstances, the last best hope for Hutu Power was to assert—in its usual simultaneous onslaught of word and action—that honesty and truth themselves were merely forms of artifice, never the source of power but always its products, and that the only measure of right versus wrong was the bastardized "majority rule" principle of physical might.

With the lines so drawn, the war about the genocide was truly a postmodern war: a battle between those who believed that because the realities we inhabit are constructs of our imaginations, they are all equally true or false, valid or invalid, just or unjust, and those who believed that constructs of reality can—in fact, must—be judged as right or wrong, good or bad. While academic debates about the possibility of objective truth and falsehood are often rarified to the point of absurdity, Rwanda demonstrated that the question is a matter of life and death. (Gourevitch, 1998, pp. 258–259)

In Rwanda today, "with an intensity that surpasses the normal clichés, there is no single history: rather there are competing 'histories'" (Newbury, 2002, p. 69). There is thus no integrated, intellectually respectable history of Rwanda to be taught:

In a 1996 visit to Kigali, I requested to be taken to a school so I could talk to a history teacher. My host, an aide to the vice-president, said this would be difficult since history teaching in schools had stopped. I asked why. Because there is no agreement on what should be taught as history, was the reply. History in Rwanda comes in two versions: Hutu and Tutsi. (Mamdani, 2001, p. 267)

Such a dichotomization of history fosters a continuing dichotomization of identities. The only way out, it might seem, is to elevate national identity over ethnic identity, to instill the ideology of the RPF, to teach all students that they are, first and foremost, Rwandans.

This is no solution, however. Hutu Power, it must be remembered, launched the 1994 genocide precisely for the purpose of protecting and preserving the Rwandan nation. Hutu Power was no less nationalistic than the RPF. The difference is that for Hutu Power the *real* nation, indigenous and natural, was the Hutu nation. The Tutsi, like the Europeans, were an alien race from the north. Some definitions of a nation are more defensible than others, and in the context of Rwandan history it is clear, I think, that the RPF definition is more justifiable than that of Hutu Power. Nevertheless, it would be a terrible mistake to indoctrinate the next generation in the view that some particular conception of nationhood is the essential basis for identity. However a nation is defined, there will be those who are identified with other nations, and who may come to be perceived as a threat to the nation in question. Under the right circumstances, nationalism of any sort can lead to genocide.

The reconstruction of history, however, need not be the replacement of one mindless nationalism with another:

> To break the stranglehold of Hutu Power and Tutsi Power on Rwanda's politics, one also needs to break their stranglehold on Rwanda's history writing, and thus history making. This exercise requires putting the truth of the genocide, the truth of mass killings, in a historical context. (Mamdani, 2001, p. 268)

The challenge is to contextualize the genocide without relativizing it, to explain it without explaining it away. If we insist on the one true interpretation, we may learn to perceive history, ideology, and identity as essential truths to be internalized from authorities. If instead we assert the equal justifiability of all interpretations, ideologies, and identities, however, ideology and identity become arbitrary and the genocide itself dissolves into a postmodern fog of cognitive and moral ambiguity. The educational and developmental ideal, I suggest, is to provide information and critique and simultaneously to encourage rational processes of coordination, reflection, and discussion. Thus might we foster identities, and selves, capable of resisting the call to genocide.

REFERENCES

Bergman, R. (2002). Why be moral? A conceptual model from developmental psychology. *Human Development, 45,* 104–124.

Berry, J. A., & Berry, C. P. (1999). (Eds.). *Genocide in Rwanda: A collective memory.* Washington, DC: Howard University Press.

Chalk, F., & Jonassohn, K. (1990). *The history and sociology of genocide: Analyses and case studies.* New Haven, CT: Yale University Press.

Chirot, D. (2001). Introduction. In D. Chirot & M. E. P. Seligman (Eds.), *Ethnopolitical warfare: Causes, consequences, and possible solutions* (pp. 3–26). Washington, DC: American Psychological Association.

Churchill, W. (1997). *A little matter of genocide: Holocaust and denial in the Americas, 1492 to the present.* San Francisco: City Lights Books.

Cohen, S. (2001). *States of denial: Knowing about atrocities and suffering.* Cambridge, UK: Polity Press.

Des Forges, A. (1999). *Leave none to tell the story: Genocide in Rwanda.* New York: Human Rights Watch.

Erikson, E. H. (1968). *Identity: Youth and crisis.* New York: Norton.

Fein, H. (1993). *Genocide: A sociological perspective.* London: Sage.

Flavell, J. H., & Miller, P. H. (1998). Social cognition. In D. Kuhn & R. Siegler (Vol. Eds.) & W. Damon (Series Ed.), *Handbook of child psychology: Vol. 2. Cognition, perception, and language* (5th ed., pp. 851–898). New York: Wiley.

Gopnik, A., Meltzoff, A. N., & Kuhl, P. K. (1999). *The scientist in the crib: What early learning tells us about the mind.* New York: HarperCollins.

Gourevitch, P. (1998). *We wish to inform you that tomorrow we will be killed with our families: Stories from Rwanda.* New York: Picador.

Janzen, J. M., & Janzen, R. K. (2000). *Do I still have a life? Voices from the aftermath of war in Rwanda and Burundi.* Lawrence, KS: University of Kansas Publications in Anthropology #20.

Jenkins, A. H. (2001). Individuality in cultural context: The case for psychological agency. *Theory & Psychology, 11,* 347–362.

Jonassohn, K., with Bjornson, K. S. (1998). *Genocide and gross human rights violations: In comparative perspective.* New Brunswick, NJ: Transaction.

Karmiloff-Smith, A., & Inhelder, B. (1974/1975). If you want to get ahead, get a theory. *Cognition, 3,* 195–212.

Kuhn, D. (1999). Metacognitive development. In L. Balter & C. S. Tamis Le-Monda (Eds.), *Child psychology: A handbook of contemporary issues* (pp. 259–286). Philadelphia: Psychology Press.

Kuhn, D. (2000). Theory of mind, metacognition, and reasoning: A life-span perspective. In P. Mitchell & K. J. Riggs (Eds.), *Children's reasoning and the mind* (pp. 301–326). Hove, UK: Psychology Press.

Maalouf, A. (2001). *In the name of identity: Violence and the need to belong.* New York: Arcade.

Mamdani, M. (2001). *When victims become killers: Colonialism, nativism, and the genocide in Rwanda.* Princeton, NJ: Princeton University Press.

Marcia, J. E. (1966). Development and validation of ego identity status. *Journal of Personality and Social Psychology, 3,* 551–558.

Marcia, J. E., Waterman, A. S., Matteson, D. R., Archer, S. L., & Orlofsky, J. L. (1993). (Eds.). *Ego identity: A handbook for psychosocial research.* New York: Springer-Verlag.

McCauley, C. (2001). The psychology of group identification and the power of ethnic nationalism. In D. Chirot & M. E. P. Seligman (Eds.), *Ethnopolitical warfare: Causes, consequences, and possible solutions* (pp. 343–362). Washington, DC: American Psychological Association.

McNeil, D. G., Jr. (2002, March 17). Killer songs: Simon Bikindi stands accused of writing folk music that fed the Rwandan genocide. *The New York Times Magazine,* 58–59.

Melvern, L. R. (2000). *A people betrayed: The role of the West in Rwanda's genocide.* New York: Palgrave.

Moshman, D. (1979). To *really* get ahead, get a metatheory. In D. Kuhn (Ed.), *Intellectual development beyond childhood* (pp. 59–68). San Francisco: Jossey-Bass.

Moshman, D. (1998). Cognitive development beyond childhood. In D. Kuhn & R. Siegler (Vol. Eds.) & W. Damon (Series Ed.), *Handbook of child psychology: Vol. 2. Cognition, perception, and language* (5th ed., pp. 947–978). New York: Wiley.

Moshman, D. (1999). *Adolescent psychological development: Rationality, morality, and identity.* Mahwah, NJ: Lawrence Erlbaum Associates.

Moshman, D. (2001). Conceptual constraints on thinking about genocide. *Journal of Genocide Research, 3,* 431–450.

Moshman, D. (in press). False moral identity: Self-serving denial in the maintenance of moral self-conceptions. In D. Lapsley & D. Narvaez (Eds.), *Morality, self, and identity*. Mahwah, NJ: Lawrence Erlbaum Associates.

Newbury, C. (2002). Ethnicity and the politics of history in Rwanda. In D. E. Lorey & W. H. Beezley (Eds.), *Genocide, collective violence, and popular memory: The politics of remembrance in the twentieth century* (pp. 67–83). Wilmington, DE: Scholarly Resources.

Prunier, G. (2001). Genocide in Rwanda. In D. Chirot & M. E. P. Seligman (Eds.), *Ethnopolitical warfare: Causes, consequences, and possible solutions* (pp. 109–116). Washington, DC: American Psychological Association.

Royte, E. (1997, Jan. 19). The outcasts: Among Rwanda's living, no one is more. shunned than a Tutsi woman who has been raped by the enemy. *The New York Times Magazine*, 36–39.

Smith, D. N. (1998). The psychocultural roots of genocide: Legitimacy and crisis in Rwanda. *American Psychologist, 53*, 743–753.

Staub, E. (2001). Ethnopolitical and other group violence: Origins and prevention. In D. Chirot & M. E. P. Seligman (Eds.), *Ethnopolitical warfare: Causes, consequences, and possible solutions* (pp. 289–304). Washington, DC: American Psychological Association.

Waller, J. (2002). *Becoming evil: How ordinary people commit genocide and mass killing*. Oxford, UK: Oxford University Press.

Wellman, H. M., & Gelman, S. A. (1998). Knowledge acquisition in foundational domains. In W. Damon (Series Ed.), D. Kuhn & R. Siegler (Vol. Eds.), *Handbook of child psychology: Vol. 2. Cognition, perception, and language* (5th ed., pp. 523–573). New York: Wiley.

Chapter 9

Culture, Selves and Time: Theories of Personal Persistence in Native and non-Native Youth

Chris Lalonde
University of Victoria

Michael Chandler
University of British Columbia

Before it finishes, this chapter ends up as a short summary of a rather long research undertaking aimed at detailing the different procedural means exploited by culturally mainstream and Aboriginal (or "First Nations"[1]) youth in their efforts to understand their own and others', personal persistence or "self-continuity" in the face of those wholesale personal changes that time and development inevitably hold in store. What was it, we wanted to know from each of them, that, "in the contemplation of their lives, links the parts to the whole" (Dilthey, 1962, p. 201)? Before coming to an account of their diverse answers to such questions, however, it is important to first attempt to get clear about what we, as well as a whole graveyard full of intellectual ancestors, have intended by the notion personal persistence, and why understanding oneself and others as somehow continuous in time has so regularly been held out as both a constitutive condition for selfhood and as a prerequisite to the maintenance of any sort of moral order.

The tightly pleated arguments to be unfolded here will be laid out in three steps. The first of these rehearses the reasons why the notion of personal persistence is so widely (and, we argue, appropriately) understood to be foundational to what self- or personhood could reasonably be taken to be. Step two—Part II—details our reasons for maintaining that the ready-to-hand reasons capable of adequately sustaining such necessary claims about the continuity of the self effectively boil down to just two: self-continuity warranting strategies that we label here as either "Essentialist" or "Narrativist" in character. Finally, in Part III, we mean to report out on evidence intended to demonstrate—and this is our main point—that the choice between these alternative approaches to the problem of self-continuity is strongly determined by one's culture of origin. We do this by describing data collected as part of a close and ongoing comparison between the claims about self-continuity offered up by several samples of Aboriginal and culturally mainstream Canadian youth.

PART I: THE PARADOX OF SAMENESS AND CHANGE

Before going on in Part II to take up what might conceivably count as solutions to the problem of self-continuity, a clear case first needs to be set out as to why experiencing oneself as personally persistent is, first of all, problematic, and, second, why solving this problem is as important as we and others go on to allege.

What renders the maintenance of self-continuity a problem, and what qualifies its solution as an identity preserving achievement, is, we argue, that properly owning one's past and future requires finding answers (often a whole train of age-graded answers) to the paradox of sameness within change—a paradox that turns on the fact that we must, on pain of otherwise ceasing to be an instance of what selves are standardly taken to be, understand our own self to somehow embody both permanence and change simultaneously (Fraisse, 1963).

Considered separately, claims for both personal change and personal sameness seem unavoidably true. Few, for example, require being convinced that each of us is, more often than not, relentlessly—even tediously—the same. The old and powerful idea that leopards do not change their spots is not only consonant with much of ordinary experience, but key to the fundamental logic of identity—a logic which requires that persons be, in some sense, sufficiently self-same to allow for their regular identification and re-identification as one and the same continuous person through time (Strawson, 1999). In short, we all regularly and happily subscribe to the idea of personal sameness because we have no choice—because of the patent absurdity of the consequences to which the rejection of this idea would lead.

All that has just been said about sameness is, of course, only the first shoe. Here is the second of what is arguably a matched pair. Life is a breakneck and, in the old phrase of Aristophenes, "whirl is king" (Schlesinger, 1977, p.

279). That is, because things are in a perpetual state of flux, selves are naturally and inevitably works in progress, forced by the temporally vectored nature of their public and private existence to constantly change or die (Gallagher, 1998). Clearly, our bodies change, our beliefs and desires change (along with our projects, our commitments and our interpersonal relationships), often seemingly beyond all recognition. If this were not so, tradition would defeat novelty, and we could neither make sense of the experience of innovation in the lives of individuals, nor of change in the history of the species (Unger, 1975).

There, in a nutshell, is the classical paradox of sameness and change, and a large part of the reason that selves lead the treacherous existence that they do. Change is inevitable, sameness is unavoidable, and working out some way of understanding ourselves as personally persistent that does not trivialize, or turn a blind eye to, either of these contradictory but necessary obligations is no easy nut to crack. Failing to do so is simply not a live option, all for the reason that any putative self that did not somehow negotiate a way of achieving sameness within change would simply fail to qualify as a recognizable instance of what selves are standardly taken to be (Cassirer, 1923). Although, as *we* take it, this conclusion is not really negotiable, coming to some better understanding why this is so is less than obvious, and requires some effort devoted to sorting out just what sort of claim actual claims of personal persistence are ordinarily intended to be.

What self-continuity is *not* is some elective "feature" (Taylor, 1991), or contingently true fact about selves that can be imagined to stand, or fall, depending on one's personal or cultural predilections. Rather, as we argue, qualifying as importantly self-same across the multiple changes and multiple phases of one's temporal existence, is no sort of disputable empirical fact at all, but an exceptionless generic, design feature or systems imperative; a normative-forensic obligation or constitutive condition of selfhood (Flanagan, 1996). In short, being understandably self-same across the multiple phases of our temporal existence is centrally and significantly what most, and perhaps all, societies think persons *ought* to be (Wilkes, 1988, p. 128).

Why this is so widely alleged to be so (e.g., Hallowell, 1955; Harré, 1979) is that every society—every moral order—requires, as a foundational condition for its continuing existence, some degree of social responsibility, which, in turn, presupposes the availability of mechanisms for both counting its members responsible for their own past actions, and for insuring some degree of commitment to an as yet unrealized but common future. In the absence of such presumptions of personal persistence it would not be possible, for example, to apply praise and blame appropriately, or to take one another's hopes or intentions for the future with any degree of seriousness. How, for example, could there be a heaven and a hell, where the good and bad are meant to languish, if people's past actions and future intentions could not be reliably counted as their own? How, for that matter, could St. Peter do a proper accounting job if persons flitted in and out of existence, and if the number of souls in the world was not reliably the same as the number of individuals originally brought into existence? If some workable measure of sameness was not to be had, that is, if there was not some proper way of reliably vouchsafing personal persistence, then the whole fabric of civic life would quickly unravel. Duties and liabilities would be unassignable, contracts and promises would be meaningless, and hopes and dreams a mystery. Consequently, self-continuity, as Wilkes (1988, p. 158) puts it, is what makes the notion of purposive behavior intelligible, and social life possible. For all of these reasons personal persistence is widely argued, even among otherwise committed cultural relativists (e.g., Geertz, 1973; Geertz & Geertz, 1975; Hallowell, 1955; Shweder & Bourne, 1982) to be "universal in the human experience" (Levine & White, 1986, p. 38), and so "ubiquitous to all of humankind" (Harré, 1979, p. 397).

None of the foregoing claims regarding the "universal" or "ubiquitous" character of presumptive personal persistence should, of course, be seen as in any way impugning the well-documented fact that, in different times and different places, various cultural groups can and have subscribed to often wildly disparate beliefs and values concerning self- or personhood (Lillard, 1998). Selves are a good deal more than the generic design features that they necessarily hold in common, and at other less top-lofty levels of analysis (Dennett, 1987; Marr, 1982; Overton, 1991), different societies obviously can and do differ dramatically in what they take to be the hardware requirements of selves, and the procedural ways in which these are instrumented (Chandler, Lalonde, & Sokol, 2000). Nor is the putative requirement that selves must necessarily persist in any way intended to legislate against the possibility that, normative expectations or not, some of the time some of the people evidently do drop the thread of their own continuous existence, or at least imagine that they have done so. Amnesias and fugue states, and conversion experiences of varying sorts presumably do happen, and in the fullness of time, many do regularly change—or believe themselves to have changed—seemingly beyond all recognition. Whether rare or commonplace, those who "suffer" such apparent lapses in persistence necessarily do so at the risk of their legitimate claims to personhood. That is, those who fail to present a winnable case for their own persistence are quickly drummed out of the corps of bona fide persons, are written off as laboring under some serious misapprehension, or, worse still, are seen as delusional (Hacking, 1999). What evidently seems required, then, if the claims about personal persistence laid out here are seen to have merit, is that all such oddities—such candidate cases of putative discontinuity—need to be understood as exceptions to a general rule, or normative backcloth of presumed sameness, that shows the rest of us to be intelligible only in view of our own past behavior and experience, and in light of our short-term and long-term goals (Wilkes, 1988). Anything less would be to abandon the "principle of charity" that allows the rest of us to proceed as if our worlds make some followable and temporally vectored sense. That, in short, is the problem that claims of self-continuity are meant to address. What, we now need to know, is the solution?

As we argue in Part II, the paradox of sameness and change, and its resolution through some followable argument for personal persistence, appears to admit to only one or the other of two broad solution strategies. One of these, which we go on to mark as "Essentialist" or entity-based, works to resolve the problem by actually embracing change, but only awkwardly and in some diminished or carefully hedged way that allows certain special identity conferring bits and pieces of the self—some indelible stain—to hide out from the ravages of time. On such accounts, what are dismissed as only superficial parts of oneself are seen to be as free and fickle and will-o'-the-wisp as they like, so long as other more central, more subterranean, more essential features of the self, often thought to lie at the very core of one's being, are understood to somehow stand outside of, and otherwise defeat, time (Shalom, 1985).

Alternatively, one can happily "give up the ghost" on any imagined "essential" part of the self thought to constitute some unchanging innermost core of one's being, and, instead, stake all claims for personal persistence on the connective tissue—the relational forms—that link together the various time-slices that together make up the archipelago of one's temporally vectored existence. On such accounts—which we have variously labeled as "Relational" or "Narrative"—nothing about the self need be understood to stand apart from time, or be wholly immune to change. Rather, self-continuity or personal "survival" (Parfit, 1971), is thought to be guaranteed by the fact that some connective thread can be found and taken up that is capable of linking earlier and later manifestations of the self into some meaningful whole.

The open question to which we now mean to turn has to do with just how these contrastive ways of thinking about sameness within change differently play themselves out in history, and in the historical lives of given individuals of different ages and cultures.

PART II: ESSENTIALIST VS. NARRATIVE SELF-CONTINUITY WARRANTS

The broad claim that we mean to defend in what follows is that whenever and wherever there is talk about wholeness or personal persistence, then only one or the other of just two vernaculars is likely being spoken. *One* of these, which we have characterized as Essentialist or Entity-based, works to marginalize change, and standardly seeks to "ground" our understanding of self-continuity by imagining some perhaps hidden, but always enduring personal *essence* that necessarily stands apart from the ravages of time, while relegating everything that is fickle and changeable to the status of a kind of ephemeral shadow of the machine.

According to what we mark out as a *second* and fundamentally different way of reasoning through the paradox of sameness within change (a way labeled here as Relational or Narratively-based), defensible claims of personal continuity are never rooted in the persistence of some fictive, atemporal part, no matter how supposedly essential or deeply tucked away in the core of one's being. Rather, on this view, personal persistence in the face of change can only be redeemed to the degree that meaningful relations—interstitial connections, if you will—can be established between the earlier and succeeding time-slices of our life. Each of these distinctive self-continuity warranting strategies is briefly hinted at below (see also, Chandler, Lalonde, Sokol, & Hallett, 2003).

Essentialist Readings of the Self

Although what has been hinted at so far in alluding to a class of Narrativist claims for personal persistence strikes many as somehow dangerously continental or otherwise suspiciously *avant-garde*, Essentialism is likely to seem as familiar as an old shoe. The reason for this, of course, is that Essentialism has reputably been the default strategy in Euro-American culture for at least 3 centuries. According to what has become the received view on this topic (e.g., Taylor, 1975, 1989, 1991; Sass, 1988), Western thought, at least since the Renaissance, can be read as a "journey into the interior" (Sass, 1988, p. 552) marked by an inward turn, away from still earlier medieval views according to which persons are imagined to have traditionally found their place in some larger meaning structure by looking outside themselves and to an all-encompassing cosmic or religious order—some Aristotelian or God-given "great chain of being" (Lovejoy, 1942) in which individual persons play some predestined but secure part. On such preEnlightenment accounts, order, harmony, value, and meaning were not to be found within one's self, but in things larger than life situated in the surrounding cosmos.

All that, of course, was then—way back then. With the Enlightenment— with the dawning of Galilean and Newtonian science—this earlier and more orderly world of fixed external meaning is widely thought to have effectively collapsed into a matrix of contingent correlations and mechanistic laws of atomic causation. In the face of this "disenchantment" or "dissipation of our sense of the cosmos as a meaningful order" (Taylor, 1989, p. 17), looking outward for sources of meaning is said to have no longer made sense. Rather, inheritors of these new insights were forced instead to turn inward to a more private realm of meaning; some "theater of the mind," where nothing was judged more reliable than our own changeable human experience or interpretations. On this now familiar account, the most famous example of which is Cartesian philosophy, the inner realms of persons, however difficult to access, came to be viewed as more trustworthy and more meaning laden than was the contingent chaos of the ambient universe. Whatever its other costs and benefits, the hallmark change of this new modern inwardness was, it is said, a heightened sense of ourselves as beings with inner depth (Taylor, 1989, p. x).

According to Taylor (1975), subsequent incarnations of this Enlightenment theme all amounted to one or another variation upon this same inward turn. One of these, which Taylor has labeled an "Autonomous" view, held that it was not only practically necessary, but morally incumbent on each of us, if we are to be free and self-determining, to build a bulwark against the mechanistic determinism of the natural world, and to freely chose our fate as individual agents—a Kantian-like understanding that still pervades much of Western thought. A second of these equally Essentialistic views, which Taylor terms *Expressivist*, and which partially coincides with Romanticism, understands each of us to possess "an inborn and inner essence that initially exists *in potentia*, and, as it were, yearns to realize itself through a natural process of self-unfolding" (Sass, 1988, p. 563). Fulfillment, on this Expressivist account, meant each person's discovery and expression of her or his own special way of being human (Taylor, 1975, p. 23). Much of the valorization of self-exploration and self-expression, again common to Western culture, obviously has its roots in this romantic counter-Enlightenment movement.

Despite their evident differences, both the Autonomous and Expressivist positions outlined by Taylor are, fundamentally, more similar than different: both maintain that the true expression of selves arises in opposition to the material and social forces that surround them, and both continue to promote an inward turn that champions individualism, self-awareness, and self-actualization against the social and material constraints of the natural world. From this now predominantly Anglo-American perspective, any reasonable account of the temporal persistence of the self necessarily begins and ends with the invention of a deeply interiorized essence, and anything else less substantive risks dissolving into what Foucault (1970) called "a dream of self-dispersal."

None of this Essentialist talk of immunity to time, however cleverly engineered to finesse the problem of sameness within change, comes without well-documented and oft-mentioned costs. By accenting inwardness, both Autonomous and Expressivist variations on essentialism foster isolation from outer nature, and an estrangement and separation from the social

world. By failing to locate a source of meaning outside the self, both promote a brand of narcissism that collapses morality into a crude form of
self-interest, and undermine the worth of anything more grand than simple
self-promotion. This is the *Malaise of Modernity* (1991) and the *Ethics of Authenticity* (1992) against which Taylor and others (e.g., Bruner, 1986;
Cassirer, 1923; Dilthey, 1962; Habermas, 1985; Harré, 1979) have written
so forcefully, and against which existential-phenomenological thinkers
such as Heidegger, Merleau-Ponty, and Sartre worked in their efforts to
promote a more outer-directed conception of human existence grounded
in a larger, encompassing external world.

Personal Persistence in a Narrativist Voice

Despite the fact that, after more than 2000 years of uninterrupted use,
Essentialism has come to so dominate Euro-American thought that it more
or less amounts to our contemporary version of common sense, it would,
nevertheless, be a mistake to suppose that it represents the whole of our (or
anyone else's) folk psychology about personal persistence. That is, not withstanding the broadly agreed on fact that Western societies are very much
steeped in an essentialist tradition, there is, just as certainly, a second, if
contrapuntal framework of understanding that works to ground identity in
the possibility of self-continuity without essence (Putnam, 1988). According
to such narrative-like or relational accounts, nothing definitive about selves
actually does survive time, or is sufficiently enduring to reliably vouchsafe
their persistence. Rather, survival is seen to be owed to whatever relations
are responsible for linking our earlier and later ways of being into some coherent pattern, or narrative structure—a connection that, as Dilthey (1962,
p. 202) put it, "can only be understood through meaning."

Selfhood, in these antimetaphysical terms, is not to be understood as
rooted in some enduring substance or transcendental essence, but as something closer to what Dennett (1992) calls a "narrative center of gravity,"
built of the stories we fashion in an effort to integrate our past, present, and
anticipated future. We are, by such lights, best seen as leaning more heavily
on the foot of change than the foot of sameness; more schematic than taxo-
nomic (Mandler, 1984); more discursive and historical than declarative and
prepositional (Bruner, 1986); more dialogical than monological
(Hermans, 1996); more local and indigenous than universal or transcendental (Habermas, 1985); and altogether as something more closely akin to
the narrative embodiment of lives as told (Spence, 1982). When obliged to
justify why selves need and deserve to be counted only once, practitioners of
this more Narrativist trade do not, as would their more Essentialist counter-
parts, begin by banking on the continued existence of some—call it now "il-
lusory"—kernel of sameness (e.g., one's fingerprints, ego, personality,

soul) that is imagined "to stand behind the passing states of consciousness and our always shifting ways of being" (James, 1891, p. 196). Rather, they begin instead by putting their money on the web of diachronic patterned relations that are understood to link up the different time slices of their own lives—linkages that are held out to be sufficient in and of themselves, to ground the possibility of self-continuity without essence (Putnam, 1988).

Like the Essentialist views that narratologists so peevishly stand on their heads, relational accounts too have their critics. Some (e.g., Car, 1986; Ricoeur, 1985; Zagorin, 1999), anxious that selfhood not be seen to dissolve into some species of literature, argue that, because lives are not amenable to just any telling, something else less story-like must stand behind and distinguish the telling from the told (Mishler, 1995). Others, still less charitably, are quick to write off proponents of such Narrative views as practitioners of "mere" rhetoric (Ring, 1987), or converts to some *en passant* French fad (Callinicos, 1989), who risk, as Zagorin (1999, p. 23) puts it, becoming "lost in the tropics of discourse."

It is not our intention here to attempt to somehow choose up sides, or arbitrate between these competing Essentialist and Narrativist views. Rather, we mean only to list them out as a way of lining up some of the culturally available resources that history provides as procedural alternatives for differently thinking about the problem of one's own and others' personal persistence through time.

PART III: ON ASSESSING THE THOUGHTS OF NATIVE AND NON-NATIVE YOUTH

Adventitiously dabbling, as we have just done, in the recent course of Western intellectual history has served, we hope, to make two points. One of these is that, at least since the Enlightenment, what Polkinghorne (1988) termed a broadly shared "metaphysics of substance," coupled with an acquired sense of "inwardness," has conspired to privilege Essentialist solutions to the problem of personal persistence, or at least it is said to have done so for those reared up in contemporary Euro-American culture. The second is that, set against this all too familiar default strategy is another at least potentially available, but countervailing intellectual tradition that privileges becoming over being by partaking in what Polkinghorne (1988) has alternatively called a "metaphysics of potentiality and actuality"—a framework of understanding that potentially favors Narrativist, as opposed to Essentialist, solutions to the paradox of sameness within change.

However representative of the general case, what these and other such Panglossian claims about whole cultures and whole epochs fail to make clear is how, precisely, the balance between such Essentialist and Narrativist thoughts actually plays itself out in real time and in the actual lives of actual individuals, or even whole communities of individuals. Our program of cross-cultural research is meant to be a beginning way of addressing such person- and community-level questions. In attempting to take up these more individuated and, consequently, more bona fide psychological matters, two procedural questions immediately arise: First, exactly *whose* thoughts should be inquired into? And second, just *how* might such an inquiry be best carried out? Fair questions, we think, in a volume meant to be all about alternate conceptions of self and mind.

Part of an answer to the first of these—the *who* question—follows rather directly from the arguments of the preceding section. If, as we have alleged, Essentialism is actually bred in the bone by Western culture, and if thoughts about personal persistence are, as claimed, alive in the minds of everyone, and not just professional philosophers, then it ought to follow that almost any run-of-the-mill Euro-American will, if pricked, fairly bleed Essentialism. That much, at least, no one would find surprising. Rather, the real challenge posed by the "who" question is not how to find live instances of Essentialist thought, but rather how best to locate a potential contrast group that might showcase the Narrativist alternative.

Our own candidate group of choice was Canada's Aboriginal, or First Nations peoples. Other, equally suitable, groups no doubt exist, but there are good reasons, other than convenience (if that is what you call it), for having chosen as we did. One such reason, or more precisely, a background condition that allows all other reasons to count, is the natural fact that First Nations are decidedly *not* Euro-American. Despite several centuries' worth of sustained attempts to forcibly assimilate them, First Nations peoples remain a set of identifiably distinct nations within Canadian society. Although individual First Nations were differentially savaged by a succession of government sponsored forced assimilation programs, all have succeeded, to varying degrees, in retaining and rebuilding much of their cultures. Although, in and of itself, "failure" or refusal to assimilate does not, of course, guarantee that Narrativist strategies would find a comfortable home in First Nations cultures, such evidence does come from other quarters. By available accounts, and in contrast to the dominant culture, Native communities, including those in western Canada, do reportedly hold a more distributed conception of knowledge and personhood (Battiste, 2002), and their claims about personal identity are widely understood to grow out of community and clan relationships in ways that are less evidently true of persons whose cultural roots grow most directly out of a Euro-American intellectual tradition (Kirmayer, Brass, & Tait, 2000). Although none of this is enough to prove a point, it was enough, we judged, to warrant our own decision to search among First Nations youth for possible evidence of a default strategy that favors Narrativist, as opposed to Essentialist, self-continuity warranting practices.

Methods and Procedures

In answer to our second question—the one having to do with *how* thoughts about personal persistence might best be gathered up for examination—we report very briefly on our own decade-long efforts to create and refine a method of getting young persons to seriously consider and speak to the paradox of sameness and change. The unabridged version of this story is long—even Byzantine—but, conveniently, is already reported elsewhere (Chandler, Lalonde, Sokol, & Hallett, 2003). Minimally, the short version comes in two parts. The first of these includes the fact that the methodology to which we eventually came consists of a semi-structured interview that requires our research participants to describe themselves, both in the present and then some years in the past, all before going on to provide reasons meant to justify why (the inevitable differences that divide their two accounts not withstanding) they still continue to regard themselves as one and the same continuous person. Part II follows a more or less identical path, but this time counterpart questions are asked, not about participants' own lives, but about the lives of various fictional story characters—where "fictional" and "various" refer to the lives of heroes and heroines of classical stories of character development (*bildungsromane*) familiar in Western and Aboriginal cultures. These stories about, for example, the lives of Jean Valjean, Ebenezer Scrooge, or "The Bear Woman," were presented either in "Classic Comic Book" form, or as short film trailers.

Importantly, this assessment approach, in contrast to more standard issue measurement strategies which presuppose that respondents harbor some declarative knowledge about this or that denotative dimension of the self, is more procedural (Wildgen, 1994), or practice based (Kitayama, 2002), and works simply by requiring participants to actively go about the business of warranting their own and others' personal persistence in the face of demonstrated change.

Scoring

Having carefully set down whatever the young participants in our several studies actually had to say on the subject of their own and others' personal persistence, we subsequently struggled to categorize their remarks in each of two ways. First, and without making a procrustean bed of the enterprise, we worked to designate each response as an instance of Narrativist or Essentialist thought, or (which effectively never came up) as something else entirely. Having settled the question of general response "Type," (i.e., having typecast each participant's account of personal persistence in, first their own lives and then the lives of at least two story characters, as three instances of either Essentialist or Narrativist problem-solving strategies) we then went on to code all such responses as reflective of what has proven to be one or the other of five ordered "Levels" of complexity.

Assuming that we are already clear enough about what is loosely intended by broad talk of responses of the Narrativist and Essentialist type, what remains in special need of careful explication is what, in this case, is meant by "Level." As proved to be the case, there was, apparent in our data, strong evidence for the existence of what amount to "canonical," if slightly homespun, versions of both Essentialist and Narrativist self-continuity warranting strategies—responses that, although falling importantly short of what might be reasonably expected from a legitimate card-carrying philosopher of mind, easily qualified as recognizable caricatures of such better polished, professionalized explanations. In the case of responses of the Essentialist type, for example, some small, but sizeable, number of our late adolescent respondents argued that although many of the evident changes in their own lives and the lives of various story characters were real enough, all of these could still be understood as superficial—or merely phenotypic—variations on another deeper lying and more essential genotypic core of sameness capable of productively paraphrasing itself in endless surface variations—an "essence" the unchanging existence of which served to justify their strongly held convictions about personal persistence. By contrast, other participants, whose general approach to the problem of sameness within change was fundamentally narrative-like in character, responded in no less canonical ways, but did so by reporting that they had identified a clear plot line running through their own autobiography that successfully laced together the various time slices of their own storied lives.

In the classification scheme eventually applied to all of our data, responses that took either of these canonical forms were coded as being at our so-called Level 4 (i.e., all but perfect) on what proved to be a 5-level coding scheme. The occasional and especially sophisticated participant who ended up actually being coded at Level 5 did so by successfully bracketing such canonical Essentialist or Narrativist forms of reasoning, suggesting that their claims about underlying essences or plotlines running through their lives were, in fact, lightly held and best understood as either provisional "theories" they were entertaining, or rough drafts they were still in the midst of sketching about the chronology of their own and others' lives. Naturally enough, responses coded at these 4th and 5th levels were the exception rather than the rule among the Native and non-Native youth on report here. This is understandably the case because young people are not ordinarily born into the world with anything like such fully-fledged ways of trying to make sense of their own and others' self-continuity in time. Instead, the large bulk of these adolescents responded in ways that amounted to stripped-down and more child-like versions of typically later-arriving canonical or provisionalized forms of Essentialist and Narrativist reasoning.

Reduced to its lowest possible common denominator, entry-level Essentialist reasoning (Level I in our accounting scheme), for example, proceeds as though selves are made up out of a simple assemblage of atomic parts (e.g., one's name, or fingerprints, or strawberry birthmark), the persistence of any of which is deemed sufficient to make you still you after all of these years. Only marginally more complex is a class of Level II or "Topological" accounts that aim to succeed by insisting that all apparent change is merely presentational, with various fixed and immutable aspects of the self simply orbiting in and out of view. Positing the existence of something like a devil on one shoulder and an angel on the other is a familiar tactic of respondents who invoke this low level Essentialist strategy. Still others, scored at Essentialist Level III, successfully factor a truncated notion of time into the equation by postulating a maturational model that allows for the possibility of latent attributes of the self—attributes that, although always present in some nascent form, have their own moments of ascendancy, each popping out (like one's beard or second set of teeth) according to some preordained epigenetic time clock.

Narrativist accounts, too, appear in a variety of scaled-down versions, the earliest Level I instance of which amounts to no more than a simple chronology. A life, seen by such lights, amounts to no more than one damned thing after another. Level II and III Narrativist responses are only marginally more complex, either lining out the various time-slices of a life like so many beads on a common Picaresque string, or treating biographies as though they amounted to no more than a deterministic chain of causes and effects.

Given that each of the commentaries offered up by the participants in our research was scored for both type (Essentialist or Narrativist) and level (I-V), and that all participants were typically asked to comment on possible continuities, not only in their own life but the lives of two fictional story characters, particular individuals or groups of individuals could display, at least in theory, any one of a wide range of response patterns. Some of these are worth listing out in advance. It could have turned out, for example, that, despite our determined efforts to elicit their best thoughts on the matter, some or all of our respondents might simply have had nothing to say that could be counted as evidence of their having seriously understood or engaged the problem we set before them. As it was, this rarely, if ever happened, with most interview protocols running to several typed pages. Alternatively, some or all of the participants in our several studies might have had *something* to say on the subject of personal persistence, but nothing that represented a natural fit with what was, at least initially, a theoretically derived scoring typology. This too, largely failed to come up, with less than

5% of the protocols collected ending up as "un-scorable." No less disruptive
to our hopes for some better understanding of the problem of personal persistence would have been a pattern of pattern-less results, suggesting that,
whatever young people might think about the argumentative grounds for
self continuity, they simply thought about these matters differently on
different occasions.

In considering this last possibility it is necessary to view the notion of
"multiple occasions" in each of two ways. First, and in the usual manner of
calculating test-retest reliability, "occasions" could be read as referring to
different testing sessions separated in time. Alternatively, the notion of
"multiple occasions" could also be taken to refer to the *content* of different
test items rather than the timing of their administration. Here, we could
count questions about persistence in the life of a story character as one item
or "testing occasion" and questions about persistence in the respondent's
own life as another, and look for evidence of inter-item consistency across
these different measurement opportunities.

Similar concerns about the stability of responses could focus, not on the
choice between Narrative and Essentialist problem-solving strategies, but
on the level of complexity of such responses. We might even predict that
measurement occasions separated by sufficient time would reveal something like a developmental progression, with responses becoming more
complex with the passage of real time. Differences in the complexity of responses that appeared across different item contents, however, would
prove (at least in our own case) theoretically troubling.

Concentrating for the moment on the *form* or type of such arguments,
the possibilities for stability would seem to line themselves out along a continuum that runs from absolute stability through utter randomness. That is,
it might have been the case that, regardless of when and how the topic is
presented, individual young persons could show themselves to be consistent in employing either Essentialist or Narrativist warranting strategies on
all occasions. A less stringent form of stability—one that allowed both strategies to co-exist within the same person—would see "consistently" replaced
by "usually." If we remain attentive to the distinction drawn between the
timing and the content of the measurement occasion, it could be that persons are consistent *within* a testing session, but inconsistent *across* sessions.
Such a finding would, then, suggest that choosing a warranting strategy,
like changing one's socks, might have nothing whatsoever to do with matters of culture. Further still, respondents, might, for example, reliably exhibit an Essentialist strategy whenever they are asked about their own
persistence and use a Narrativist approach to the persistence of others (or
vice versa). At the far end of this continuum we would reach a point where
we could find no rhyme or reason behind the use of these strategies by
individual participants.

Within this set of possibilities, our own theoretically driven expectations with regard to the question of stability were as follows:

1. Both strategies would be available to many or most of the young persons tested—that is, participants would show some understanding of both forms of reasoning.
2. Many or most of the participants would strongly favor one strategy over the other—that is, each young person would have what might be called a "default" strategy.
3. Across testing sessions and across test content, all or most individuals would cling to the same default strategy.
4. The complexity (not the form) of the response would be relatively stable *within* testing sessions (i.e., complexity would not vary widely whether questions were being posed about the continuity of self and others).
5. Complexity would be observed to increase "longitudinally" *across* reasonably long stretches of developmental time.
6. The default strategy in evidence would be shown to differ between the cultural groups.

Participants

Finding samples of young persons best suited to the testing of these half dozen predictions required special attention to matters of culture and demography. Our first challenge, having decided to pursue the possibility of cultural differences between First Nations and non-Native youth in British Columbia, was to find some way of taking "representative" samples from within these cultural groups. Here, history and geography conspire against success. British Columbia, where our research was conducted, occupies more than 10% of Canada's large land mass and is home to nearly 200 distinct First Nations communities comprising dozens of diverse languages and cultural traditions. In the face of these logistical barriers, we elected to narrow our focus to just two Native communities: one urban and one rural. The task of locating a 'comparison' sample of non-Native young people within British Columbia (i.e., representative of Euro-American culture and otherwise comparable to First Nations youth) is equally complicated given the multicultural mosaic of BC's urban centers and the fact that the history of First Nations people renders the usual set of socio-economic matching variables inappropriate. In the end, solving this "control group" problem involved selecting youth from within a school system that catered primarily to the third-generation descendents of a white European immigrant group.

Although data collection in all of these settings is still ongoing, the sample to be reported on here consisted of a total of 220 young persons between the ages of 12 and 20, of which 91 were drawn from an urban Native community, 92 from a rural Native community, and 37 non-Native participants. These groups did not differ significantly from one another with respect to their composition by gender or age.

Finally, with these participants in place, we also felt it necessary to put in place a set of additional control procedures. For example, it was judged important, given the fact that our cap was set on identifying possible cultural differences, to employ procedures for establishing that our participants were indeed committed to, or felt themselves to be fully-fledged members of, their respective cultural communities. To this end, we employed several questionnaire measures meant to variously assess "ethnic identity," "ethnic orientation," and levels of "acculturation." Similarly, to ward off the possibility that differences between the groups might result from contrasting linguistic styles or abilities rather than more deeply rooted differences in ideas about personal persistence, we subjected the transcripts of our interviews to a series of text analyses meant to estimate linguistic and conceptual complexity.

Results

Responses for each participant from each of the three scorable sections of our interview protocol (self and two stories) were categorized according to type (Essentialist versus Narrative), and assigned to one of the five levels of complexity just outlined. By way of reminder, we made six predictions about the results of these classification efforts. First, we anticipated that the type designation of Essentialist or Narrativist would not prove to be a person-sorting exercise. That is, we assumed that it was not only possible, but even likely that individual participants might have both of these problem solving strategies in their repertory. We also anticipated that, across variations in test content, and across testing sessions, most young people would strongly favor (i.e., employ as a default option) one of these strategies at the expense of the other. The available data clearly support these predictions: 75% of the participants employed the same type of argument throughout their interview, whereas only a quarter were observed to use both Essentialist and Narrativist warrants. When re-interviewed after an interval of 18-24 months, 70% of a small longitudinal subsample ($n = 23$) of our Native participants consistently used the same warranting strategy that they had employed during the initial interview. We take these findings to mean that, although "access" to both sorts of warranting strategies is frequently demonstrated, most participants do have a default strategy that is regularly exercised across occasions and across time.

We also laid out a set of expectations regarding the complexity, or level of the responses. One of these concerned performance at any given point in time. Here we predicted that during an interview, complexity would not vary importantly as a function of whose personal persistence (self or other) was being inquired into. Again, our findings lend support to these expectations. Better than half (58%) of our participants showed no variability in level assignments across the three available scoring opportunities, and for a further quarter of the sample all of their responses fell in at least adjacent levels. Although not perfect, this degree of consistency indicates that, ordinarily, most of our participants employed not only the same type of reasoning across content, but also did so at the same level of complexity.

Although we predicted that each participant's type of reasoning would remain relatively constant over time, we also anticipated that the level of complexity would increase during the course of development. Analysis of our longitudinal data reveals that, after removing those participants who were already at ceiling on the measure (i.e., at Level 5), fully two-thirds of participants were observed to employ higher levels of reasoning at the second interview than they had at the first. The remainder of our participants who failed to show this developmental pattern were evenly split between those who showed a measurable but trivial decline over time, and a small group of our youngest participants who remained at Level 1 on both testing occasions. In short, for most of these young persons, an interval of 18 to 24 months between interviews appears sufficient to reveal measurable increases in the complexity of their reasoning.

All of the preceding was meant to lay the groundwork for a discussion of the real point of our assessment efforts—the search for possible cross-cultural differences. We not only anticipated that our participants would give voice to some form of commitment to the proposition that persons in general, and they in particular, *ought* to be seen as persisting through time and despite change, but we also expected them to do so in ways that were largely consistent with what we envisioned to be the main and contrasting currents within their respective cultures of origin. We did find such a difference, and will, in short order have more to say about its size and shape, but it is important to first stress that finding a reportable difference between groups drawn from different cultures is not at all the same thing as finding a difference that is attributable to culture. Before leaping to any such conclusion it is important to be especially confident of two things. First, we needed strong assurances that our respondents accept and value the cultural designations that we used to recruit them—that is, that they recognize themselves as members of their respective cultural group and take that membership as a cornerstone of their identity. With this in hand, we would then need solid evidence that any observed difference was not the result of some systematic, but coincidental set of noisy background variables that work to divide the groups, but only in culturally and theoretically uninteresting ways.

Here, most importantly, is what we found: 76% of non-Native participants employed Essentialist warranting strategies; and 87% of Native participants employed Narrativist strategies. The Urban and Rural Native communities, as it turned out, did not differ from one another in the frequency of Narrative or Essentialist ratings, nor was the type of strategy used associated with age or gender: culture was, then, the only grouping variable that showed a statistical association with type of reasoning.

As previously noted, the first test of our faith in these results turns on the always suspect designations Native and non-Native. As such, we were more interested in what individual participants took themselves to be, and whether they especially valorized their ethnic identity, rather than how they were classified for census purposes. Although available measures of ethnic identity are not without certain inherent shortcomings, we deemed it important to make some effort to assess whether or not our First Nations participants—and most particularly, those First Nations youth who appeared to employ "counter-cultural" Essentialist warranting practices—expressed any strong affiliation with their culture of origin. That is, our having picked out our contrast groups by focusing on their Aboriginal or non-Aboriginal status, although clearly of interest, might well have proven a matter of little personal relevance to our young participants. As a way of examining this prospect, a subset of our Native participants were given a 130-item ethnic identification scale composed of items drawn from several established measures that had been developed or adapted for use with First Nations youth. Items included ratings of levels of participation in traditional activities and practices as well as endorsement of Native and non-Native cultural values and customs. Any doubts that we might have had about the depth of commitment to Native ways on the part of our First Nations participants were dispelled by the extremity of their responses: in our sample, all things Native were uniformly judged to be of value and "highly true of me." This was equally true of the minority of Native youth who employed Essentialist warrants as it was for the majority, who responded in more Narrativist ways. Whatever else might divide these contrasting groups, it is not to be found in the depth of their attachment to Native culture.

Although all of our Native participants reported that they were comfortably identified within their First Nations culture, it might still have been the case that responsibility for the observed relation between Narrativist practices on the part of Aboriginal youth and the Essentialist practices of non-Aboriginal participants lies not, as we imagined, in the contrasting views of personal persistence held by members of these different cultural groups, but rather in some more mundane difference in the ways in which these young persons use language, particularly the language they use to describe their self-concept. Perhaps, one might imagine, Essentialist talk is simply more conceptually complex or somehow argumentatively "better" than Narrativist talk. Perhaps what we are calling Narrativist responses are simply Essentialist answers offered by those without a special talent for abstraction, or, alternatively, that Essentialist responses are simply Narrativist answers put forward by those without an ear for plot. Or perhaps First Nations youth, living as they do in what some might mistakenly see as a "collectivist" enclave within an "individualist" nation, are simply marked by a heightened concern for interdependence and community that somehow colors all talk of "self" in collectivist hues. Narrativist and Essentialist self-continuity warranting strategies would, on such a reductive account, simply amount to a new set of labels for the tired individualism–collectivism dichotomy that has, of late, come under increasing suspicion (Fiske, 2002; Kitayama, 2002; Miller, 2002; Oyserman, Coon, & Kemmelmeier, 2002; Turiel, 2002).

The business of ruling out these various reductive interpretations for the finding that Native and non-Native youth regularly employ different default strategies in reasoning about their own and others' personal persistence involved several alternate assessment procedures and analyses. First, to test the reductive prospect that what passes for Essentialist and Narrativist responses strategies are, when unmasked, really only differences in linguistic complexity, we subjected the transcripts from our interviews to a set of text analyses that estimate the linguistic sophistication of the participant. No reliable differences emerged between the Native and non-Native youth, nor between Essentialists and Narrativists on any of 10 different markers of linguistic competence (Pennebaker & King, 1999). Complexity was (as anyone might predict) positively correlated with age, but even with age partialled out, complexity, it turned out, was best predicted by our level of reasoning assignments. That is, more sophisticated language ability was most strongly associated, not with the type of reasoning used, but with higher levels of reasoning.

Even if, as proved to be the case, linguistic skill is distributed evenly across the cultural groups, it might still have been the case that Native and non-Native youth simply differ in the ways that they use language to describe the self. That is, our terms Essentialist and Narrativist could simply refer, not to differing ways of warranting personal persistence, but to more incidental differences in the attention devoted to self and others in talk about persons. For example, Essentialists might exhibit an "idiocentric" focus on their own personal qualities, attitudes, beliefs and traits, whereas the talk of Narrativists might have proven more "allocentric" in its focus on interdependence and responsiveness to others. Testing this reductive prospect was accomplished by asking a subset of our participants to complete Kuhn and McPartland's (1954) famous *Twenty Statements Test* (also known as the "Who Am I?" Test) in which respondents are asked to complete twenty sentence stems that begin "I am ..." The resulting responses were then scored for the presence of idiocentric and allocentric statements. No reliable differences in the proportions of these statement types were found between the cultural groups or between Essentialists and Narrativists. In other words, neither group showed a tendency to disproportionately concentrate their attention, either on subjective psychological traits or other-oriented characteristics.

Further evidence in support of this same conclusion comes from our participants' performance on Singelis' (1994) measure of independent and interdependent self-construals. Again our cultural groups and our assigned groupings of Essentialist and Narrativist did not differ in their ratings of statements that stress the importance of internal states, feelings, and traits (independent self-construal) or the external or public dimensions of self in roles and relationships (interdependent self-construal).

Where the groups did differ—and where we had good reason to suspect that they might—was in their implicit theories of personality and in particular in the ways in which those theories make room for the possibility of personality change. Responses to Dweck's (2000) *Implicit Theories of Personality Scale*, reveal that Essentialists endorse a static or entity view of personality in which enduring traits effectively withstand change. Narrativists, by comparison, hold a more "process"-oriented view in which personality is understood to be malleable. These positive findings are perhaps best seen, not as some additional control measure, but as the results of a multimethod approach aimed at triangulating on what was originally intended by our designation of some protocols as narrative-like, and others as more essentialistic.

In summary then, it appears that, like their elders and a whole raft of their intellectual ancestors, young persons are not only committed to the necessary conviction that personal persistence is a critical requirement of personhood, but also make serious attempts to resolve the paradox of sameness and change in their own and others' lives in ways that shadow the Essentialist and Narrativist traditions evident in the broader course of intellectual history. Most First Nations youth employ Narrativist strategies. Most culturally mainstream youth employ Essentialist strategies. These default strategies are neither wholly dictated by culture (some 15-25% of youth employ the problem-solving approach common to the "other" culture), nor are persons reliably marked by having access to just one strategy (25% show the ability to use both strategies even if one is preferred). These cultural differences are not the result of background differences in linguistic sophistication or conceptual complexity, or ethnic identification, nor do they reduce to differences between the ways individualists versus collectivists are prone to talk about matters of selfhood. Essentialists and Narrativists do not differ in the extent to which they endorse idiocentric and allocentric statements, or independent and interdependent conceptions of identity. They do show a tendency to differ, however, and in just the way one would predict, in their implicit theories of selfhood, with Narrativists championing personality change and Essentialists favoring enduring immutable traits. The clear conclusion supported by all of these analyses is that culture is very strongly associated with (but does not fully determine) whether one adopts a Narrative or Essentialist strategy for resolving the paradox of personal persistence and change. We take these distinctions between Native and non-Native ways of warranting personal persistence to be reflective of the fact that constructing such arguments is neither a completely private and personal affair, not wholly dictated by social environments or cultural practices.

ENDNOTE

[1]In keeping with common practice in Canada, the term "aboriginal" is used here to refer to indigenous persons in general, whereas "Aboriginal" refers to several specific groups within Canada: Inuit, First Nations, and Métis. The Inuit were formerly referred to as "Eskimo," and First Nations were once termed "Indian." The Métis have their origins in intermarriages between the First Nations and European settlers.

REFERENCES

Battiste, M. (2002). *Indigenous Knowledge and Pedagogy in First Nations Education—A Literature Review with Recommendations.* Report prepared for the National Working Group on Education, Indian and Northern Affairs Canada, Ottawa, ON.

Bruner, J. S. (1986). *Actual minds, possible worlds.* Cambridge, MA: Harvard University Press.

Callinicos, A. (1989). *Against post-modernism.* Oxford: Polity Press.

Car, D. (1986). *Time, narrative, and history.* Bloomington: Indiana University Press.

Cassirer, E. (1923). *Substance and function.* Chicago: Open Court.

Chandler, M. J., Lalonde, C. E., & Sokol, B. (2000). Continuities of selfhood in the face of radical developmental and cultural change. In L. Nucci, G. Saxe, & E. Turiel (Eds.), *Culture, thought, and development* (pp. 65–84). Mahwah, NJ: Lawrence Erlbaum Associates.

Chandler, M. J., Lalonde, C. E., Sokol, B., & Hallett, D. (2003). *Surviving time: Aboriginality, suicidality, and the persistence of identity in the face of radical developmental and cultural change.* Monographs of the Society for Research in Child Development.

Dennett, D. C. (1987). *The intentional stance.* Cambridge, MA: MIT Press.

Dennett, D. C. (1992). The self as a center of narrative gravity. In F. S. Kessel & P. M. Cole (Eds.), *Self and consciousness: Multiple perspectives* (pp. 103–115). Hillsdale, NJ: Lawrence Erlbaum Associates.

Dilthey, W. (1962). *Pattern and meaning in history: Thoughts on history and society.* New York: Harper.

Dweck, C. S. (2000). *Self theories: Their role in motivation, personality, and development.* Philadelphia, PA: Psychology Press.

Fiske, P. A. (2002). Using individualism and collectivism to compare culture—A critique of the validity and measurement of the constructs: Comment on Oyserman et al. (2002). *Psychological Bulletin, 128*(1), 78–88.

Flanagan, O. (1996). *Self expressions: Mind, morals and the meaning of life.* New York: Oxford University Press.

Foucault, M. (1970). *The order of things: An archaeology of the human sciences.* New York: Pantheon Books.

Fraisse, P. (1963). *The psychology of time.* New York: Harper & Row.

Gallagher, S. (1998). *The inordinance of time.* Evanston, IL: Northwestern University Press.

Geertz, C. (1973). *The interpretation of cultures; selected essays.* New York: Basic Books.

Geertz, H., & Geertz, C. (1975). *Kinship in Bali.* Chicago, IL: University of Chicago Press.

Habermas, J. (1985). Questions and counterquestions. (J. Bohman, Trans.). In R. J. Bernstein (Ed.), *Habermas and modernity* (pp. 192–216). Cambridge, MA: MIT Press.

Hacking, I. (1999). *The social construction of what?* Cambridge, MA: Harvard University Press.

Hallowell, A. I. (1955). *Culture and experience.* Philadelphia. PA: University of Pennsylvania Press.

Harré, R. (1979). *Social being: A theory for social psychology.* Oxford, UK: Blackwell.

Hermans, H. J. (1996). Voicing the self: From information processing to dialogical interchange. *Psychological Bulletin, 119*(1), 31–50.

James, W. (1891). *The principles of psychology.* London: Macmillan.

Kirmayer, L., Brass, G., & Tait, C. (2000). The mental health of aboriginal peoples: Transformations of identity and community. *Canadian Journal of Psychiatry, 45*(7), 607–616.

Kitayama, S. (2002). Culture and basic psychological processes-Toward a system view of culture: Comment on Oyserman et al. (2002). *Psychological Bulletin, 128*(1), 89–96.

Kuhn, M. H., & McPartland, T. S. (1954). An empirical investigation of self-attitudes. *American Sociological Review, 19,* 68–76.

Levine, R. A., & White, M. I. (1986). *Human conditions: The cultural basis of educational development.* New York: Rutledge & Kegan Paul.

Lillard, A. (1998). Ethnopsychologies: Cultural variation in theories of mind. *Psychological Bulletin, 123,* 3–32.

Lovejoy, A. O. (1942). *The great chain of being: A study of the history of an idea: The William James lectures delivered at Harvard University, 1933.* Cambridge, MA: Harvard University Press.

Mandler, J. M. (1984). *Stories, scripts, and scenes: aspects of schema theory.* Hillsdale, NJ: Lawrence Erlbaum Associates.

Marr, D. (1982). *Vision: A computational investigation into the human representation and processing of visual information.* New York: W. H. Freeman.

Miller, J. G. (2002). Bringing culture to basic psychological theory—Beyond individualism and collectivism: Comment on Oyserman et al. (2002). *Psychological Bulletin, 128*(1), 97–109.

Mishler, E. G. (1995). Models of narrative analysis: A typology. *Journal of Narrative and Life History, 5*(2), 87–123.

Overton, W. (1991). Competence, procedures, and hardware: Conceptual and empirical considerations. In M. Chandler & M. Chapman (Eds.), *Criteria for competence: Controversies in the conceptualization and assessment of children's abilities* (pp. 19–42). Mahwah, NJ: Lawrence Erlbaum Associates.

Oyserman, D., Coon, H., & Kemmelmeier, M. (2002). Rethinking individualism and Collectivism: Evaluation of theoretical assumptions and meta-analyses. *Psychological Bulletin, 128*(1), 3–72.

Parfit, D. (1971). Personal identity. *Philosophical Review, 80*(1), 3–27.

Pennebaker, J. W., & King, L. A. (1999). Linguistic styles: Language use as an individual difference. *Journal of Personality and Social Psychology, 77*(6), 1296–1312.

Polkinghorne, C. (1988). *Narrative knowing and the human sciences.* Albany: State University of New York Press.

Putnam, H. (1988). *Representation and reality.* Cambridge, MA: MIT Press.

Ricoeur, P. (1985). History as narrative and practice. *Philosophy Today, 29,* 213–222.

Ring, M. (1987). *Beginning with the pre-Socratics.* Mountain View, CA: Mayfield.

Sass, L. A. (1988). The Self and its vicissitudes: An "archeological" study of the psychoanalytic *avant-garde. Social Research, 55*(4), 551–607.

Schlesinger, A. (1977). The modern consciousness and the winged chariot. In B. Gorman & A. Wessman (Eds.), *The personal experience of time* (pp. 268–288). New York: Plenum.

Shalom, A. (1985). *The body-mind conceptual framework and the problem of personal identity.* Atlantic Highlands, NJ: Humanities Press International.

Shweder, R., & Bourne, E. J. (1982). Does the concept of the person vary cross-culturally? In A. J. Marsella & G. M. White (Eds.), *Cultural conceptions of mental health and therapy* (pp. 97–137). Boston, MA: D. Reidel.

Singelis, T. M. (1994). The measurement of independent and interdependent self-construals. *Personality and Social Psychology Bulletin, 20,* 580–591.

Spence, D. (1982). *Narrative truth and historical truth: Meaning and interpretation in psycho-analysis.* New York: W. W. Norton.

Strawson, G. (1999). Self and body: Self, body, and experience. *Supplement to the Proceedings of Aristotelian-Society, 73,* 307–332.

Taylor, C. (1975). *Hegel.* Cambridge, MA: Cambridge University Press.

Taylor, C. (1989). *Sources of the self.* Cambridge, MA: Harvard University Press.

Taylor, C. (1991). *The malaise of modernity.* Concord, ON, Canada: House of Anansi Press.

Taylor, C. (1992). *The ethics of authenticity.* Cambridge, MA: Harvard University Press.

Turiel, E. (2002). *The culture of morality: Social development, context, and conflict.* Cambridge, UK: Cambridge University Press.

Unger, R. (1975). *Knowledge and politics.* New York: Free Press.

Wildgen, W. (1994). *Process, image, and meaning: A realistic model of the meaning of sentences and narrative texts.* Philadelphia, PA: John Benjamins.

Wilkes, K. V. (1988). *Real people: Personal identity without thought experiments.* Oxford, UK: Clarendon Press.

Zagorin, P. (1999). History, the referent, and narrative: Reflections on postmodernism now. *History and Theory, 38,* 1–24.

Part IV

THE SOCIAL CONSTRUCTION OF SELF

Chapter 10

A Preface to the Epistemology of Identity[1]

Theodore R. Sarbin
University of California, Santa Cruz

I begin my chapter with a sketch of the evolution of my thinking about the concept of identity. It was in the early 1960s that I realized that the work on the concept of self (to which I had been a contributor [Sarbin, 1952]) seemed to have reached a dead end. Although many psychologists had accepted the idea of the social origins of selfhood, they were reluctant to give up their attachment to Cartesian mentalism. Rolf Kroger, Karl Scheibe, and I (1965) tried to make a fresh start by latching onto the concept of social identity. We prepared a working paper that featured a three-dimensional model of the transvaluation of social identity. Scheibe and I continued to develop the model and some years later published it as the centerpiece in a book that we edited under the title *Studies in Social Identity* (Sarbin & Scheibe, 1983). The titles of a few of the contributions suggest the direction of the work: The Victorian Governess: Status Incongruence in Family and Society; Loneliness and Social Identity; The Psychology of National Identity; Rebels and Sambos: The Search for the Negro's Personality in Slavery; The Self-Narrative in the Enactment of Roles; and A Metaphor for the Identity of Tragic Heroes. The contributors were not all psychologists, one was a specialist in Shakespeare, another a historian, another an anthropologist, still another an authority on Talmudic studies.

This was a period during which Erikson's seminal ideas (1963) were being further developed, mostly by psychologists working at the crossroads of

233

psychoanalysis and developmental psychology. The center of interest was identity formation in adolescence. Hypotheses about epistemology flowed from the mentalistic tradition with its universalistic and ahistorical ontological premises. Our approach was contextual, we prescribed no model course of identity development outside the contexts provided by local, social and cultural conditions.

Earlier work in ethnography (Linton, 1936) had made use of the categories: ascribed roles and achieved roles. We converted these categories into a "status" dimension with ascribed statuses at one end, and achieved statuses at the other. Locating (or positioning) an actor on this dimension, and on two other dimensions, valuation, and degree of involvement, provided the model for construing a social identity. The system worked quite well in illuminating the problems of social deviance, the reasons for the success or failure of institutionalized systems of conduct reorganization, the legitimization of aggression, the nature of group loyalty, the impact of total institutions, and the nature and consequences of social danger.

From this list of achievements, it is clear that our focus was on social psychological phenomena. Our model was a heuristic device to account for the contextual features of identity formation—a useful device for psychologists and other social scientists to formulate the identity of Others. In order to understand identity as a self-reflexive process, we had to look closer at a set of constructions that had not heretofore been studied in depth, namely, the narrative (or poetic) construction of world making, including the narrative (or poetic) construction of self-identity.

It is from the narrative perspective that I examine the epistemology of identity. The perspective suggests a journey with a starting point, a problematic passage, and a destination. For the present journey the destination is an understanding of how knowings and believings influence the construction of identity. A traveler who undertakes this journey is beset with many perils and uncertainties, not the least of which is the recognition that identity is not a name for a discrete point on a map. Rather the label "identity" can refer to a range of differentiated possibilities. The journey is beset with other potential difficulties in that the destination is a fiction—an indispensable fiction, to be sure—for which conventional time and space coordinates are nonexistent.

Social psychological writers have generally regarded identity as equivalent to social identity—how an actor positions himself or herself in the social ecology. The term *identity* is used in two ways: the first, self-identity—which can be likened to autobiography—is reflexive, the actor fashions a role for self from his or her believings and imaginings. For example, before embarking on his ill-fated Russian campaign, Napoleon looked eastward and declared "I am Charlemagne," at the moment metaphorically asserting his identity.

The second meaning can be likened to biography—constructing an identity of another person. We formulate the identity of our co-actors through attention to their expressive behavior, mode of speech, dress, facial features, and so on. Psychologists have been creative in developing technical devices the purpose of which is to describe the identity of a client or patient. The California Psychological Inventory, for example, provides the interpreter with a profile that serves as the basis for describing the identity of the test-taker. A user of the Rorschach test, similarly, composes an identity from the respondent's verbal responses. A psychoanalyst constructs an identity of an analysand from free associations, dream reports, and other cues given off during the therapy hour. These are all examples of methods employed to form an identity portrait of an Other. In this chapter I concentrate on self-identity, deferring until another time a discussion of the many theoretical issues connected with the identity formation of the Other.

Helpful in formulating the epistemology of identity is the ethological conception of *vigilance*. When an animal, human or other, registers inputs through vision, hearing, olfaction, and so on, it tries to match the inputs with available constructions. In the world of nature, the effort might be represented by the question: Is the stimulus event to be classified as benign or hostile? It is as if the animal were to ask the question "What is it?" and reflexively "What am I in relation to the stimulus event." Survival would depend on making the correct inference.

Using the concept of vigilance as a prototype, I define social identity as the locating or positioning of self in the social ecology. Social identity, then, is the composite of voiced and unvoiced answers to the implied question; "who am I?" made in the context of finding answers to the reciprocal question "who are you?" Following the implications of the vigilance model, formulating a response to the "who am I?" question must take into account the construction of the actor's answers to the implied "who are you?" question. That is to say, the answers are for the most part conditional on the social context Because we live in a story-shaped world, the implicit identity questions are reformulated as "in what story or stories am I taking part?"

In addition to living in a social ecology, we inhabit a moral ecology—a world of ethical codes, deportment standards, and moral rules. A person in the midst of a moral dilemma will engage in discourse (with self or others) that centers on constructing answers to the moral identity question, "what am I in relation to ethical codes?" usually phrased as "am I doing the right thing?"

We also inhabit a transcendental ecology—a world of abstractions, often but not exclusively religious terms and symbols. Examples of such constructed abstractions would include departed ancestors, deities, spiritual entities, and devils. A devout Christian, for example, in trying to understand the implications of the Easter story, would focus on seeking answers to such a transcendental identity question as "what am I in relation to the life and death of Jesus?"

A complete discourse on the epistemology of identity would incorporate the positioning of self in these ecologies as significant aspects of one's identity-building efforts. In this chapter, I focus on social identity, the positioning of self in the social ecology.

To understand how the believings and imaginings come together to fashion a social identity, the talented writers on self and identity began their conceptual work, sometimes unwittingly, from the perspective of grammar. To communicate about experience in which the grammatical units "I" and "me" were involved, James, Mead, Cooley, Baldwin, and Freud, among others, "substantiated" first person pronouns. They coined such unlikely constructions as "the I," "the me," "das Ich," "le moi," "the ego," and so forth. These constructions were created to illuminate the concept of self. More recently, discourse analysts have favored "identity" as a term to designate constructions emerging from the use of expressed or implied first person pronouns.

The "substantiating" pioneers of self and identity did not have available recent work on language processes, especially writings that demonstrated the influence of linguistic forms on epistemic actions. We now know, for example, that any substantive term is ambiguous or lacking in meaning in the absence of expressed or implied predicates. This observation is certainly relevant to first person pronouns. Uttering the pronouns "I" and "me" (without linguistic context) would be like offering bits and pieces of unformed metal in settings where established currency is the norm. The variability of the properties assigned to the pronoun "I" is illustrated in such simple sentences as "I hate snakes," "I am jealous," "I ordered him out," "I love her," "I am thirsty." In each sentence, the pronoun "I" takes on meaning from its associated predicate. Thus, the properties of the "I" of one sentence are not the same as those of the other sentences. The properties we would assign to "I" in the sentence "I am a servant of the Lord" would be radically different from the properties we would assign to "I" in the sentence "I love coconut crème pie," even if spoken by the same person. From these remarks, it would follow that identity is constantly recreated in discourse, both from the perspective of the actor (self-identity) and from the perspective of dialogue partners.

In my introductory remarks, I pointed to the problematic nature of the traveler's quest for identity as a singular destination. From the examples given so far, it is clear that identity is a protean construction, that the actor is many identities depending on ever changing social contexts. This observation flies in the face of the common usage of the term *identity* as reflecting a sense of permanence or self-continuity over time. The *Oxford English Dictio-*

nary shows that the root *ident* is the combining form for the Latin *idem* meaning "the same." The first of this dictionary's definitions is "the quality or condition of being the same in substance, composition, nature, properties, or in particular qualities under consideration; absolute or essential sameness, oneness." This construction is that of a continuous entity that is transcultural and persistent. In contrast, the protean construction of identity allows for change and novelty, the form and dimensions of which are products of participation in particular cultural settings.

Michael Chandler regards the two constructions as constituting a paradox (Chandler, 2000). Whatever contrarieties give substance to the notion of paradox, they are dissolved when we shift epistemological perspectives from *either/or* to *both/and*. The apparent permanence of identity constructions arises from the inescapable premise that identities are embodied, that a space-occupying body is the central reference for constructing inferences about identity. Although bodies do change as the result of maturation, diet, exercise, aging, and so on, it is indubitable that Peter's body today is essentially the same body that he remembers as the site for the development of various identities over the years. William James (1890) claimed that the corporeally experienced body is the persisting foundation for identity formation. When a person goes to bed at night as Peter, he does not awaken in the morning thinking that he is his twin brother Paul. His roles, values, and dispositions—aspects of identity—are certainly changeable but he still identifies his bodily location as the site for his participation in the varied activities that provide the basis for his life narrative.

We could assign the label "social identity" to the protean construction—the particular ways in which self-narratives are shaped by social determinants. This would include gender, occupational, kinship, and national identity, among other features. We could assign the label "human identity" to the construction that emphasizes persistence and continuity. An alternate way of resolving the paradox would be to define human identity as the (usually unvoiced) answers framed to the implied question: *what* am I? and social identity as the answers framed to the implied question: *who* am I? In a classroom exercise, for example, to the *What am I* question, a high school student wrote " I am an elaborate bit of protoplasm" In another place, he said "I am a body and a mind." To the *Who am I* question, he answered in the language of conventional social roles: "I'm a senior at Rawlings High School, the son of Ernest and Carrie Bledsoe, and shortstop on the varsity baseball team."

These observations suggest that identities are languaged, products of discourse. The knowings and believings that are assembled to fashion a self-identity arise in discourse, sometimes with imagined others, sometimes with actual others. The others, the discourse partners, are integral to the creating of an identity. The actor is expected to construe the identity of the

Other. For example, to observe the rules of politeness an actor must first establish the identity of the Other.

The development of a self-identity, then, takes place within a context of relationships. Immersed in a world of social relationships, we are at the same time immersed in a story-shaped world. Other people are actors in our everyday life dramas, some have central roles, others are bit players. The interactive nature of conduct provides referents for second person pronouns, implied answers to covertly voiced "who are you?" questions. At the same time the interactions create the conditions for self definitions, for answering the "who am I?" questions. Thus identity-building is necessarily, if unwittingly, a collaborative enterprise.

I resist the temptation to look for "cognitive variables" or for "developmental stages" to account for the discursive actions that are instrumental in self-identity formation. Rather, I see identity development as intimately tied to narrative. The metaphor "poetics of identity" better connotes the framework for identity development. I make the claim that the development of identity is a *storied* enterprise no less than the later telling about it is *storied*.

Narratives are fashioned from imaginings and from empirically derived constructions, such as, "facts." An ongoing problem is how to identify the social contexts that favor assigning credibility to the constructed imaginings The distinction made by the logic-of-science philosopher, Hans Reichenbach (1938), is informative. He wrote of the context of discovery and the context of confirmation. The construction of knowings in the context of confirmation is governed by rules and conventions; (acquiring the rules and conventions is of course related to one's experiences). In the context of discovery there are no rules. Therefore, a person (scientist or other) could construct hypotheses (imaginings) from authority, from idle daydreaming, from transient sensory inputs, from stories, from scientifically established theorems. Don Quixote is the paradigm case. Exemplifying the context of discovery, he fashioned a self-identity from imaginings stimulated by tales of chivalry. He failed to employ the context of confirmation, a condition that provided humor and pathos for the reader of the novel.

A constant dialectic is ongoing between imaginings and believings. The believings help to screen the kinds of information that serve as the inputs that stimulate imaginings; imaginings become the raw materials for story-shaped believings. Note my use of gerunds rather than the traditional nominative forms. The nouns "belief" and "imagination" facilitate the construction of cranial objects; the gerunds, "believings" and "imaginings" facilitate the construction of actions, of doings, of shaping life narratives.

To make concrete the claim that identities are the products of poesis—the practice of assembling bits and pieces of experience to form a story—I offer a brief synopsis of an autobiographical account taken from an anthology (Pellegrini & Sarbin, 2002). This anthology demonstrates the poetics of identity for 17 authors. Each fashioned a narrative of a critical father/son episode that had lasting effects on his social and moral identities. The poetics of identity involves the framing of one's efforts to locate one's self intelligibly in some storied context. Such framings are influenced by the library of stories one has acquired from books, orally told accounts, pictured portrayals, fantasies of cultural heroes—all acquired from family or cultural sources, the individual putting idiosyncratic touches on any particular formulaic story (Sarbin, 1986).

The anthology contains father-and-son incidents that were critical in forging a *self identity*. These narratives explicitly or implicitly center on events serving to answer the ever-present identity question that takes the form, as mentioned before, of *"who am I?"* and by extension *"who am I to be?"*

The memoir contributed by Julian Rappaport, a distinguished professor of community psychology, may be taken as an example of the poetic construction of identity. His response to a traumatic event at age 10 was pivotal in the development of his self-identity. With two playmates, he was playing a game in the breezeway of the housing project in which the participants lived. Each would toss a baseball card against a brick wall, the player who threw the card closest to the wall was the winner and would keep all the cards thrown on that particular play. Barry, one of the playmates, tossed a treasured hard-to-get card of a famous pitcher. On this occasion Julian's card was the winner. As he ran to the wall to gather up his winnings, he was accosted by Barry's father who demanded the valued card. Julian refused. Barry's father struck Julian with a baseball bat and forcibly took the card. Julian ran home and reported the incident to his stepfather who, predictably, refused to take any action. That night Julian resolved that he would have to take care of himself because he could not count on others. He decided he would be like his father who had died about 6 years before. His mother had told him that he looked like his father. Julian remembered little of his deceased father but transformed disconnected scraps of information into a story. Someone had mentioned that his father liked to read books. With very little in the way of concrete facts, he poetically constructed a portrait of his father as an intellectual. He decided to use his construction of his father as a model. He abandoned the common practice of collecting baseball cards and forsook playing in the breezeway. Instead, he frequented the public library where he read books of all kinds. In addition to creating a portrait of his father as an intellectual, he formed a physical image. From knowledge that his father as a young man had shoveled coal in the boiler room of a merchant marine vessel, Julian fashioned a fantasy of strength and stamina, replete with bulging muscles. The latter image helped to make more vivid the imagined presence of his father. The imaginings of his father both as an intellectual and as a physical being were poetic constructions that became part of a sacred story. In one dramatic moment, he forged an identity for himself modeled after the imagined story of his deceased father. The centrality and the long term influence of this poetic construction qualifies as a major force in his identity development.

To be sure, not every person can tell such an explicit story. Others tell of identity-shaping influences that are less dramatic. With constant exposure to stories, from bedtime tales to television drama to urban legends, children (and adults, I might add) are constantly immersed in stories, some of which may serve as guides to forming a self-identity.

I close with a bit of information that provides a kind of historical warrant for my claim that narrative is the appropriate root metaphor to guide explorations into the epistemology of identity. Our modern words "knowing" and "narrating" have a common etymological ancestry. Both can be traced to a common root—the Sanscrit *gna*. Somewhere along the line, two lexical forms emerged, "knowing"—to denote a private form of poesis, and "narrating"—to denote a public form.

ENDNOTE

[1] I am indebted to Ralph Carney and Gerald Ginsburg for their critical reading of an earlier draft. This chapter is revised from a paper read at the 30th annual meeting of the Piaget Society, Montreal, Canada, June, 1999.

REFERENCES

Chandler, M. (2000). Surviving time: The persistence of identity in this culture and that. *Culture and Psychology, 6*, 220–240.

Erikson, E. (1963). *Childhood and society.* New York: W. W. Norton.

James, W. (1890). *Principles of psychology.* New York: Holt.

Linton, R. (1936). *The study of man.* New York: Appleton Century.

Pellegrini, R., & Sarbin, T. R. (Eds.). (2002). *Between fathers and sons: Critical incident narratives in men's lives.* Binghamton, NY: Haworth Press.

Reichenbach, H. (1938). *Experience and prediction.* Chicago: University of Chicago Press.

Sarbin, T. R. (1952). A preface to the psychological analysis of the self. *Psychological Review, 59*, 11–21.

Sarbin, T. R. (Ed.). (1986). *Narrative psychology: The storied nature of human action.* London: Sage.

Sarbin, T. R., Scheibe, K. E., & Kroger, R. O. (1965). *The transvaluation of identity.* (Unpublished working paper).

Sarbin, T. R., & Scheibe, K. E. (Eds.). (1983). *Studies in social identity.* New York: Praeger.

Chapter **11**

The Social Construction of Persons

Rom Harré

INTRODUCTION

To see human development aright one must already have an account of the product, the mature human being. It is depressing to see how much of the spirit of behaviourism lingers on into an era that pays lip service to cognitive psychology as its working paradigm. For someone like myself, with a background in the physical sciences, the behaviourist legacy is visible in mistaken ideas about the physical sciences as ideal types to emulate, together with a persistent positivistic empiricism that vitiates a great deal of expensive and time consuming research.

To put the matter bluntly: science is impossible without metaphysics. Main stream psychology in North America is laden with implicit metaphysics of a very unsatisfactory kind. We must let our metaphysical presuppositions be explicit, examined and their consequences drawn out.

The many streams of dissent[1] that are converging on a new paradigm are animated by a common metaphysical presupposition: *that in normal circumstances human beings are active agents*. The general methodological principle that inspires my attitude to the theory of human development, is that whatever we have to say about the processes of maturation must be consistent with the new paradigm conception of the person as actively engaged with others, real and imaginary, in the joint production of the stream of life. Our point of view must be social and dynamic.

241

The shift in emphasis can be seen very clearly when we reflect on the difference between the role of our understanding of neural mechanisms and processes in the two paradigms. If we are still thinking in terms of human action as responses to stimuli then the neural mechanisms become mediating processes, and the concept of "person" is made redundant. If we think in terms of active agents performing tasks then the neural mechanisms become tools that the agent makes use of in performing the tasks that local circumstances might require. In this paradigm the concept of "person" is preserved, and so most of our moral intuitions and legal demands are maintained. We can also understand how engineers can create prosthetic devices, such as palm top organizers, that we can use to do some of the jobs that we used to use our brains for.

DISCOURSE AND ACTION

The turn toward discourse as the major focus of psychological research opens up some intriguing dimensions, not least that the techniques of analysis should be turned on the discourses of psychology itself. It is, after all, a cluster of human practices, and ought to be subject to the same kind of scrutiny in search of some understanding of the projects, rules, meanings and intentions discernible in this form of life.

The general framework of the new style psychology, in its many varieties, does seem to include the idea that psychological phenomena, such as remembering, deciding, reasoning, classifying, and psychological attributes ascribed to individuals in the old scheme, such as self-esteem, are one and all aspects or properties of the flow of joint action produced by the relatively skilled performances of the human actors involved. Discourse, perhaps more tightly specified as "conversation," becomes both an empirical concept, and a metaphor for analyzing other uses of symbols than the verbal. Individuals have skills, and use them to jointly create psychological phenomena. Among the products of skillful action are persons, created and maintained discursively.

THREE GRAMMARS

The management of life within systems of norms, conventions, customs, rules, and skills, can be concretely imagined for our purposes by metaphorically extending the notion of rule-following as a device for expressing standards of correctness in every domain. This technique must be used with discretion because we do not want to fall into the mistake of mainstream cognitive psychology of re-inventing the Cartesian mind by inserting a domain of cognitive processes between managed action and the neural processes by which it is realized. To talk of tacit rule-following can only be a metaphor that supports the methodological technique of writing down one's hypotheses about the relevant norms, customs and conventions as systems of rules. With this caveat in mind we can turn to Wittgenstein for another metaphor, his use of the concept of a "grammar."

The root metaphysical presupposition of every science is its conception of the fundamental agents that power the dynamic flow of events in its domain. It is convenient to identify distinct grammars by reference to the categories of agents that each presupposes. It seems to me that human beings in the third millennium in the part of the world we inhabit manage their lives within three main discursive frames, or grammars.

There is the discourse of popular chemistry with its commitment to a domain of molecules. Allergies, food fads, red wine drinking, medication, environmental pollution, and so on are conceived and where people are actively engaged, they are managed by a discourse constrained by a molecular or M-grammar. People happily talk about "free radicals" and "flavonoids." Women study the oestrogen content of contraceptive pills. The term *pheromone* is catching on, and so on.

Then there is the organismic or O-grammar of popular biology and medicine, in which the active entities are organisms. If we follow such popular figures as Desmond Morris and E. O. Wilson this grammar would dominate our self-reflective discourses as human beings. This grammar is becoming pervasive in the popular press, for example.

There is a third grammar which the best efforts of biochemists, dieticians, behaviourists, and sociobiologists has not yet dislodged. This is to be seen in many of discursive genres of everyday life in the Western world. It dominates the law courts, for instance. It is still the root of popular morality, although that is under assault from the medical model that rewrites moral failings as illnesses or genetic malfunctions. This is the person or P-grammar grounded in the presupposition that the basic active entities of human life are persons. Any debate in the courts about the degree of responsibility the accused might have for his or her actions must juxtapose the P-grammar with one or other of the alternatives, M or O. Even such a simple act as asking someone what they meant by what they said presupposes the P-grammar. Only persons are managers of intentionality.

By the use of the P-grammar we can create discourses and other flows of symbolic actions that display intentionality, that is are meaningful to ourselves and others, actions we could revive the word *conduct* to describe. At the same time an implication of this way of construing human activity is that everything we do can, if the circumstances demand it, be subject to assessment as correct or incorrect, proper or improper, elegant or clumsy, and so on. These dichotomous phrases express norms. The term *norm* is used to refer to ideal forms in psychology but it may be used in sociology to refer to what is usual or normal. This ambiguity ought at least to be noticed.

PERSONHOOD: THE P-GRAMMAR IN DETAIL

Although everywhere the human organism is very much the same—and O-grammars are universally applicable—persons are culturally and historically diverse. The P-grammar, in which person figures as the ultimate the activity of which is taken as primitive, must also be diverse.

One useful device with which to study the P-grammar is to pay attention to personal pronouns. First and second person pronouns are sensitive to fine shades of cultural difference, whereas third person are less so. For instance everyone is aware of the difference between the English "you" and the French (and other language) informal and formal second person, *tu* and *vous*.

However to set this discussion in motion we must first sketch, however roughly, the outlines of the grammar of two other expressions, one of which is available only to English speakers, the words *person* and *self. Moi même* or *mi mismo* do other work, more or less similar to the role of "myself." "Person" has always had a flavour of a being that is visibly public, from its roots in the Latin *persona*, a mask. The mask is displayed to others. I have suggested that we can simplify the grammars of the cluster of "person" and "self" usages by adopting a standard model expressed in the little schema:

$$P = \{S_1, S_2, S_3\}$$

where S_1, S_2 and S_3 stand for three major uses of the word *self* in English.

The use I have labelled "S_1" is the device we use to identify the spatio-temporal singularity we identify as the abstract core of our personal identity. This is the sort of usage in which one talks of "the self—the core of one's being." Each person is a self in that sense. It is necessarily implicated with consciousness because each person is centered as a singularity in a field of perceived things and remembered events.

By S_2 I mean the total set of attributes of some individual person. This does not usually include bodily attributes like height or weight, skin or eye color and so on. The self in this sense is complex, because it must include not only the attributes I actually have but also those I believe I have. These may be and usually are different. The beliefs I have about myself are also attributes of myself, that is of myself as a person. Some are occurrent, fully realized at the time at which the attribution is made. Others are dispositional, manifested only on certain occasions and under certain circumstances. S_2 is rendered yet more complex by the fact that both the actual attributes of a person and that person's beliefs about their attributes are in flux, some changing more rapidly than others. Although there are some additions to the totality, there are also some losses.

A third sense of self has been popularized recently, partly from the usage by Erving Goffman (1964), for the public manifestation of certain of my personal attributes, myself as I present myself to others. This includes my personality of the moment, agreeable, amusing, erudite, and good-natured for example. Other personalities are no doubt available for other persons and other occasions. It also includes displays of character, such as fortitude, honesty, and so on, qualities that have a moral tinge.

S_1 is largely immune from cultural influences because it is a feature of human embodiment. Generally speaking it is singular. S_3 is largely a social product being produced with and for others, and necessarily making use of a publicly recognizable repertoire of conventional forms of display. Generally speaking it is multiple. Almost everyone has a repertoire of personas with which to display personality and character appropriate to the situation in which the display is called for.

The question of the multiplicity and variability of Self$_2$ has been much discussed recently, usually in a way which suggests a deep confusion between this sense of self and the two other major uses I have highlighted. Each person has aspects of self which are invariant, such as singular embodiment and one field of consciousness, and aspects which are unstable and variable, such as one's beliefs about oneself. Couple this with the relativity of displays of selfhood and even of capacities to remember certain events in one's life to situations and the possibilities of confusion and bad analyses multiply.

Much of this analysis can be found in the writings of William James. I do not find much room myself for his "spiritual self," but it is evident in a fourth grammar, the S- or Soul-grammar with which many people still organize their lives and their discourses.

THE EXPRESSION OF PERSONHOOD

How is the unity and singularity of personhood as it is in our cluster of cultures expressed? Phenomenologists have studied how it is experienced, but how their intuitions could be shared by others is not obvious. Among Wittgenstein's most profound investigations concerned the grammar of the words we use to express our personal feelings, our bodily states one to another. He distinguished carefully between expressing my feelings and describing yours. The constructionist account of personhood deals with the same issue in respect of the personal experience of personal unity and continuity and the means for its public expression. In experiencing myself as a singular being I am not inwardly studying an entity, my self. There is no such entity—there are only persons. My sense of unity and continuity is grounded in the shape of the fields of perception and action. I experience myself as located in space among other beings, and as continuous in time, that is have the power to recollect my past and to foresee my future. My singularity of personhood cannot be constituted by memories and forecasts because it is that very person the existence and integrity of whom is presupposed in the possibility of taking some experiences as memories and others as daydreams and yet others as forecasts, hopes and so on. As Wittgenstein might have put it personhood is part of the frame, presupposed in all that I think, feel and do, not part of the picture, that is not part of what I think, feel and do.

How is this aspect of the frame of my life expressed? Surely by such grammatical devices as proper names, pronouns and other referring expressions. The intimate relationship between the first person pronouns and the sense of self as a continuing unity and singularity suggests that it is to that topic that the psychologist must turn. The forms of experience are to be found in the forms of their expression.

Wittgenstein (1953), in one of his most powerful paragraphs, sketched in a few words a fundamental account of how expressive devices are learned. Using the example of the word *pain* he pointed out that a child could never acquire this word directly as a name for a sensation by pointing to an exemplar as neither the child nor its caretaker could display the bad feeling in public space to be attended to by both. Learning the use of the word *pain* must be quite different from learning the use of the word *sheep* or *spoon*. Wittgenstein's insight arose from his realizing that there were natural expressions of major psychological states, such as being in pain, that were part of the ethology of human kind. A child learns the word *pain* as an alterative form of expression, replacing weeping or groaning or rubbing the spot. Thus that use of the word falls under the same "grammar" as the natural expression. In particular there is no gap between the feeling and the expression because if there was no tendency to express oneself this way it would not be that feeling.

My thesis is that the expression of the singularity of personhood follows the very same pattern. Natural expressions of a sense of self such as reaching for something from where one is and similar acts are replaced by words, such as "I want …" or "Gimme …." These have just the same expressive function as the reaching and fall under the same grammar. They are not descriptions of a singularity other than the point of view from which the embodied person acts. In particular they do not denote Cartesian egos, residing somehow in concordance with the singular body. There are just embodied persons. So we must now turn to examine the grammar of first person pronouns and other similarly expressive grammatical devices like the inflections of the verbs of romance languages.

THE GRAMMAR OF SOME PERSONAL PRONOUNS

Using the principle that there are expressive devices by which basic psychological features of human cognition are presented publicly and which are integrally bound into a unity with what they express, a principle derived from Wittgenstein's Private Language Argument, we pay very close attention to the use of personal pronouns (Mühlhäusler & Harré, 1992).

One must begin by making a fundamental distinction between two classes of pronouns, the anaphoric and the indexical. Anaphoric pronouns do indeed, in a straightforward sense, stand for names or pronouns. They are used to maintain an external reference for a discourse without repeating over and over again the relevant proper name or definite description. This is the characteristic role of the third person. "The President took his golf club and he smote the ball mightily. It fell into the rough and he was annoyed with himself." The personal "he's" and the "it" that carries through the reference to the ball maintain the external reference or denotation of the subjects of the sentences and clauses that lay out the story. Whatever the original proper name or referring expression points to is also the referent of the successive anaphoric pronouns.

However, the first and second person "pronouns" are not functioning pro-nouns, nor are they any kind of proper name, though persons are their domain. To see the role of indexicals in general it is helpful to look at the grammar of a nonpersonal indexical "now" or "here." How do we know which spot in space is being referred by the word *here*? We have to know where the speaker was located at the moment of speaking to know. Thus the word *here* indexes what is said with a place very near the speaker, just as the word *now* indexes the content of the speaker's utterance with the moment at which it was uttered. Thus "Put it here" indexes the command with a place near the speaker, whereas "Do it now" does the same for the time aspects of the content of the command and the moment of its utterance, that is that the obeying should be simultaneous with the utterance or nearly so. "I" and "me" index the content of what is said as this speaker's. It might be location in space and time as an embodied being. It might be the social force of what is said with the moral or social standing of the speaker, and so on. "I" does not refer to the speaker since it is not a referring expression at all. So "I need the pencil as soon as possible" indexes the need with a place in space and time, namely the location of the speaker's body. And "I'll take up the collection" indexes the social force of the promise with the speaker's moral standing and reliability. If that is not generally thought to be up to scratch someone may say, "No, I'll do it."

"You" behaves in a similar fashion for the addressee. Not so long ago there was a choice between "thee" and "you," "thine" and "yours." These alternatives have survived in various forms in other European languages, in the general T/V distinction. T/T discourse is informal and/or intimate whereas V/V discourse is formal or remote. V/T is condescending whereas T/V is deferential.

With both varieties of indexical pronouns the word does a certain kind of work, indexing the content of what is said with aspects of the speaker or addressee. Some of these are spatio-temporal, some are moral and some are expressive of relative social standing. In neither person do indexical pronouns refer to anything substantial and invisible, any more than "here" and "now" refer to abstract places or moments at which the speaker or addressee happens to be located. These places and times are always relative to one who is speaking or being addressed. We could not tell someone to go and stand "here" over the phone nor could we tell someone to start singing tomorrow at "now."

THE SOURCES OF PERSONS

Do persons just emerge naturally from the organic soup of the biosphere? Not so. They are artifacts, manufactured according to certain patterns and principles by other people. They are as much products as books or video-recorders or garden tools. They come in standard and deluxe versions. And, like any other class of manufactured goods, there are factory rejects. Generally speaking, families are the main people factories. There are many customizing services on offer, to give a special character to otherwise standard models.

This may sound like a playful metaphor but I mean it rather seriously. I believe that only when we begin to see individual human development in this light will the fundamental processes become visible. The "manufacturing" trope is a powerful analytical model, an analogue that makes visible much that has been overlooked. If the sort of selves we are manufactured to be are brought about in the processes of learning to make the Wittgenstein switch from natural expression of singularity of personhood to verbal expressions we must ask how this learning is accomplished. This takes us to the work of Vygotsky, and also, most importantly, William Stern, the originator of the personalist point of view in psychology.

The wealth of insights to be found in the writings of Vygotsky (1968) are surely very well known by now. I want to highlight one such insight only, and to elaborate it along dimensions of my own. The developmental process as Vygotsky understands it, is rooted in a phenomenon he calls "being in the zone of proximal development." A skill at that stage, is not fully mastered by the learner, who makes inadequate efforts at performances. The teacher, adult, sibling or whosoever is at hand completes the actions of the learner, along the lines that the teacher thinks the learner is striving. The learner then imitates the contribution of the teacher, and at the same time, more definitively settles what it is he or she was trying to do. For various reasons I prefer to call this developmental process *psychological symbiosis*. A task is fully developed only in the mature world, is completed by an infant, for example, by the supplements provided by the other. The work is done by neither, but by the dyad, which becomes the active psychological agent, responsible for the shaping and execution of the task.

So far so good. This is all orthodox Vygotsky with a slight change in terminology. But let us peer into the nursery, the workshop, the kitchen, and so on where dyads are engaged in projects and achieving them through psychological symbiosis. We will surely soon become aware of an asymmetry. In each dyad there is a junior and a senior member. These are positions in the terminology of Positioning Theory. They exist as clusters of rights and duties. Both junior and senior members of a Vygotskian dyad are locked into a local moral order via the positions they soon come to occupy. The junior member has a right to proper and appropriate supplements from the senior and a duty to respect the senior member's expertise. Reciprocally the senior member has a duty to provide the supplements as they are required in the proper form, or by describing them or both, and a right to be obeyed without protest or innovation. To understand the Vygotskian picture of development we need to combine a analysis of the components of a skilled performance and how they are redistributed between junior and senior member of a dyad as time goes by with an analysis of the relevant positions which endow the symbiotic partners with sufficient social dynamics to push through the project of acquiring a skill.

Although Vygotsky did not say so, it is evident to everyone who reads *Thought and Language* that the phenomena we have been describing can occur at any time of life. All that is required is a disparity in degree of expertise between the partners in a dyad, and a local moral order that facilitates the transfer of skills through psychological symbiosis. Goffman describes some striking cases in his essay Face work in *Interaction Ritual* (Goffman, 1964). Those who are seen by others and by themselves as forming a group may provide supplements to complete a performance by one of the members that is inadequate by local standards. Goffman sees this somewhat cynically as falling under the rubric "We must improve this fellows performance, otherwise we will be seen as the sort of people who hang around with this socially incompetent wretch."

CONCLUSION

We now have the materials to draw together a comprehensive account of what it might mean to insist on the thesis that selves are socially constructed. Patently one must learn the repertoire of public presentations that are proper in one's local milieu. Less obviously, but clearly emerging from Wittgenstein's account of the expressive aspect of language and other symbolic systems in displaying one's inner life in public, there is the role of pronoun systems in this expressive activity in so far as it concerns personhood.

It is the singularity of self that is expressed with these means. Each of us is located at a singularity in space and time, as an embodied being. Thus we have good reason to think that both S_1 and S_3 are "selves" that are made publicly visible through discursive activities, by means of which they are literally constructed, that is manufactured in joint action. S_2, the totality of our attributes, including among those attributes our beliefs about our attributes, in so far as such psychological phenomena as memories are involved, are also socially constructed. The distinction between memory and fantasy is a socially inculcated distinction, not evident in the phenomenology of reflection on one's mind's deliverances. With Vygotskian psychological symbiosis as our generic developmental point of view we can see how these aspects of personhood could be the products of a kind of industrialisation, the production of the right kind of people for the task of carrying on the life of our village.

ENDNOTE

[1] I have in mind discursive psychology, cultural psychology, social constructionism in so far as it falls short of postmodern excesses, and so on.

REFERENCES

Goffman, E. (1964). *Interaction ritual*. Harmondsworth, UK: Penguin Books.
Mülhäusler, R., & Harré, R. (1992). *Pronouns and people*. Oxford, UK: Blackwell.
Vygotsky, L. S. (1968). *Thought and language*. Cambridge, MA: MIT Press.
Wittgenstein, L. (1953). *Philosophical investigations*. Oxford, UK: Blackwell.

Chapter 12

Improvisatory Accident-Prone Dramas of (What Passes for) a Person's Life

Amélie Oksenberg Rorty
Yale University

A colleague of mine—let's call her Zoe—recently retired. She had just become a grandmother, and the department decided to celebrate the two events with a party in her honor, to be held late in the afternoon on the last day of term, just after all the grades had been sent to the Registrar. Only minutes before the celebration was to begin, Zoe finished making the last supportive and encouraging comments on her students' barely literate, hastily manufactured papers. After the first two rounds of drinks and cheddar cheese bits, the rituals of such occasions began: appreciative, flattering speeches and jokes were made; toasts to her future joys of grandmothering were offered; gifts—flowers for her, toys for her grandchild—were proffered. In truth, Zoe was a grim, crotchety, lantern-jawed codger who had never minced words, speaking her mind ever since she began talking at 15 months ... and continuing to do so without stop ever since. Although her colleagues knew that she matched W.C. Fields in her animus against children, they cooed and gurgled at the great delights of grandparenting. Instead of accepting all this with the grace and gratitude customary to such occasions, Zoe flew into a rage. She called her colleagues hypocrites for pretending that she had been an affably cooperative companion and for projecting a detestable vision of her future. With some embarrassment,

251

everyone said their good-byes, wished her well and went off to supervise their children's Little League games. The story quickly became the focus of much discussion. It entered departmental lore and everyone, even new-comers who had never met Zoe, had their own plausible theory—some called it a narrative—to explain Zoe's behavior. Some thought that Zoe's origins—her being the tenth child of a devoutly Catholic Haitian family—featured in her reactions. Others thought that although her origins—and her experience of the prejudices commonly directed to Haitian immi-grants—were deeply formative, they played virtually no significant part in the events of the party.

Taking Zoe to represent Anyone and Everyone, what does her story tell us about understanding individual persons, their characteristic thoughts and traits, their life histories? What does it tell us about the identities of per-sons and theories of the mind?

By way of locating the parameters of an interpretation of the philosophic and psychological significance of Zoe's story, I would like to summarize their heuristic directions. I must perforce present them informally, crypti-cally, and dogmatically. Certainly they are contestable; certainly they need elaboration; certainly they require justification. I hope you will forgive my continuing to speak anecdotally rather than scientifically or technically. Al-though these reflections are speculative, ungrounded in any experimental basis, they are intended to be empirical, in the larger and original sense of that term, as it invites anyone's and everyone's confirming reflection on their experience.

The moral of Zoe's story seems to be that at any given time, a robust explanation of a person's mentality—the pattern of her salient percep-tions and motives, emotional responses, configuration of habits—re-flects complex interactions among many independent parameters. As a culture is a battleground of competing forces whose relative powers are in dynamic imbalance, so is the self an attenuated field of dramatic ac-tion, counteraction, revolution. Neither cultures nor persons are, in any proper sense of the term, *basic metaphysical entities*. "A" culture has no def-inite boundaries: there are invasions, trade routes, exiles, immigrants. Similarly "a" person—even an embodied person—is not a self-sustain-ing organism, let alone a well-formed, well-narrated organism. Physi-cally, it is a loose collection of organs that sometimes collaborate, sometimes fail. Each claims dominance, and accidentally sometimes suc-ceeds in getting primary focus, as circumstances—food supplies, noise, bombs, hate and love—allow. Psychologically, a person is a loose collec-tion relatively independent, multilayered dispositions and habits, some "hard-wired," others acquired from a diversity of sources and occasions.[1] Different personae, different aspects of "the" self emerge as dominant as situations call them forth.

To explain Zoe's reactions, to understand what is salient to her, we need to know something about:

1. her body, her constitutionally based but interactively, dynamically changing physiology;
2. her historically, politically, and subculturally based characterological dispositions, often at odds with one another;
3. the contingencies of her personal experiences;
4. the accidental vicissitudes of her present situation, and
5. a set of paired, counter-poised cyclically alternating traits that form a loosely self-regulating homeostatic system.

To give flesh to these bare bones, let's examine our explanatory parameters one by one.

1. Zoe's outburst expressed one among a set of relatively enduring lifelong character traits, some of which have a strong organic base: It seems her irascibility is associated with a severe hormonal imbalance. What is (in the medical textbooks of her culture) classified as a constitutional disorder has recently been magnified by her going on an all-protein diet of genetically altered beef.

The full account of a person's mentality—the salient features that govern and explain her interpretations of situations, her actions and reactions, perhaps her proprioceptive sense of herself—includes a comprehensive profile of her physical constitution and the vicissitudes of its present condition. Subculturally variable as they may be, many psychological attitudes reflect physiological changes: the hormonal changes of "adolescence" bring new patterns of attentional salience. Similarly, childbearing and childrearing—and also significantly many occupations (those of coal miners, deep sea divers, computer programmers, airline attendants) bring physical changes and specializations as well as characteristic interests and preoccupations. A person's work affects circulation, muscular tension or atrophy, sleep patterns, exercise, diet. Although these of course do not directly affect the substantive details of perception, affect, motivation and cognition, they do set directions of presumptive salience. As individuals experience such socially charged physical changes, the range of their typical experiences change, and vice versa. Although these do not determine a person's interpretations of—and reactions to—events, they do set salient "in your face" constraints on experience. You do not have to be disabled or very old to know that body interactive affects psychology. Being an infant, short, pregnant, or (what in our culture is considered) overweight is enough. Although such psycho–physical conditions provide an essential explanatory feature of mentality and behavior, they fall outside our primary concerns. Let's bracket them in our discussion.

2. Zoe's response occurred within a specific highly structured event, a liminal ritual with stereotypic scripts, encoded for numerous subcultures of American academic institutions, for age and gender and even for field. (A retirement party for an MIT physicists differs dramatically from one for an anthropologist at St. Aloysius College in El Rancho, Texas.) The staging of the retirement event—the speeches, the gifts of flowers, and toys—express Zoe's colleagues' stereotypic assumptions about age- and role-based stages of development and patterns of gender interests. Those assumptions were so deeply embedded in their practices that they blocked nearly everything Zoe's colleagues knew about her individual character and tastes. Would they have given flowers and toys to Abe, whose temper and tastes were similar to Zoe? And if not, would the event and its aftermath have the same sorts of consequences?

By now, we have a rich anthropological literature on differences in the ways that cultures model stages in the lifespan. Novels give us rich descriptions of the further subcultural fragmentation and differentiation: Balzac and Zola give us finely articulated descriptions of the differences between the mentality of the haute bourgeoisie of Paris that privileges and molds *une femme comme il faut* and *un pere de famille* and the mentality of a Provencal peasant or a factory worker in Alsace. Jane Austen, Trollope and D'Israeli chronicle the finely attuned contrast between the ideal types projected by Anglican parishioners in rural England and those marked by the political aristocracy of London society. Dreiser and Edith Wharton attest to the differences between the mentality of upwardly mobile youth and that of conservative Manhattan high society. Marxists have traced even more finely refined class-differentiation within such subcultures: some have argued that a consumer dependent economy propels adolescent—if not actually infantile—salient patterns of attitudes and habits. Feminist theory and sociology add gender significant subscripts to socially and economically differentiated subcultures; and both role and personality theories distinguish yet further relevant differences. With these manifold subcultural additions, and the realization that any individual is constituted by a wide array of distinctive "identity markers," the attempt to characterize a person's mentality—the characteristic patterns of perceptual, cognitive, emotional, motivational salience—has no shortcuts. A finely articulated list of the character-forming "identity markers" that might be relevant to a robust explanation of a person's behavior—a list that would include Zoe's being a Haitian immigrant, the tenth child of a devout Catholic school teacher, and an inconsolable widow—is mind-boggling long.

Zoe acquired many of her identity markers through the sheer contingencies of her individual experience: her commitment to a certain style of generous teaching began derived largely from the influence of a devoted faculty member in her undergraduate college. Zoe was well on her way to becoming an airline hostess when her English professor invited her to be a teaching assistant. As it happens, that invitation—and its subsequent dramatic consequences—was quite accidental. The professor had intended to extend the offer to another student, who—as luck would have it—was absent on the last day the selection had to be made. To be sure, some identity markers are under voluntary control, but many are not. And of those that can be deliberately chosen and cultivated, many can only be altered by changing other interconnected traits. Some alterations have wide-ranging ramified consequences, others have very little effect. Out of such contingencies are identities formed; out of such accidental occurrences do the multifaceted mess that we, in this time, in this place, are wont to call "the self."

Americans tend to treat the active capacity for choice, for voluntary self-construction as a developmental advance. To most Europeans, such first person pronouncements are active only as an exercise in self-deceptive illusion, made all the more glaring when they are also sparked by an earnest sensitivity to the dialogical, interactive character of "self"-construction. Such historically, strongly politically/ideologically charged theories/narrations reveal more about the conventional language of self-ascription and self-description than they do about a person's experience. They may—or may not—coincide with what an astute observer sees about us; and they may—or may not—coincide with what we ourselves inarticulately feel about the profound constraints on self-imagery.

There are even more accidents in the improvisatory drama that is a so-called person's so-called life. The configuration of dominance and recessiveness of "identity markers" varies with those of other parameters. As if this were not enough, the pattern of Zoe's actions and reactions also reflects her hypersensitive perception of the contingent reactions of her fellows. The focus and language of self-description—the prominence of this or that identity marker—varies with context and audience. Identities we have wholesale; and when a person's psychological economy is in jeopardy, they come with a generous discount.

And of course all this zooms by faster than the eye can blink or the tongue can wag when we respond to the subtle responses of our fellows in our multiple gossip groups, modifying our thoughts, perceptions, reactions en route. Hegel taught us to see the power of the powerless, to see that the power relation—mutually constraining as it is—is a moment in a dynamic dialectic that can (in principle) move toward civic life ... although rarely in the course of an individual's life-time. Call this action if you wish; call it reaction if you prefer; call it socialization or social construction if you will; call it role negotiation if you prefer. In each case, what matters—and it matters greatly, because classification affects mentality—is that we specify the perspective and effects of each classification. That having been done, explanations are not arbitrary. We are not hostage to the ill-fortunes induced by carefree of postmodernism.

3. Zoe's action emerges from the dialogical collision of multiple modes of thought. In all innocence, Zoe's colleagues enacted their assumptions about the mentality of a newly retired grandmother. Similarly acting in character, Zoe reacted against being cast in what she experienced as a set of painfully inappropriate roles. To understand Zoe's temper tantrum, we must take into account the active—the reactive—interaction between the vast array of Zoe's own "identity markers" and the stereotypes projected by her colleagues.

Zoe's colleagues acted on the basis of an implicit normative theory, one that projects a set of age or stage-related ideal types, configured as narrative trajectory of a lifespan. As they simplify it, the ideal type of each stage is characterized by a mentality, by patterns of salient perceptions and concepts, a field of emotions, moral attitudes and motives. Each stage (infancy, childhood, adolescence, early middle, and late maturity [sic!]) has its formative conflicts, and optimal strategies for their resolution. Peak maturity is characterized as stable and generative; the gradual movement to geriatric age has its own preoccupations, its idealized strengths and foibles. The severity of this latently teleological pattern is typically softened by characterizing the strengths and weaknesses—the virtues and vulnerabilities—of each stage. Such coercive stereotyping may be softened, but it remains normative. Truth be told, Zoe experiences the assumptions of her colleagues' age and stage stereotypes as constricting and coercive. She resents the fact that by their standards, her character is seen as deviant or defective: "an infantile personality," "frozen in adolescence."

In truth there is no clear correlation—and certainly no isomorphism— between the trajectory of projected life stages and the dramatic vicissitudes and vagaries of attitudinal changes. It is not unusual—nor is it precocious— for a 10-year-old to express the insights and carry the gravity of a 50-year-old or to experience the losses and nostalgia of a 60- year-old. A 47-year-old quite reasonably frequently has the moods, perceptions, attitudes and actions of a (chronologically-measured) 10-year-old. It is neither pathological nor a mark of exceptional vitality for a 75-year-old person to have the ambitions, the desires and hopes of a 25-year-old. Fifty-year-old departmental tyrants express the many personae of the children they were and remain when they are on vacation with the family. What's more, they are sometimes controlling tyrants when it comes to deciding where to dine during holidays; quite 6-years-old during departmental squabbles. These are not embarrassing regressions, nor slightly pathological distinctions between the public and the private domains, but the life sustaining force of the chameleon soul within.

Such "cross-over" attitudes are commonly classified exceptional mosaic moments. We treat them as prescient or regressive responses to atypical circumstances. But this is a mistake, a serious and grievous mistake. When developmental patterns set the norms of psychological maturation, they camouflage and misrepresent the subtle and complex workings of the mind; they inappropriately constrain interactions; they block the adaptive dynamics of sensitive responses; they produce false and falsifying speech and gestures. Stereotypic expectations of the mentality of chronological adolescents often lead to profound misunderstandings. More seriously, they can produce the tragic melodramas of self-fulfilling prophecies. Similarly, we tend to project severely limited roles and expectations of the chronologically elderly: they must endure our patronizing tone, our all too demeaningly helpful attentions, our curtly or abruptly detaching them from the collective work in which they have been engaged all their lives; our withdrawal if they do not meet our expectations of being nurturing, serene, and wise. Result: the psychological damages of the terrible loss of communication, the terrible sense of loneliness and unreality. Stage theory is a procrustean operation: it leaves its subjects—and the word is pregnant with its history—crippled.

Far from being regressive, aberrant, or pathological, layered age-indifferent "cross-overs" are frequent, normal standard issue human equipment. Without them, we would be rigidly fossilized, our deeply empathic communication limited to a cohort of (deeply boring, mutually mirroring) age-mates, incomprehensible to our children and grandparents. Ironically enough, what saves us from the normative imperial, politicized power of stage theory identity is the wild cacophony of our multiple voices, the blessed contentious chaos of our shifting, contingent multiple identities.

4. The strength of Zoe's reaction was, at least in a part, a fortuitous response to the contingencies of the day. Adaptive to circumstance as she is, a different day—a different gathering—might well have prompted a very different reaction.

Our interpretations and reactions, views and attitudes are affected by variations in the minutiae of interactions: irony or admiration on an interlocutor's face, the fear of exclusion, loss and solitude. A period of relentless optimism can elicit skeptical reactions; enough frivolity can evoke stern gravity. Many of our basic reactions take this reactive flickering improvisatory dramatic form: making comments on student papers, offering and responding to a toast, preparing a paper for delivery to a learned society, designing a curriculum or a playground, planning a meal, selecting a Supreme Court justice, hanging paintings for an exhibition … and adding a new turn to the argument of a philosophy paper.

We are engaged with our fellow players in the counterpoint of the ongoing improvisatory dramas of our lives.[2] The events that emerge from these improvisations are in their fine-grain details, dynamically collaborative.[3] Each "moment" or "stage" opens new alternatives and sets new problems; each moments tests and shifts dominance and recessiveness, action and counteraction. We are rarely able to foresee the configuration that will emerge from our interactions. Our original intentions may be dramatically reframed—their aims and options redefined—by the momentum of the interchange. Players are often propelled into exchanges that do not reflect their original intentions. Sometimes the very fact and tonality of opposition can, independently of its content, impel us to exaggerate our roles and attitudes: we become less able to hear or understand our fellows. They can become further entrenched, insistent on their positions. Consider the sobering examples of the ways that dynamic interactions between antagonists can move them to express—and destroy—their characters. Each protagonist impels the other to an ever more antagonistic—and self-destructive—response. (Think of Achilles and Menelaeus, Creon and Antigone, Lear and his daughters; think of your favorite examples of intolerable dynamically explosive political antagonisms, whose interactions propel players to act out of character, in deeply damaging ways.)[4] Zoe may have hoped to continue participating in the activities of the department, to be occasionally asked to direct a thesis, to be invited to seminars and picnics. The accidents of her vitriolic outburst may have endangered what could have been a continuing relation, perhaps a relation that, given Zoe's character, would remain testy, but a genuine relation for all of that. Whether the exclusion that followed her outburst leaves her profoundly depressed or impels her to explore inventive and productive activities will—as usual—depend on the accidents of her temperament and her future encounters. We shall have to wait and see.

Sensitivity to interactive improvisation does not always end in harmony. Even when they are not initially antagonistic, players can become so strongly focused on what they perceive as neglected aspects or issues that they sweep aside shared aims and assumptions. Because they attempt to complement or supplement (what they perceive as) neglected lacunae in varieties of stereotypic stage, gender, "identity marker" scenarios, their responses often becomes exaggerated and exclusionary. Once under way, such exchanges can lead to relatively irreversible positions and postures. Apparently irresolvable differences disagreements can arise out of the accident-prone dynamics of dramatic role playing. Ironically, even discussions that end by moving participants farther apart are nevertheless subterraneously collaborative: the articulation of each position is marked, affected by those of others in the drama.

It would be pretty to think that all dialogic sensitivity to subcultural contexts could be called "growth" and "development," that it could enhance what we—in this time, in this place—like to think of as autonomy, a more sensitive and discriminating choice and civic activity. There is no reason to think that the course of a person's life forms a parabola, still less an upward learning arc, sparked by a life force called "will" by Kantians, "mutual adaptation" by Dewey-minded Bakhtinians. There is every reason to think that a person's life is one damn thing after another, luck in and luck out.

5. Zoe's response was a moment in a cycle of periodical, luck-bound rhythmically alternating counter-poised traits. Having generously and patiently extended herself for her students just beyond her means, the paired trait of her brusque, blunt irritability exploded.

The psyche has its own alternating rhythms. Like other cyclical processes—those for sleep and waking, muscular activity and rest, sociability and solitude, nourishment and satiation, sexuality and abstinence—psychological rhythms are sensitive to the merest accident of environmental changes. And, like the alternations of other homeostatic systems, those of the psyche respond to the measures of consonant rhythms. Some paired dispositions reinforce or enhance one another; others tend to be mutually inhibiting. So, for instance, heightened physical activity typically realigns the default cycles of sleep and nourishment. And so it is for many other (less obviously organically based) paired psychological activities and attitudes. Elation and sorrow, confidence and insecurity, trust and distrust, impulsiveness and caution, naivety and sophistication, resentment and forgiveness, greed and generosity, outrage and indifference, stubbornness and adaptability, merriment and melancholy are responses to experience. Besides being rooted in the complexities of a person's character, they have a momentum and rhythm of their own. Independently of their being responses to immediate experience, they also have a discernible periodic dynamic.

At any given time, at any given age, we are all ages at once; and at any given time, the paired oppositions of traits continue their own periodic rhythms; and at any given time, our dialectical relations to fellows impel us to what the world might wrongly call infantilism or sagacity. And at any given time, chance, accidents, contingencies mark our interpretations, our reactions. Half a day of being "childish" is usually enough even for a 6-year-old American; and several days of the wildest Texan "adolescent" swings of mood usually trigger the sobriety of a 59-year-old. A week of carrying the cost-benefits responsibilities of a 47-year-old CEO prompts a weekend of spiritual retreat or the fantasies of a 27-year-old or the carefree play of a 12-year-old. Soldiers under fire at the front are preoccupied with the dangers that face them: their perceptions and responses are suited to their situation. But even in the heat and fear of battle, the soldier is struck by ageless ironic detachment, by an "adolescent" sense of mischief, by a child's tender pity.

There may well be universal patterns in what we may laughingly call "a person's life." Most of us do begin life as infants, grow taller and stronger, acquire language and a range of skills; in one way or another, we do all participate in recognizable patterns of social life. And so forth and so on. Certainly conventional chronology maps some significant patterns of organic changes, that can, for some very general purposes, be charted as "developmental stages" toward what is culturally and normatively marked as maturity. Certainly conceptions of prime human activities—reproduction and (culturally variable) ideals of social attitudes or productivity—form large scale patterns that can be developmentally traced. But these universal patterns are far too general to help us understand the independent rhythms, the dynamics, the cyclical dramas of the alternations of psychological attitudes. The more solidly universal the model/pattern, the less it explains the particularity of events; the more universal the theory/narrative, the more its explanatory power depends on the details of differential information.

What do these brief, disjointed observations indicate about identity and models of the mind?

A person is not an integrated system, not a unity with a central pan-optical core. (Synchronically) an individual is, at any given time, an assorted collection of over-lapping but not systematically organized perceptual, emotional, cognitive, motivational traits. (Diachronically), the gestalt patterns of an individual's traits vary with circumstances. They are sometimes tightly, sometimes loosely organized. Their relative dominance changes with a large range of variables, some strongly predictable, statistically law-like; others are erratic; and yet others are acquired accidentally, fortuitously. There is no correlation between the entrenchment of a trait and its relative dominance or effective strength. A trait may be relatively permanent but recessive and/or weak; an accidentally acquired trait may be highly dominant or strongly ramified. Varieties of traits can be classified by a range of distinctive parameters. Such a classification is not systematic: it is neither exhaustive nor exclusive.

You may well wonder what has been gained by introducing a myriad distinctions, parameters of explanation. "Parameters of what, explanations of what?" you might well ask.

Zoe's colleagues offered numerous plausible, relatively well-grounded theories—and even more sensible, evocative narratives—to explain her outburst. Many of their explanations were nested within a variety of stage/developmental theories. What do generic stage/developmental theories—ranging as they do from those that chart the logical dependence of concepts, to those that trace a temporal sequence of the acquisition of specific cognitive skills or competence (like "developing a theory of mind"), or to those that track stages in the expression of emotional and moral attitudes—explain? Some are openly teleological; others are implicitly normative; others characterize the strengths and weaknesses, the virtues and vulnerabilities of what they project as distinguishable life-stages; yet others profess normative neutrality. Even culturally specific, presumptively non-normative theories remain extremely general: they do not purport to explain, let alone predict individual behavior. Nor do they claim to be statistically reliable. Most such theories present themselves as nonstatistical analytic constructs of ideal types; others announce themselves as normatively neutral empirical studies.

Differ as they do in their focus, in their aims and methods, generic development theories present us with ideal types, types that attempt to understand the mentality—the saliences—and the skills that seem roughly typical of age and stage classifications. The lessons we have extracted from Zoe's story complicates the typology of generic stage/developmental theories. It attempts to provide a more robust understanding of events and actions of everyday life by introducing multiple parameters of "identity markers." Our heuristic guidelines are diverse: they prompt us to look in a number of different directions, to dialectical improvisations and to the vicissitudes of contextually-based cyclical alterations. The multiplicity of our parameters—the myriad of identity markers—should not make us skeptical about understanding our fellows. Although these accounts made no pretense of predicting Zoe's behavior on any specific future occasion, they place it in a general frame, one that provides heuristic counsel for explaining the responses of anyone roughly in her situation. To be sure, we have abandoned the luxury of working within the frame of a reductive, taxonomically encompassing theory; but we are none the worse off for that. Far from propelling us to skepticism, the multiplicity of identity markers, the contingencies of interactive dramas, the shifting rhythms of counterbalanced paired contraries provide us heuristic guidelines for understanding one another reasonably well.

I'd like to end by bringing you up to date on Zoe's story. After the fiasco of the party, and her profound distaste for the conventional cultural scenarios of retirement—gardening, volunteering, and grandmothering—she took up stunt flying. Although she remained blunt, out-spoken, and irritable, those traits became far more recessive than they had been when she was cast in the role of a supportive conscientious teacher in a drama set in contemporary American academic life. When last heard from, she was planning a solo non-stop cross-Pacific flight.

ENDNOTES

[1]I shall refer to "traits," "dispositions," "habits," "mentality," "states," "conditions," terms that many scholars have worked hard to define and distinguish. For our purposes, for the time being, I'll use these locutions generically, interchangeably, believing that doing so does not blur or mask the phenomena we shall explore.

[2]See Mikhail Bakhtin, *The Dialogic Imagination* (C. Emerson & M. Holquist, Trans.; Austin: University of Texas Press, 1981) and his *Speech Genres* (C. Emerson & M. Holquist, Eds.; Austin: University of Texas Press, 1981); Wolfgang Iser, *Languages of the Unsayable* (New York: Columbia University Press, 1989); and "From Exasperating Virtues to Civic Virtues." *American Philosophical Quarterly*, 1996, pp. 303–314.

[3]See Jonathan Adler, "Moral Development and the Personal Point of View," in *Women and Moral Theory* (E. Kittay & D. Meyers, Eds.; Totowa, NJ: Roman & Allenheld, 1986); Annette Baier, *The Commons of the Mind* (Open Court, 1997), and my "Witnessing Philosophers," in *Philosophy and Literature,* 1998, reprinted in *The Many Faces of Philosophy* (A. O. Rorty, Ed.; Oxford, 2003).

[4]For discussions of the compatibility of accident and inevitability in such dramas, see Bernard Williams, *Shame and Necessity* (Berkeley: University of California Press, 1993); Bakhtin, op. cit. For a metaphysical theory that attempts to explain these phenomena, see Spinoza, *Ethics,* Bks. III and IV; and A. O. Rorty, "From Exasperating Virtues to Civic Virtues," *American Philosophic Quarterly,* 1996, pp. 303–314.

Author Index

Note: *f* indicates footnote, n indicates endnote

263

Subject Index